EL MUNDO ZURDO 8

SELECTED WORKS FROM THE 2019 MEETING OF THE SOCIETY FOR THE STUDY OF GLORIA ANZALDÚA

EDITED BY
ADRIANNA M. SANTOS, RITA E. URQUIJO-RUIZ, AND NORMA E. CANTÚ

aunt lute books

San Francisco

Aunt Lute Books, P.O. Box 410687, San Francisco, CA 94141
www.auntlute.com

Cover art: © 2019 Liliana Wilson, "Forastera sin planeta"
Cover design: Amy Woloszyn, Amymade Graphic
Text design: Amy Woloszyn, Amymade Graphic Design
Senior Editor: Joan Pinkvoss
ProductionTeam: Shay Brawn, Sharon Emanueli, Bianca Hernandez-Knight, Maria Minguez, Sharon Page Ritchie, Emma Rosenbaum, Maria Minguez, and Frida Torres

Library of Congress Cataloging-in-Publication Data

Names: Mundo Zurdo (Conference) (8th : 2019 : Trinity University, San Antonio, Tex.) | Santos, Adrianna Michelle, editor. | Urquijo-Ruiz, Rita, editor. | Cantú, Norma E., 1947- editor.
Title: El Mundo Zurdo 8 : selected academic and creative works from the 2019 El Mundo Zurdo conference and meeting of the Society for the Study of Gloria Anzaldúa / edited by Adrianna M. Santos, Rita E. Urquijo-Ruiz, Norma E. Cantú.
Description: San Francisco, CA : Aunt Lute Books, [2022] | Includes bibliographical references.
Identifiers: LCCN 2022039287 (print) | LCCN 2022039288 (ebook) | ISBN 9781951874032 (trade paperback) | ISBN 9781939904393 (ebook)
Subjects: LCSH: Anzaldúa, Gloria--Study and teaching--Congresses. | Anzaldúa, Gloria--Influence--Congresses. | Anzaldúa, Gloria--Philosophy--Congresses. | Mexican-American Border Region--Social conditions--Congresses. | LCGFT: Conference papers and proceedings. | Literary criticism.
Classification: LCC PS3551.N95 Z78 2019 (print) | LCC PS3551.N95 (ebook) | DDC 818/.5409--dc23/eng/20220817
LC record available at https://lccn.loc.gov/2022039287
LC ebook record available at https://lccn.loc.gov/2022039288

Printed in the U.S.A. on acid-free paper 10 9 8 7 6 5 4 3 2 1

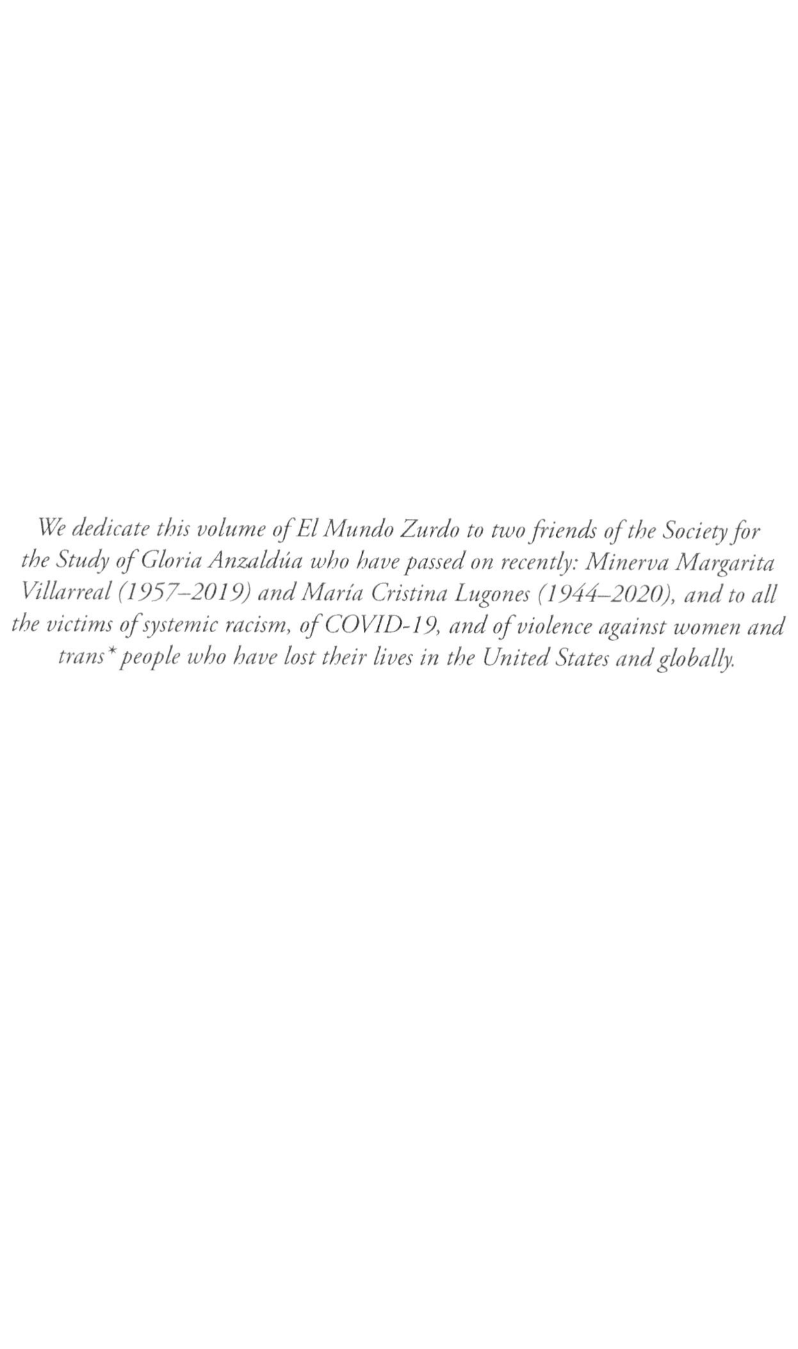

We dedicate this volume of El Mundo Zurdo to two friends of the Society for the Study of Gloria Anzaldúa who have passed on recently: Minerva Margarita Villarreal (1957–2019) and María Cristina Lugones (1944–2020), and to all the victims of systemic racism, of COVID-19, and of violence against women and trans people who have lost their lives in the United States and globally.*

PREFACE

JOAN PINKVOSS

Gloria Anzaldúa would have turned 80 in 2022 and what a year it would have been for her. Not only did the 5th edition of *Borderlands/La Frontera* come out, both in print and eBook, but the much-awaited critical edition of her work, edited by Ricardo F. Vivancos-Pérez and Norma Cantú with an afterword by AnaLouise Keating, came out in late 2021.

However, the big news for 2022 is that four different translations of *Borderlands* are coming out in the fall of this year: in French (Éditions Cambourakis), German (Archive Books), Italian (Edizioni Black Coffee) and in its Mexican re-release of Norma E. Cantú's Spanish translation (including the translations of her poetry by Claire Joysmith) (UNAM).

Gloria Anzaldúa has increasingly come to the attention of the larger feminist world outside the U.S. There clearly is a need within many cultural populations for her insightful writing as it pertains to the "outliers" of their own societies.

Perhaps this would not have come as a surprise to Gloria, who, in her concept of the new mestiza, clearly understood the need to include all who signed on for a socially just world; who understood the complexity of such a coming together and offered us metaphors, images and visions to help us get there; who showed us the way out of the everyday dualistic, capitalistic, ego-centric world. She knew that the work would be ever on-going. And most important of all, that it would be in and of the community, not exclusively done in the academy.

This is the very work of scholars, poets, artists and activists who come to the SSGA conferences. It is what makes the chronicling of that work in the *El Mundo Zurdos 1-8* so important: evidence that, in all its complexity, it still goes on and is still necessary—reminding us of the myriad ways the SSGA participants are carrying it forward. As clearly seen in the excellent organization by the editors, *El Mundo Zurdo 8* is especially rich in the variety of ways it touches on all parts of Gloria's own writing: her theoretical work, her art, her connection to community and to healing, and in her belief in the importance of individual historia.

Those of you who had the opportunity to see Gloria at a reading or event, know how much community meant to her. How she approached her community interactions with great humility, lack of ego, and was completely equal-footed. During the book signings that followed her events, she would actively listen to each of those in line till the end of their story and stay until the last book was signed—sometimes into the late hours and undoubtedly at some cost to her own health.

That's why it is especially important to me to see the two essays in the first section that describe activities in the Rio Grande Valley communities. Gloria, who as many of you know, was not allowed to write her thesis at Pan American University (now UT RGV) on the Chicano movement as she had intended, would, I believe, be truly gratified by knowing how she is part of the Valley community.

In 2019, many folks came together in New York City for an 8-hour reading of the entire manuscript of *Borderlands*—word for word—put together by the lesbian cultural activist and writer Sara Schulman, who felt a new generation of readers needed more exposure to Gloria's important work. In the brief initial comments by colleagues and friends, it was made clear how much Gloria had influenced their own work. I know this would have made her happy to hear. Gloria never, never wanted to be a star. Her leadership was of an entirely different nature—she wanted her ideas and her work to be what mattered.

And so they do. And so does this work between the covers of *El Mundo Zurdo 8*. Moving us all forward.

—Joan Pinkvoss, editor of *Borderlands* and Gloria's friend

ACKNOWLEDGMENTS

We would like to acknowledge Joan Pinkvoss at Aunt Lute Books, the Society for the Study of Gloria Anzaldúa at the University of Texas at San Antonio, Trinity University, the Esperanza Peace and Justice Center, and all who attended El Mundo Zurdo 2019 and who supported the work of the Society for the Study of Gloria Anzaldúa during the difficult time of the COVID-19 pandemic. Thank you to the contributors whose work first impressed us during the El Mundo Zurdo 8 conference and who have entrusted their work to us for this volume.

Adrianna: I would like to express my sincere gratitude to the entire team who stewarded this manuscript from conference to publication. We completed the entire manuscript in a pandemic thanks to a lot of grace. I would especially like to acknowledge my coeditors who modeled compassion, diligence, and respect, true to Anzaldúa's legacy. Finally, I would like to honor the indigenous ancestors and current caretakers of this land from which much of the inspiration for Anzaldúa's writing emerged. It has been a great honor to be entrusted with this important work and I look forward to continuing it. ¡Adelante!

Rita: It is my honor to continue to "do work that matters" (such as this book) with my dear amigas/coeditors, Adrianna Santos and Norma E. Cantú, as well as with the kind folks at Aunt Lute Books and our diligent colleague Sharon Emanuelli. To all the contributors who exercised their patience and gifted us their brilliance: ¡Mil gracias! To my partner Marisela "Sela" Chávez and to our dearly departed animalís, Ori (Perrótoro) Chávez and Corbatín "Tin Tin" (Chipi): Your profound love and understanding have sustained and nurtured me during these most challenging times. I am forever grateful. A mis tres familias, Urquijo Ruiz, González, y Porter: Gracias de todo corazón. ¡Seguimos adelante!

Norma: I am ever grateful to the many guides and helpers along the way who provide support in innumerable ways: at Trinity University, Lupita Domínguez, Corrine Castillo, and work study students Natasha Sahu and Kimberly Granados; at home, Elsa and Elvia, along with Tito and Mia. Gracias, also, to everyone at Aunt Lute Books—Joan, Shay, María, and others—and to the amazing copyeditor Sharon Emanuelli, without whose work this book would not be what it is. A shout out to the amazing team who curated the art exhibition and the conference presentations in 2019. To my extraordinary coeditors, Adrianna Santos and Rita Urquijo-Ruiz, colleagues and friends whose patience, diligence, and grace helped usher this project forward: ¡Gracias!

CONTENTS

PART II: TELLING LIVES: TESTIMONIOS, AUTOHISTORIA, ORAL HISTORY, AND AUTOETHNOGRAPHY

PART III: PHILOSOPHY, THEORY, CULTURE

PART IV: HEALING, POETRY, AND ART

INTRODUCTION

INTERPLANETARY CITIZENSHIP

ANZALDÚAN THOUGHT ACROSS COMMUNITIES, HISTORIES, CULTURES

ADRIANNA M. SANTOS, RITA E. URQUIJO-RUIZ, NORMA E. CANTÚ

When the Anzaldúistas[1] first gathered in 2007 at the University of Texas at San Antonio, a mere three years after the passing of Gloria E. Anzaldúa in 2004, we had not yet formed the Society for the Study of Gloria Anzaldúa (SSGA) nor had we intended to host subsequent gatherings under the name El Mundo Zurdo (EMZ). But after witnessing the incredible response to sessions on Anzaldúa at various national gatherings such as the National Women's Studies Association, American Studies Association, and Modern Languages Association meetings, creating a space for scholars, students, and activists to gather and celebrate Anzaldúa's legacy became a priority. We, the editors of this volume, reside in San Antonio, Texas, a frequent home of the EMZ conference. Much of the intellectual and community engagement that happens at EMZ reflects the local culture, which resonates in the details of this introduction.

Because we deemed an annual meeting to be too labor intensive, the idea emerged of a recurring meeting every 18 months on the weekend closest to May 15, the anniversary of Anzaldúa's passing, and closest to November 1–2, the

1 Anzaldúistas are scholars, artists, students, and activists who seek to keep Anzaldúa's ideas alive and honor her memory.

traditional Día de los Muertos celebration. From the beginning, the conferences held in May included a trip to the Río Grande Valley where Emmy Pérez, Stephanie Álvarez, and the Anzaldúa Legacy Project (led by Lina Suárez and others) hosted an event at the cemetery in Hargill. The same group, led by Emmy Pérez, later hosted El Retorno, an event held on the campus of the University of Texas Río Grande Valley (UTRGV) that featured an art exhibit, a poetry reading, and a keynote speaker, all centered on Anzaldúa. Each time, attendees of EMZ went to Hargill and then to UTRGV in Edinburg. Most traveled by bus, some drove in their own cars, and often the group stopped at the shrine to Don Pedrito Jaramillo, located in Falfurrias, Texas. El Retorno by UTRGV annually draws local artists, scholars, and writers to a one-day celebration of Anzaldúa by her community in the very place where she shaped her ideas and her life. An invited keynote speaker addresses the crowd during a luncheon, followed by a poetry reading by local authors and an art exhibit.

Figure 1. Flyer for El Retorno, UTRGV, 2019
Photograph: Randy P. Conner, Gloria Anzaldúa
Graphic design by Arnulfo Daniel Segovia

In 2019, SSGA held its eighth El Mundo Zurdo Conference on October 31–November 2, the weekend of Día de los Muertos, on the campus of Trinity University. The committee chose the theme, *Interplanetary Citizenship: Anzaldúan Thought Across Communities, Histories, Cultures,* after a lengthy discussion of the government policies that had been forcing the separation of families and the criminalization of asylum seekers at the US-Mexico border. The conference sponsored an art exhibit at the Southwest Workers Union gallery, and then we met at the Trinity University campus for workshops, panels, roundtables, a marvelous lunch, and many one-on-one and group pláticas.

Figure 2. Flyer for El Mundo Zurdo 8, Trinity University, 2019 Artwork: Liliana Wilson, Forastera sin planeta, 2018. Acrylic and colored pencil on paper. 30 inches x 30 inches.

LA OFRENDA

At every El Mundo Zurdo gathering since 2007, a committee has been charged with building an ofrenda, or altar, to Anzaldúa. In 2019, we believed it was most appropriate for the ofrenda to be in the heart of the community, as part of the annual Day of the Dead celebration at the Esperanza Peace and Justice Center, the organization that first invited Anzaldúa to San Antonio in 1989. The 2019 ofrenda was created by SSGA members Antonia Castañeda, Cecilia Amanda Macias, and Adrianna M. Santos, and was inspired by the Anzaldúa Archives at the University of Texas at Austin. From research, we knew that Anzaldúa's own home altar items reflected her life and work, reverence, activism, a sense of humor, desire, creativity, geography, mysticism, and more. They included such things as figurines, small clay pots, masks, rattles, candles, altar cloths, buttons, magnets, crystals, cards, incense, and rugs. Our ofrenda was part of an exhibit that was open to the public during the Esperanza's annual community celebration at Casa de Cuentos in the historically Mexican American west side of San Antonio. The ofrenda featured flores, rebozos, nopales and sávila, crystals, books, una tortuga, and candles. It included items similar to those that adorned Gloria's own altares as well as photos and flyers from past events. We asked for donations of artifacts from committee members, their families, students, and communities.

We know that altars were important for Anzaldúa and we sought to honor that aspect of her spiritual activism. The following quotation, which is further explained in the recently published critical edition of Anzaldzúa's most cited work, now takes on a new meaning with our lives being lived on screen and spending so much time in virtual meetings to create and preserve our much-needed connection. "I sit here before my computer, Amiguita, my altar on top of the monitor with the Virgen de Coatlalopeuh candle and copal incense burning. My companion, a wooden serpent staff with feathers, is to my right while I ponder the ways metaphor and symbol concretize the spirit and etherealize the body. The Writing is my whole life, it is my obsession" (*Borderlands: Critical Edition*, 2021).

THE ART EXHIBIT

Because Anzaldúa used images in her work and due to her keen interest in supporting Chicana artists, we believe it is imperative to curate and hang an exhibit that accompanies the conference theme at each EMZ. Therefore, as we have done since 2007, we held an exhibit of artwork submitted by local and national artists around the theme of the 2019 El Mundo Zurdo. Curated by Rebel Mariposa, Jess Gonzales, and Eliza Pérez, the event was held in a community gallery space at the Southwest Workers Union Hall. The participating artists included Alexandra Robinson, Andrea Rivas, Anel Flores, Cordelia Barrera, Cynthia Jane Treviño, Elva Salinas, Estafania Trejo, Jesusa María Vargas, Juan C. Escobedo, Julie Treviño, Karen Bravo, Kieran Myles-Andrés Tverbakk, Laura Ríos Ramírez, Liliana Wilson, María Alvarado, Maritza Torres, Mónica J. Alaniz-McGinnis, Sara Smith, and Sarah Castillo. Mindful of Anzaldúa's support for Chicana artists, we have included the artwork submitted by some of the participants in this volume of El Mundo Zurdo as well as by artists who responded to our call for artwork.

INTERSTELLAR NEPANTLA
transcending dreams, realities, and dimensions

Exhibit opening: Thursday, October 31, 2019 6 p.m.
The Movement Gallery
1412 E Commerce St, San Antonio, TX 78205

Curated by Rebel Mariposa, Jess Gonzales, and Eliza Perez

Art exhibition in tandem with the 2019 El Mundo Zurdo: Borderlands,
an International Conference on the Life and Work of Gloria E. Anzaldúa
presented by The Society for the Study of Gloria E. Anzaldúa

Figure 3. Flyer for *Interstellar Nepantla*, Southwest Workers Union Hall, San Antonio, 2019
Artwork: Jesusa Marie Vargas, *Mexicanidad and the Otherness #8*, 2018
Black and white film photograph on fiber paper, 8 inches x 10 inches

OTHER SACRED SPACES

The Anzaldúa conference privileges nonacademic ways of knowing and being in community. We open each year with a welcome that includes a blessing and a limpia by a local member of an Indigenous group, often performed outdoors, weather permitting, as it did that crisp October morning in South Texas in 2019. At this particular gathering, we also featured a variety of workshops that invoked a spiritual and creative connection to nature and collective action. For example, in one workshop titled "Coyolxauhqui ReMembered," Laura Ríos and Cecilia Aragón came together to offer a demonstration of how the roles of researcher and performing artist recreate Danza Azteca to address the subject of a new formulation in Chicana indigeneity. The audience participated in a dance tradition through improvisational physical movements, music, chant, and ceremonial blessings, per Elisa Diana Huerta's concepts of "embodied knowledge" and "sensuous identifications" (Huerta, 2009). Woven into the performance, Aragón offered insights into the historical, philosophical, spiritual, and contemporary additions, as Ríos performed the choreographic foundations. The ceremony honoring the Día de los Muertos tradition included marigolds, chanting, drumming, music, and dance, and focused on healing through movement. There was also an invitation to plant the seeds of the marigolds in our own jardines to blossom in the spring to continue inspiring and beautifying our perennial "work that matters."

ONE YEAR LATER

As we began drafting this introduction in the fall of 2020, we found ourselves in a different world from the one in fall 2019 when we mingled in San Antonio. Little did we know that in a few months, such a gathering would not be possible as the country and the world battled COVID-19. Since March 2020, we have seen the devastation and the utter destruction of what was our way of life. The pandemic continues to wreak havoc on communities, families, and countries, especially on individuals and communities from underprivileged environments. COVID-19 and its variants have ravaged the Mexico-US border. The poor and Latinx areas of Texas have been especially affected. It has been a devastating time for all of us with well over a million dead reported in the US and nearly 6½ million reported worldwide. The fact that Black, Indigenous, and People of Color (BIPOC) were most immediately and disproportionately affected reveals the systemic racism that exists in the United States, especially in regard to health care. The inequities abound and, not surprisingly, the pandemic impacted those who live in poverty—the unemployed and the working poor—people who have limited or no access to health insurance, and those with preexisting medical conditions like heart disease, diabetes, and obesity, all of which are found in higher numbers in Black and Brown communities. Moreover, many BIPOC work in areas deemed essential and thus are more likely to be exposed to the virus. The impact on the financial stability of these workers who lost their jobs and their homes due to the pandemic has been devastating.

At the same time that the country is grappling with a collective grief, illness, and financial uncertainty, police violence against communities of color has risen to the forefront of the national and global consciousness like never before. While Black Lives Matter activists have been advocating for change for over a decade, the recorded and widely broadcast murder of George Floyd in 2020 made the problem visible for a mainstream White audience. To make matters worse, the Trump administration's family-separation policy at the border ripped children away from their parents, exposing them to abuse and trauma in detention centers for indefinite lengths of time. Even now during the Biden administration, hundreds of children have not been reunited with their families. This outrageous, immoral, yet "legal" situation taints their families' futures as apparently the mechanisms were not put in place to make reunification possible. Anzaldúa's work continues to resonate at this time. We remain hopeful, although, regrettably, we acknowledge that the situation continues to worsen as Haitian and Central American migrants attempt to cross the Mexico-US border, fleeing violence, (un)natural disasters, and economic instability. All of these issues are compounded by the COVID-19 pandemic that has hit people of color the hardest.

Recent events have forced us to ponder the changing cultures of education, scholarship, and organizing, and have brought opportunities along with challenges. This pandemic has encouraged the use of technology at an accelerated rate to bring people together for both celebratory and educational purposes. In the face of isolation, grief, and loss, online events afforded us the opportunity to gather in a novel way. For example, "'Work that Matters': Jotería Celebration in the Río Grande Valley," a roundtable hosted by Verónica "Lady Mariposa" Sandoval that featured César L. De León, Stevie Luna, Amanda Victoria Ramírez, and Victor Cruz was part of the thirteenth annual "El Valle Celebra Nuestra Gloria" event (part 2), hosted by UTRGV's Center for Mexican American Studies on October 2, 2020. In addition, editors Margaret Cantú-Sánchez, Candace de León-Zepeda, and Norma E. Cantú, as well as several contributors to the new book *Teaching Gloria E. Anzaldúa: Pedagogy and Practice for Our Classrooms and Communities* (2020), came together on October 22, 2020, in an online panel to discuss the volume's practical application and inspiring ways to deploy Anzaldúa's transformative theories through meaningful action.

The virtual events that centered Anzaldúa and her work this past year have allowed an even wider audience to gather; this accessibility and community emphasis allowed for more potential global connections overall. The transborder nature of these events invites us to consider a kind of virtual nepantla within a twenty-first-century context. Planned at the 2019 El Mundo Zurdo, a 2020 gathering in Puebla, Mexico, had to be reimagined as a virtual event. Faculty from the Benemérita Universidad Autónoma de Puebla, the Tecnológico de Monterrey, and the Universidad Nacional Autónoma de México hosted two events in the fall of 2020: "Tiempos Nepantla / Nepantla Times: A Celebration of the Life, Work and Legacy of Gloria Anzaldúa" on September 26, and a Day of the Dead celebration called "Ancestral Futurities: Memory, Tempo & Contrapunto, Nepantla Times 2020," held on October 31. More than fifty participants offered words of remembrance, read creative work, or sang songs during these virtual events. Additionally, in January 2022, the Library Association of America honored Gloria Anzaldúa with a Literary Landmark installed on the grounds of the University of Texas Río Grande Valley.

These events have continued to bring people together to celebrate the life and work of Anzaldúa even, and perhaps especially, through dark times. She can refer us back to the Coatlicue state and what we might learn from this time of withdrawal, grief, rage, and transition. As vaccines are distributed across the globe and new variants of the virus emerge, we continue to lose beloved members of our families and community to disasters both natural and human-made. The steps toward racial healing necessary to move us to another world, a world that Anzaldúan scholars envision, continue to push us forward. The pandemic has given us new experiences through which to ponder nepantla, the in-between spaces. In these times of transitions, we believe Anzaldúa's work can offer us some tools and continue to teach us new lessons about ourselves, our communities, and our world.

THE CONTENT

This volume gathers selected academic and creative works from the 2019 meeting of the Society and recognizes the importance and sustained impact of Anzaldúa's work. We have divided the productions for these edited conference proceedings into distinct categories that align with the conference tracks in EMZ. As in Anzaldúa's work, it is difficult to categorize many of the essays in this collection. This means that some could fit into various sections because they are fluid. We, however, organized them so that each work speaks to the one next to it, emphasizing the manner in which Anzaldúan thought travels across communities—from the personal to the political, from the academic to the activist, from the creative to the spiritual.

Part I. Anzaldúa in and out of Academia: Theory & Pedagogy begins with a written account of the opening plenary panel, "Honor a Nuestra Gloria:

Remembering Gloria Anzaldúa in the Río Grande Valley," in which Stephanie Álvarez, Emmy Pérez, and Sergio G. Barrera, participants in a unique partnership project, shared their experiences as part of a workshop sponsored by Aunt Lute Books (Chapter 1). Next is a detailed pedagogical exploration of theory and praxis called "Using Anzaldúan Thought to Decolonize the Teaching of Composition, Literature, and Creative Writing at a Hispanic-Serving Institution," by Candace K. de León-Zepeda (Chapter 2). The following chapter, "Towards a New Consciousness: On the Revolutionary Power of Latinas in Academia," by Chelsea R. Barron Dávila-Conaway and Jacqueline Cantú Contreras, presents a collaborative narrative of two scholars whose work challenges academia, arguing that "it is imperative that Latinas in the academy draw on the work of contemporary Latina scholars working to challenge existing systems of domination." They conclude that "engaging in acts of solidarity with Latina scholars and resistance against White-normative culture will empower Latinas to disrupt the systems of subordination that seek to disempower them" (Chapter 3).

Then Erika Zavala, in her personal essay, "The Trojan Burra Mula of Gloria Anzaldúa: Characterizing the *Other* and Facing Challenges in Education," seeks to reconceptualize and metaphorically interpret the *Trojan Burra Mula* at the core of Anzaldúa's project as an exposé of "the subaltern woman and her challenges during her journey as a student in a hegemonic world" (Chapter 4). In "La Facultad and Decolonial Pedagogy: Teaching Valerie Martínez's *Each & Her*," Cecilia Amanda Macias explores how "decolonial pedagogies can help reframe epistemologies, and prior experiences of both teachers and students, so that violence of both the text and the classroom are openly acknowledged, discussed, and critically negotiated." By focusing on Martínez's text, Macias offers a case study for demonstrating how violence must be addressed and confronted beyond the classroom discussion. As she argues, "Necessary to the critical conversations related to content that confronts violence" is the unpacking of violent content in a text. But it must not stop there. As Macias writes, "Within transformative pedagogy, there is still room for la facultad, deeper senses and sensibility, but the inclusion of a call to action gives developed emotional sensibility a greater purpose" (Chapter 5).

The section concludes with "'Queering Cuentos: Borderland Intergenerational Narratives through Anzaldúan Scholarship'—Anzaldúan History, Lesson Plans, Writing Prompts, and Reflections of the 2019 Aunt Lute Summer Programming in the RGV," by Verónica "Lady Mariposa" Sandoval. The essay arose from the 2019 El Mundo Zurdo opening plenary session titled, "*Borderlands / La Frontera* in the Río Grande Valley: Poetry & Art Workshops Beyond University Walls." In it, Sandoval describes her experience creating and facilitating writing workshops in the Texas Río Grande Valley at the invitation of Aunt Lute Books editor Joan Pinkvoss as part of their education and outreach initiatives in the region. The chapter offers insight into the use of Anzaldúan theory in service to community, creativity, and pedagogy (Chapter 6).

Part II. Telling Lives: Testimonios, Autohistoria, Oral History, and Autoethnography brings together authors who are participating in the legacy of storytelling and theorizing from personal experience, history, creative expression, and social observation in the tradition of Anzaldúa. The chapters include literacy narratives, personal essays, academic research, reflections, creative nonfiction, and the in-between. The theme of border-crossing threads every chapter in the section, including the crossing of linguistic, geopolitical, sociohistorical, personal, political, and philosophical borders.

To begin this section, Alia Hazineh, Theresa Jbeili, and Kathleen Thomas-McNeill use ethnographic research methods and testimonio in their research study about immigrant women who cross the Canadian border, a less explored geographical area of study. Their essay, "The Gendered Construction of Border-Crossing into Canada: Immigrant and Indigenous Women's Life Histories," nuances our understanding of border-crossing experiences from one country to the other as it participates in Anzaldúa's cutting edge reframing of gender binaries and third spaces through personal narrative (Chapter 7).

Several of the other chapters in this section are personal essays. Yvette Chairez, for example, engages Anzaldúa's autohistoria-teoría in her chapter titled "Trauma as Nonordinary Reality: Using Anzaldúan Thought in Recuperating Painful Memories." The author recounts memories of an abusive family member and makes sense of them through the lens of Anzaldúa's concept of "nonordinary" reality (Chapter 8). Further exploring familial dynamics and narrative, in "The Generational Disconnect: Being My Parents' Navigator," Angie Contreras explores the concept of nepantla as applied to the experiences of first-generation US Latinx Americans who thrive in the borderlands despite the pressures of acting as translators and helping their immigrant families navigate the challenges of border-crossing (Chapter 9). Last, "Who Can Publish Autohistoria-Teoría with the Anger It Deserves?: Unclassified Lloronas and the Academic Text" by Smadar Lavie questions the types of "transnationalism" and language that are acceptable in academia and how Anzaldúa's grassroots, immigrant communication remains marginalized within the ivory tower (Chapter 10).

Part III. Philosophy, Theory, Culture explores the interconnectedness of Anzaldúa's contributions to these three fields of study. The first essay, "La Mexicana en la Chicana: Sources of Anzaldúa's Mexican Philosophy," by Alexander Stehn and Mariana Alessandri, offers an exploration of Anzaldúa's use of philosophical constructs rooted in Mexican philosophical thought. The essay is divided into three sections. In the first, the authors define the terms "*Mexican* and *philosophy* in conversation with Anzaldúa's work," then they "examine the Mexican philosophical sources that Anzaldúa cites in *Borderlands / La Frontera*," and finally they present the "other major Mexican philosophical influences on Anzaldúa . . . found in the archive" at the Nettie Lee Benson Library, University of Texas at Austin (Chapter 11). Javier Alejandro Camargo Castillo's chapter, "Gloria Anzaldúa: Intersticios entre las fronteras de Iberoamérica, la filosofía y la paz," also draws on Mexican philosophical tradition to explore the philosophy of peace. The author analyzes how epistemological tools deepen the reassemblage of a researcher in peace studies as they go through a self-transformation, a reinscription of oneself that articulates a spiritual practice alongside political activism (Chapter 12). In a turn back from the creative to the personal within the academy, Mauricio Patrón Rivera's "Geographies of Translation" recounts the author's project of translating Anzaldúa's *Borderlands / La Frontera: The New Mestiza* into Spanish. Rivera offers a look into the challenges and potentials for transformation that arise from translating *this* text and identifying such work as an "act of bridging" and an opportunity to briefly inhabit the Other (Chapter 13).

Next, Bernardita M. Yunis Varas's chapter, "Articulating Methodologies for a Dissertation Project: Embodied Experience to Tell a Story of (Colonial & Forced) Migration," explores the author's "identities as a diasporic Palestinian and Chilean immigrant in the United States," to arrive at methodologies that serve her well. For her project, she chooses "Anzaldúan thought and Indigenous and women-of-color feminisms [to] provide the tools for doing this work of recovery, discovery, reclamation in just, nonviolent, life-giving ways." In recovering her familial history, Yunis Varas selects a methodology that "must acknowledge and connect with other fights for survival and resistance." She aims "to reclaim and expose the stories of [her] peoples as Palestinian and Latinx communities whose lives been displaced and erased" while outlining and developing a methodology that allows her to achieve her recovery goal (Chapter 14). Then, Gloria Vásquez Gonzáles employs a cultural studies approach that she reshapes using Anzaldúan thought to delve into the Tejano music industry. With "*Las Invisibles*: The Women of the *Tejano* Music Industry," structured as a case study, Gonzáles uses the Anzaldúan concepts of cultural tyranny, borderlands, *nepantla*, *Coatlicue*, *Coyolxauhqui*, *la facultad*, and *mestiza consciousness* to understand the ways in which "*Tejanas* experienced the *Tejano* music industry" (Chapter 15).

This section closes with a chapter by Samantha Ceballos, "Nepantlera of Blackout Poetry: A Conversation on Art as Healing." This personal essay states that the author has "found a way to kick-start [her] writing, create a work of art, and most importantly, a way to heal the wounds [she] accrues daily" (Chapter

16). Calling herself a "Nepantlera of Blackout Poetry," she states: "I use Blackout Poetry to piece myself back together so that I may continue working to change the world by changing myself." Thus the section ends with a blueprint for putting the ideas and practices into action.

Part IV. Anzaldúa and Healing: Art, Music, and Poetry, as the final section, brings together the creative works and cultural production born out of Anzaldúa's work. As we have done at EMZ since 2007, we honor the work of artists by including their artwork in poetry and prose readings, as well as in an exhibit during the conference. The short fiction and artwork included in this section focus on the border reality of the artists and the way they connect their work to Anzaldúa.

Erika Garza-Johnson's poetry starts the section off with insight and humor. In her poem "Shade," Garza-Johnson hilariously details the life of a jaded or "hate filled witch" who does everything wrong. In "These Walls," many of the negative phrases used against women and people from the borderlands are enumerated. The piece closes with a positive outlook on "walls" as protection for the unsheltered. In "Coatlicue Status," the poet presents us with a woman who is ready to "heal" herself from her self-inflicted wounds (Chapter 17). María L. M. García, in her artist statement as well as in her two poems "About the Medio (Found Poetry in *Borderlands*)" and "En el Medio," articulates the struggles of accepting the term *artist* for oneself when art is not part of our daily life. García dares those of us who inhabit the "middle" of the borderlands to not only survive, but to thrive and to live "sin fronteras" (Chapter 18).

In their creative piece, "Who Am I?: Understanding My Borderlands Using Poetic Inquiry," by Soph/Spencer Margulies, who identifies as a "third culture individual," they recount their experiences as the child of a former US diplomat, exploring the intersections of nonbinary gender, movement across national borders, and light-skin privilege (Chapter 19). José David "Pepe" García Gilling rewrites a scene from the film *The Treasure of Sierra Madre* in "'We Don't Need No Stinkin Badges!' Remake" by listing many of the Hollywood stereotypes assigned to Latina and Latino actors; the poem ends with a call to "¡acción!" (Chapter 20). Christen Sperry García in "///borderlands///arte///remezcla/// pedagogy///entre///el valle///HSI///san diego///" utilizes images (such as a red and blue tortilla and a "patriotic concha") and poetry to detail the lives of people living in nepantla who work at an Hispanic-Serving Institution (HSI) while being from two worlds/cultures and three languages (Spanish, Spanglish, English) at once (Chapter 21).

In "Cases," Isaac Chavarría engages Anzaldúa's views and sentiments regarding the terrible treatment, in life and even in death, of "los atravesados." In this case, Chavarría highlights how the undocumented immigrants who inhabit the South Texas borderlands for fleeting moments, remain there forever as their spirits haunt the physical sites of their death. In "La Llorona del Valle," this mythical figure's victims help irrigate the Río Grande Valley in order to mitigate her insatiable hunger and in turn, help feed the people from the barrio-colonias (Chapter 22). In the tradition of blending academic and creative work, Ethan Trinh's poem "To you, Gloria E. Anzaldúa" was written as a reflection on the conference proceedings and highlights the conversational relationship that the poet has cultivated with Anzaldúa as they have been inspired to display vulnerability in their academic writing (Chapter 23).

Our anthology closes with selected works of visual art from some of the participants in the EMZ art exhibit. Octavio Quintanilla, Juan C. Escobedo, Maritza Torres, Julie Treviño, Kieran Myles-Andrés Tverbakk, and Jesusa Marie Vargas each explore their views, liminality, and borderlands/nepantla identities by engaging Anzaldúan concepts, language, and theory (Chapters 24–29).

Each contribution to this volume takes up the call for a hybrid methodology and dives into the personal as a form of knowledge creation. Some essays focus on the more immediate interpersonal relationship(s) to self, while others place their work in the context of the collective or community spaces. All authors, poets, and artists, however, engage in the important acts of border-crossing and storytelling that Anzaldúa has brought forward and that we celebrate at each EMZ conference. We offer you our "work that matters," dear reader, as a cultural/literary, long-lasting artifact for you to enjoy and share with others as Gloria E. Anzaldúa intended: en comunidad.

April 2022

WORKS CITED

Anzaldúa, Gloria. *Borderlands / La Frontera: The New Mestiza: The Critical Edition*. Edited by Norma Cantú and Ricardo F. Vivanco-Pérez, Aunt Lute Books, 2021.

Margaret Cantú-Sánchez, Candace de León-Zepeda, and Norma E. Cantú, eds. *Teaching Gloria E. Anzaldúa: Pedagogy and Practice for Our Classrooms and Communities.* University of Arizona Press, 2020.

Huerta, Elisa Diana. "Embodied Recuperations: Performance, Indigeneity, and *Danza Azteca*." *Dancing across Borders: Danzas y bailes mexicanos*. Edited by Olga Nájera-Ramírez, Norma E. Cantú, and Brenda M. Romero, University of Illinois Press, 2009.

PART I

ANZALDÚA IN AND OUT OF ACADEMIA: THEORY & PEDAGOGY

HONOR A NUESTRA GLORIA

REMEMBERING GLORIA ANZALDÚA IN THE RÍO GRANDE VALLEY[1]

STEPHANIE ÁLVAREZ, EMMY PÉREZ, AND SERGIO G. BARRERA

In her last published piece, "Let us Be the Healing of the Wound: The Coyolxauhqui Imperative—La sombra y el sueño," Gloria Anzaldúa states that "for women of color, home and homeland have not been safe places—our bodies

1 We are deeply indebted to the work the community has done for so long to honor Gloria Anzaldúa in the Río Grande Valley. We are particularly grateful for the generosity of Noemi Martínez and Lina Suarez not only for their work but also for their willingness to share materials and stories and to exchange messages to ensure we were able to tell the most complete story possible. There is no doubt that there are gaps in this history and for that we apologize as documenting the work of activists, writers, community workers, and in particular, femmes and Women of Color, is quite difficult given too many factors to list. Please know any omissions are not done purposefully. In fact, we as authors are sure we have not documented some of our own work. Two of us, as women of color and mothers overburdened with service, rarely also have time to document. This essay is to honor all of the tireless work done by so many people, overwhelmingly mujeres, to honor Gloria Anzaldúa on shoe-string budgets, and at times, no budgets. Most often, no recognition is offered to them. However, know that we see you—the community benefits from your work. You do work that matters y sí vale la pena.

are constantly targeted, trespassed, and violated" (308). Unfortunately, even though it was written almost twenty years ago, this statement still holds true today, and although we have witnessed efforts to legally and socially protect and serve women of color, many are still "targeted, trespassed, and violated" emotionally, physically, psychologically, and intellectually. However, Anzaldúa reminds us, "May we do work that matters. Vale la pena, it's worth the pain" (314). Many often cite this phrase, but very few include the second piece: "it's worth the pain." Nonetheless, it is important to acknowledge that aspect of the work because Anzaldúa wrote as a queer woman of color doing work that matters even if it too often went unrecognized. This is not unlike many women of color, and Latinas and Chicanas especially, who have resiliently endured the struggles through painful paths traversing their institutions, communities, and in many instances, their familias. This essay is an effort to continue the Anzaldúan call for "work that matters" by paying homage to and writing into the archive not only nuestra Gloria but also the work of the community organizers, artistas, intellectuals, educators, students, and mujeres of the Río Grande Valley—the Borderland Anzaldúa writes about—who have bulldozed through institutional barriers in order to continue celebrating their borderlands, nuestra frontera.

Gloria Anzaldúa was born and raised in the Río Grande Valley (El Valle) and much of her writing and theoretical musings emerged from her lived experiences en El Valle. For this reason, many mujeres who are familiar with her work are from El Valle, reside in El Valle, or both, have for many years committed themselves to honoring her legacy in the Río Grande Valley. The work of these mujeres demonstrates the depth to which the Valley cares about Anzaldúa and they are determined to raise awareness about her work so that others may benefit from it and take pride in knowing that one of the greatest writers of our time is from El Valle. This paper in many ways emerged from the desire not only to document the invisible labor of mujeres but also to dispel the notion that El Valle does not do enough to honor its homegirl. Many of us have heard academics and community members, both outsiders and those from El Valle, murmur that not enough is done to honor Anzaldúa or what a shame it is that "nobody" in El Valle knows who she is. However, we attribute this to the gendered and invisiblized efforts of our labor.

As most know, this invisiblization of Chicana/Latina efforts has been a persistent tradition driven by a controlled narrative voice in US history, which is why Chicana/Latina feminists have dedicated their work to raising awareness about the important sociopolitical contributions of mujeres in history through acts of *testimonios* and remembrance. Maylei Blackwell, in *¡Chicana Power!*, states that Chicanas' strategies include "remembering themselves in time and place, being whole under erasure, creating new terrains of memory in which to forge a vision of history, a history in which Chicanas and their communities have a central role in creating a better world" (11). Thus, our collective remembrance leads us to think that there is no single geographic location in the world that has done more to recognize Anzaldúa than South Texas; the Society for the Study of Gloria Anzaldúa Association (SSGA) and the Río Grande Valley. However, while the SSGA is a collective organization it is important to note that in the case of the Río Grande Valley the majority of these efforts were undertaken by community members first and then faculty and not unified under any one organization. There are no national news stories about this work, only a few local ones, but the impact has been felt. Despite the lack of media coverage, our activism in the Río Grande Valley has remained consistent. These heroic Chicana feminist efforts have been led by many mujeres and its jotería even when there has been little to no institutional funding to memorialize Anzaldúa and spread her gospel.

BUILDING BRIDGES, BUILDING COMMUNITY

Some of the earliest work to honor Anzaldúa began with CAFÉ Revolución (Community Activists For Equality) and Voices Against Violence founded by poet and *zinester* Noemi Martínez around 2004. Martínez learned about Anzaldúa through zines[2] and then used the zine platform to spread knowledge about her through CAFÉ Revolución and Voices Against Violence. In a 2008 interview, Martínez says that "CAFÉ Revolución started out as a traveling café, where we would take our coffee mugs and have discussions and poetry readings," and explains that the group is "comprised of community activists and other community groups with different agendas, but we intersect in many of them." Martínez also reveals that they "organize[d] a yearly Voices Against Violence vigil in October . . . including poetry, speakers, and survivor-led discussions." Martínez and Priscilla "Lina" Suarez collaborated on other projects including "Homenaje a Nuestras Muertas and Mujer Fest." Through these venues they created zines, and for two consecutive years the main person honored was Gloria Anzaldúa. This spiraled into and intersected with the *Gloria Anzaldúa Legacy Project.*

Lina Suarez and Noemi Martínez founded the *Gloria Anzaldúa Legacy Project* (GAL) in 2007 as a means to spread awareness about Anzaldúa and her writings. Important to note was the desire to interject Anzaldúa's work within disability discourse since the majority of this work was coming from outside of the Valley. Moreover, Martínez observes that many who were/are discovering their disabilities identified with Anzaldúa as chronically ill and see themselves in

---

2 Some of the zine authors that Martínez learned about Anzaldúa from include: Athena Tan's Framing Historical Theft; Mimi Thi Nguyen's *Race, Race* and *Evolution of a Race Riot* (which was a compilation zine written by people of color); Sabrina Margarita Alcantara-Tan's *Bamboo Girl*; Bianca Ortiz's *Mala Zine;* and *Mamasita,* among others.

her work (personal communication). A few days after Anzaldúa passed away in 2004, Cherríe Moraga wrote the first entry on the "Web Altar for Gloria" and invited others to contribute as well as to make physical altars for Gloria. On the web altar (which Suarez learned about on MySpace), Suarez wrote, "Anzaldúa's words have thundered my many ancestors within me, opening the windows that were not yet used as a girl, taking her hope that we (Chicanas) comprehend the importance of the rattlesnakes in our veins." She also wrote "I am undoubtedly grateful to this courageous woman. Not only did she pave a road for Chicana writers of South Texas, but for Chicana writers in their entirety." Indeed, Suarez would create many altares in the Valley for Gloria and continues to do so to this day.

It is important to also note that both Suarez and Martínez did not learn about Anzaldúa in Valley institutions. Suarez learned about her as an undergraduate at the University of Michigan. Martínez revealed during the 2018 event El Retorno: El Valle Celebra Nuestra Gloria, held at UTRGV, that she took GED and college classes on the same campus (then University of Texas Pan American [UTPA]) in the '90s and did not learn about Anzaldúa: "I was so angry because here was a queer Chicana writer . . . but I was not taught her here in the Valley, so it [Gloria-related activism] was like a spark that we created, and we wanted to see both in the community and on campus how can we celebrate and honor someone who was like us, someone who came from here" ("El Retorno").

As Suarez and Martínez recall, few people in the Río Grande Valley knew who Gloria Anzaldúa was at that time and most of those who did were scholars and professors at UTPA. As Suarez relates, the Río Grande Valley and Anzaldúa's family knew that she was a writer and professor but did not fully understand the impact of her scholarly writings for our region. At that time, a local poet, Daniel García Ordaz,[3] had written several articles in the *McAllen Monitor* about Anzaldúa. This instilled in Martínez and Suarez a lot of orgullo because it was completely unexpected. Later, García Ordaz would join Suarez and Martínez in GAL. Nevertheless, at the same time they were disappointed about her not being recognized at her alma mater, UTPA, formerly Pan American College. Moreover, her books were scarce in the Valley and there did not seem to be a way to promote her literature within the community. Suarez recalls that "after we had a successful Homenaje a Nuestras Muertas [which came about after the Voices Against Violence events] in 2006, it encouraged us to start the legacy project." (personal communication). She also notes that professors such as Emmy Pérez,

3 See Verónica Sandoval's essay "Queering Cuentos: Borderland Intergenerational Narratives through Anzaldúan Scholarship" in this volume of *El Mundo Zurdo* for more information on García Ordaz's community work in the RGV.

Rob Johnson and others from UTPA encouraged them to continue work they had already begun, though this work was clearly in progress already.

On April 26th, 2007, GAL hosted its first event honoring Gloria at the McAllen Public Library Palm View branch, Remembering Gloria: A Night of Poetry! Suarez and Martínez wanted to invite Anzaldúa's family to come, but had no idea where to start so they went to the phonebook and searched for the surname in the two or three pages dedicated to Hargill. One entire page was made up of Anzaldúas. Suarez chose the very first name, called, and it was a teenage boy who answered. She recalls talking to him and telling him,

> I know this sounds pretty weird. But I work here at the library and I wanted to see if maybe you knew someone that's related to Gloria Anzaldúa. And so the kid right away gets very excited. He's like "oh okay her sister, that's my tía. Her sister lives right next door." And so I just heard him like he put the phone down, and he went running. And within two minutes he came back and he's like "yeah she said that you could call her"... he gave me her phone number. And I sat on that phone for about three hours with Hilda Anzaldúa. She doubted me because of the fact that she had so many people just wanting to know and kind of getting personal information about Gloria (personal communication).

Hilda Anzaldúa would reveal to Suarez that a lot of writers and professors and journalists had been going out to the family to try to get information about Gloria. Unfortunately, they did not have any pictures left of Gloria to share because they naively trusted someone who said he was writing a biography about Gloria. They gave him, a professor from UTPA (whose name we do not know), all the pictures and so they do not have any baby pictures of her. A great distrust had developed between the family and the community, yet the efforts of Suarez yielded positive results. At this first event on April 26, 2007, at the McAllen Public Library, Janie Anzaldúa, Gloria's sister-in-law, attended.

GAL connected activists, professors, scholars, and community members wanting to learn more about Gloria Anzaldúa. GAL held events and published zines to teach others about how her work relates to the community and how it all ties back. GAL and CAFÉ Revolución were very interconnected and on July 28, 2007, CAFÉ Revolución hosted MujerFest: This Bridge We Call Home at the McAllen Creative Incubator, which hosted workshops, classes, discussions, films, poetry and art (Martínez, Personal Archive). While MujerFest was not exclusively dedicated to Anzaldúa, it was a community platform to spread knowledge about Anzaldúa and her work. A few months later, from September 15 to October 19, 2007, GAL, with the assistance of UTPA Special Collections archivists Virginia Gause and George Gause, curated the exhibit ¡Gloria Presente! in the UTPA library corridor through which thousands of students pass daily.

Figure 1. Lina Suarez (left) with Janie Anzaldúa, 2007
Photograph courtesy of Lina Suarez

At this time neither Martínez nor Suarez were students at the university, yet they chose the university setting for the exhibit in order to expose more students to Anzaldúa. Even then, knowledge of Anzaldúa was not as widespread as they would have liked and only a handful of professors were teaching her work. The exhibit displayed Anzaldúa's books, images, quotes, and art, as well as mixed media pieces inspired by Anzaldúa, to raise awareness on campus about who she was and the fact that she was from the Valley. GAL would follow-up with a second Remembering Gloria: A Night of Poetry at the McAllen Public Library Palm View Branch on April 10, 2008. Additionally, GAL also created at least three zines dedicated to Anzaldúa, *Our Gloria: Homenajes* (2008), *Homenaje a Nuestras Muertas: Gloria Anzaldúa Legacy Project* (2009), and *This Bridge We Call Home: Finding Gloria* (2009).

Through GAL, Suarez was

> able to see Gloria's legacy to the Valley in a way that she has connected us and given us a circle of community where we have writers, activists, visual artists and educators who have all, because of Gloria, become a circle that we could always go back to even if we are very different otherwise, but it's in community. Somos una familia. She's made a familia that wasn't there

Figure 2. Gloria Anzaldúa Legacy Project, zine, *Homenaje a Nuestras Muertas*, 2009
Photograph courtesy of Stephanie Álvarez

> when Gloria was in the Valley. It's something beautiful. Some of us will leave, some will come back, but she's helped us recognize that our roots are very important and our ties to our community are very important. That has been her legacy with the Gloria Anzaldúa Legacy Project. That has also been the legacy of GAL that we were able to connect with so many different organizations (personal communication).

There is no doubt that GAL's presence in the community laid a tremendous foundation for honoring the legacy of Anzaldúa. On May 16, 2008, GAL hosted the event, Honoring Gloria, Reading Gloria, Seeing Gloria, to remember the passing of Anzaldúa at her resting place, the Hargill Cemetery. They invited the public to read, write, and meditate. Martínez would read from her "Letters to Gloria" collection. Attendees were encouraged to bring their own letters and submit them to be included in the zine *This Bridge We Call Home: Finding Gloria* (2009). This zine, as described by GAL, was produced by CAFÉ Revolución as the "third issue of the first zine devoted to la Mera Nepantlera. A zine created by the folks she influenced; from the place she grew up in the borderlands. How her writing helped shape Chicana feminism, how it created a new consciousness and gave voice to her generation and future generations—and how this allowed others to find their voice and articulate through their bordered tongues" (Martínez and Suarez). GAL's visits and readings at Anzaldúa's gravesite would soon become a yearly tradition as many were impacted by their work and moved by the community's deep commitment to honoring Anzaldúa and sharing her legacy with others. One of the people moved by the GAL Project and their members was poet and UTPA assistant professor Emmy Pérez.

In 2006, Emmy Pérez joined the creative writing faculty at UTPA to teach poetry in the new Master of Fine Arts (MFA) program and became part of the familia Suarez speaks of. She had been living and working in El Paso prior to moving to the Valley. Soon upon her arrival, she came to know poets in the community at readings and events, including a Writing to Heal event she hosted on campus with visiting writer Michelle Otero. She began to contemplate how she could help spread awareness about Anzaldúa on campus beyond the classroom, where she was teaching *Borderlands / La Frontera* in her Mexican American Literature courses. Of course, professors at UTPA had already been teaching her work—professors such as Guadalupe Cortina, Edna Ochoa, Rob Johnson, and likely others as well. Each year, more professors began teaching her work. In 2007, Pérez was invited to participate in the GAL Project's first Remembering Gloria: A Night of Poetry. A year later, she applied for campus funding to bring Norma E. Cantú, founder of the Society for the Study of Gloria Anzaldúa Association, to give a talk on campus about Anzaldúa and her own work. Funding proved difficult and there were various delays, but on April 14, 2008, Cantú came to UTPA to give a talk titled "Living en la Frontera: Gloria Anzaldúa and Border Theory," along with a reading from her critically acclaimed autoethnography *Canícula: Snapshots of a Girlhood en la Frontera*. The UTPA Ballroom was full. Students and community members responded positively and had many questions and there were long lines to speak with Cantú afterwards. Pérez also invited Verónica "Lady Mariposa" Sandoval to share her poetry. At this event, Pérez asked Cantú her opinion on "how we at UTPA could honor Gloria?" Cantú's response was to hold an annual event, and so, Cantú's presentation would be the first of what would become a long compromiso on the part of Pérez to honor Gloria en El Valle. Another community organization that would prove important to honoring Gloria Anzadúa was the Valley International Poetry Festival (VIPF), organized yearly by Daniel García Ordaz. VIPF ends their annual community poetry festival with a visit to Anzadúa's resting place in Hargill, led by Lina Suarez. Additionally in 2009, VIPF would cosponsor, along with Art That Heals, South Texas College, UTPA's Creative Writing MFA

Program, the UTPA Mexican American Studies Programs and Writers Bloc,[4] a film screening of *ALTAR: Cruzando Fronteras, Building Bridges* including discussions with producer and director Paola Zaccaria at three different locations in the Valley. Artwork by Celeste De Luna and Beatriz Guzmán Velásquez was on display. Anzaldúa's mother attended the film screening held at UTPA. It was a very special moment and the continuation of Anzaldúa's family attending events in her honor throughout the Valley.

EL RETORNO

The following year, 2009, Pérez (in consultation with Cantú) invited Norma Alarcón to give a talk on the UTPA campus just before the SSGA's El Mundo Zurdo 2009 Conference on the Life and Work of Gloria Anzaldúa, held in San Antonio. Pérez also collaborated with Cantú and the SSGA in determining how to link the event in the Valley with the event in San Antonio. Alarcón's talk "Becoming MeXican@ with Gloria Anzaldúa," would be open to the public, including students, and to attendees of the SSGA conference who registered in advance and were willing to travel to the Valley, either by the bus chartered by the SSGA or by other means. Emmy Pérez, Verónica Sandoval—a Graduate Assistant in the MFA program at the time—and Stephanie Álvarez would be the primary organizers of the event from the university. However, GAL Project members cosponsored and collaborated in significant ways, along with community members, including several UTPA creative writing and art students and some faculty, beginning with a meeting at Pérez's home and through many emails and on their own. Erika Garza-Johnson, Noemi Martínez, Lina Suarez, Lauren Espinoza, Celeste de Luna, and Beatriz Guzmán Velásquez are just a few of the mujeres who helped make it all possible. Student artist Beatriz Guzmán Velásquez generously made an original drawing of Gloria that would be used in the poster and displayed at that and subsequent events. Student poet Lauren Espinoza contacted Valley graphic designer and poet Jessica Salinas, another of Pérez's former students, who designed the event poster and program from their residence in Austin. In Pérez's recollection, for the event title, Erika Garza-Johnson suggested "El Retorno" from the section in *Borderlands / La Frontera* and Martínez added "El Valle Celebra Nuestra Gloria," which immediately took hold as the annual title, and which we also retroactively applied to the first event with Cantú in 2008.

---

4 Art That Heals is a charitable organization founded in 2005 by Daniel García Ordaz to provide arts and HIV/AIDS programming. Art is used as a tool to encourage good health among those who are HIV-positive. Art That Heals has collaborated with GAL at different times. Writers Bloc was a student organization for creative writing.

The 2009 event would establish the tone for many others to come. The GAL Project and community poets and artists primarily organized the ceremony at Valle de la Paz cemetery in Hargill as they had made similar trips before, beginning with their May 16, 2007, event: Honoring Gloria, Reading Gloria, Seeing Gloria. Erika Garza-Johnson, who grew up in Elsa, near Hargill, once commented to Pérez with her signature humor, "that's what we Mexicans do, go to the grave" to honor others. Garza-Johnson had also attended Anzaldúa's funeral in 2004. At the time, Garza-Johnson was just learning about Anzaldúa's work, but recalls writer David Rice stating, "we need to go to her funeral." In the same interview with Pérez, she says, "I wanted to go back to her book and I really wanted to know who she was. . . . [The funeral] opened my heart to her; . . . it opened up the world actually."

At El Retorno 2009, Suarez created an altar for Gloria at the site. That morning, Valley participants met SSGA members as they deboarded the chartered bus from San Antonio near the entrance of the cemetery. These SSGA members had arrived early to San Antonio for El Retorno before the El Mundo Zurdo Conference, led by Cantú. In earlier planning for the day, Edna Ochoa, poet and professor, had suggested a brief selection from Anzaldúa's poem "Arriba Mi Gente" that we included in the program for all to chant if they chose while taking the short walk to the grave site led by local poets, including Sandoval. Once at the gravesite, Suarez and other community poets read selections of Anzaldúa's work and Ochoa performed a ritual piece called "Danza de Serpientes." Participants were also encouraged to share why they traveled to the gatherings that day, which is always a very meaningful highlight of meeting at Valle de la Paz before moving on to the institution.

Participants then traveled to the UTPA campus in Edinburg for the luncheon featuring Alarcón as keynote speaker. The event also included original artwork by local artists and local poets who read their work in advance of Alarcón's talk. Pérez always insists on including local poets and artists as it is an opportunity for students and visitors to witness the legacy of Anzaldúa's influences, "theory in the flesh." Furthermore, this campus event would not exist without them. They are the heart and soul of El Retorno, as is the GAL Project, and we recognize their labor in multiple settings and honor their creative work. While El Retorno has been held every year since 2008, the SSGA conference occurs every eighteen months, in the fall and spring. Since 2009, each time the SSGA conference falls in the spring, a trip to Anzaldúa's grave site has been organized primarily by Pérez, Cantú, Suarez, Garza-Johnson, and Sandoval (before she moved out of state for doctoral studies), as well as others. Pérez, along with several sponsors at first and later with the Center for Mexican American Studies (CMAS), organized the speaker visit and luncheon.

Figure 3. Poster for El Retorno: El Valle Celebra Nuestra Gloria #2
Illustration: Beatriz Guzmán Velásquez, *Gloria Anzaldúa*, 2009

As previously mentioned, another reason for Pérez to continue the annual event was that, to her knowledge, Anzaldúa was never invited to speak at her alma mater. This idea of not being honored in one's home region as a scholar/writer/artist became a focus of repair and celebration for many of our subsequent invitations. Therefore, her efforts have also concentrated on inviting Chicanas, mostly Tejanas, as speakers, and in particular, mujeres from El Valle like Aída Hurtado, Sonia Saldívar-Hull, and María Herrera-Sobek, to bring them "back/retornar" al Valle. This is to help ensure other Chicana scholars or artists from the Valley will not go unrecognized by the institution and, at the same time, to honor Anzaldúa's work along with theirs.

The first El Retorno events came to fruition without institutional release time for faculty to do the work and without easy access to sufficient funding. The effort was truly a manifestation of mujerista movidas that included the generosity of time and purpose by student and community member volunteers who were integral to the events' success. Furthermore, it cannot be stated enough that the GAL Project's community-based events and on-campus exhibit prior to El Retorno were integral to Pérez's urgent sense of purpose to do more public work on campus *with institutional funds and resources*, however minimal. These efforts are aligned with the history of cultural and community-based needs that many mujeres have labored for. María Cotera, one of the founders of Chicana por mi Raza Digital Memory Collective (a digital archive dedicated to the collection, curation, and preservation of the labor of mujeres during the Chicano Movement) states, "We had to do something to bring attention to this history because the contributions of that generation were quickly receding from public memory as a result of scholarly neglect" (489). This neglect continues to erase and discredit the efforts; stories, experiences, and intellect of many women of color for many institutions do not emphasize or acknowledge community work.

The scholarly neglect became apparent to Pérez via the question of funding. In 2007, Pérez consulted with her colleagues Jennifer Mata and Kamala Platt. At the time, Mata, with whom Pérez had collaborated earlier in the year, was the coordinator for the Gender and Women's Studies program on campus. Mata suggested the possibility of applying for UTPA's competitive faculty development funding. Pérez proposed bringing Norma E. Cantú for a talk on Anzaldúa and poet Diana García for one on service learning. After she applied for the funds, the council asked Pérez for the lecture dates. Pérez contacted Cantú and García to ask for their preferred dates, thinking that would complete the funding request. As it turned out, the requests were initially denied because "conference-like" activities were not funded. However, the proposals had been presented as faculty development talks to help more faculty teach Anzaldúa's work and learn more about service learning in detention centers with García. Pérez was most disappointed because they had requested she contact the speakers in advance of knowing whether the proposal would be funded. She felt it had been a sign that the proposals were about to be accepted—the last step. In fact, one presenter was about to purchase her flight when she contacted Pérez for confirmation. After receiving the denial, she contacted a campus administrator to explain the situation, and how it would reflect poorly on the university and herself to now have to tell presenters they were not coming after all. Thankfully, the administrator understood the situation and funded the proposals.

For the second event, Pérez was able to secure some minimal funding from the MFA program's start-up funds. Álvarez had just started directing the Mexican American Studies program in her first year as an assistant professor and had a budget of $2000.00. However, her commitment to ensuring the students at UTPA know about Anzaldúa motivated her to secure $500 from the $2000 budget each year for the annual event. After faculty and students led a movement on campus for greater funding in 2012, the total CMAS budget increased significantly to $30,000 and Álvarez increased that permanent commitment of $2000 for El Retorno, which remains intact. In 2009, both Pérez and Álvarez would hustle for additional funding from the Department of Modern Languages and the Dean of the College of Arts and Humanities at different times. For the second event in 2009, with no administrative assistance whatsoever and a very limited budget, Verónica Sandoval and Álvarez somehow figured out how to feed everyone. While Emmy Pérez has taken the lead in organizing the campus event since 2008, the 2011 event was organized by Álvarez and her first Anzaldúa class as they created an exhibit for El Retorno. To date, there have been more than thirteen El Retornos celebrated at the University of Texas Pan American / Río Grande Valley.[5]

There was also great interest in Gloria Anzaldúa in the Philosophy Department, which was developing its focus in continental philosophy, Latin American philosophy, and feminism. In 2007, Philosophy faculty member Cory Wimberly began to contemplate a speaker series focusing on Gloria Anzaldúa and her theories. He held a meeting with faculty members Pérez, Álvarez, Ochoa, and Guadalupe Cortina to get their feedback. In 2008 the series was formalized and the naming rights secured from the trust for two years by Adriel Trott. When the naming rights were acquired, it was very clear that the series was limited to issues pertaining to Anzaldúa's work, which was construed broadly in terms of race, gender, border theory, intersectionality, queer studies, and political philosophy. Acquiring the rights through the trust would be quite simple as they supported the idea. However, getting the approval from the university would prove to be extraordinarily difficult in terms of both bureaucracy and a lack of understanding why anyone would want to name the series after Gloria Anzaldúa if she had not donated any money. Nevertheless, on October 9, 2009, The *Gloria Anzaldúa Philosophy Series* hosted its first talk by Gregory Papas of Texas A&M, College Station, titled "Being in the Border is an Opportunity and Not a Fall from Grace." The series has hosted one to two talks per year since 2009 and received funding consistently from Philosophy and the Center for Mexican American Studies. On other occasions, funding has come from

5 For a complete list of events please see Appendix 1.

CAVE (Center Against Violence and Ethics), LGBTQ Alliance, and the Office of the Provost. From 2008–2013, Adriel Trott organized the series and from 2013–2019, Cinthya Paccacerqua did so.[6]

LA GLORIA GETS HER OWN CLASS

Another area in which El Valle has attempted to make an impact in honoring Anzaldúa is in the classroom and with the collaboration of Río Grande Valley student activism. As mentioned previously, many professors on campus teach her works in their classes. However, in November of 2010, a group of Chicana Graduate students petitioned for assistant professor of Spanish Stephanie Álvarez to teach a single author course on Gloria Anzaldúa (Álvarez et al.). These students were in her Spanish course on the Nuyorican poet Tato Laviera. The group was led and organized by Orquidea Morales, now herself an assistant professor of American Studies at University of Arizona. Álvarez said that she could probably offer this in the fall, or maybe the summer. However, students insisted that this was not an option as they were graduating, and so it needed to be done in January. Álvarez doubted the likelihood of it being approved. Nevertheless, she told them if they could get ten students they could likely petition the Chair, Glenn Martínez, to offer the course. Martínez, a sociolinguist and Valley native, also studied Anzaldúa and was never one to get in the way of student learning. He was always flexible and creative when it came to helping faculty and students and approved the course. Álvarez was not scheduled to teach that semester because she had had a teaching overload the previous semester. Nevertheless, she knew what this meant to her students. This would be the first-ever course solely on Anzaldúa taught at the institution. We find it extremely important to also document the efforts of students of color, especially of Chicana students, for as Carlos Muñoz Jr. states, "the work of New Left scholars in the 1980s continued to promote the false image that history centered on white radical middle-class youth" (14). Student activism, especially non-white student activism, has continued to be erased, whitewashed, and neglected in multiple realms when in reality they have been spearheading diversity, equity, and inclusion efforts in academia since the 1960s, before these initiatives became institutionalized.

Using a decolonial approach to teaching, Álvarez asked students to collaboratively design the syllabus the first day of class. After all, they wanted the class, so what did they want to get out of it? Aside from the traditional readings one might gather from a typical graduate seminar and *pláticas*, what emerged were the same desires expressed by GAL and Pérez; to create more awareness among the

6 For a complete list of talks hosted by the Gloria Anzaldúa Philosophy Series, including the presenters and their titles, please see Appendix 2.

community about Anzaldúa, her ideas, and in particular, her poetry. What could they do to make that happen? The class then settled on the creation of an exhibit for the public as part of the university's annual FESTIBA: Festival of International Books and Art. The exhibit consisted of posters with quotes from Anzaldúa's *Borderlands / La Frontera: The New Mestiza* paired with glifos found in her archives, posters of poems from the same book, displays of her books, a computer playing music videos that students felt connected to Anzaldúa's work, a look book, a comment book, and a poster featuring three of her yearbook pictures from Pan American University, making it obvious to everyone that she had attended the university herself. On opening night, the students and Álvarez spoke about Anzaldúa and read from *Borderlands*. It was a very emotional evening and some students could not get through their readings. The exhibit lasted five days and numerous professors indicated that they had taken their students to the exhibit. Some fifty-five people left comments, all positive, in la libreta de comentarios. The posters remained up until 2016. The event opened the door for future courses on Anzaldúa at UTPA (Marci McMahon in 2011, Cinthya Saavedra in 2018, Cynthia Paccacerqua in 2020). In 2018, a stand-alone course was proposed by Stephanie Álvarez and was accepted unanimously by the Graduate Studies council as MASC 4335: Gloria Anzaldúa remains in the course catalog today.

OUT OF THE IVORY TOWER AND BACK INTO THE PUBLIC SPHERE

In 2007, Suarez obtained a position at the McAllen Public Library where she currently serves as their marketing coordinator. Her influence on the discussions, vision, and events at the library are deeply felt throughout the community. In the last five years, there has been an explicit attempt on behalf of the McAllen Public Library to make Anzaldúa's legacy visible. The first began subtly in 2015, when Dr. Cathryn Merla-Watson from the University of Texas Río Grande Valley and poet César L. de León were invited to deliver a workshop on Queer Poetics. In it, participants explored the intersecting issues of gender, sexuality, race, and identity in the work of local queer Chicanx poets, including (but not limited to) Anzaldúa, de León, and José Antonio Rodríguez. Focused on themes of trauma and healing, the workshop was facilitated as a Socratic seminar. After the workshop there was an open-mic session with de León in which participants shared their poetry. Then, in 2018, to commemorate the thirtieth anniversary of the publication of *Borderlands / La Frontera: The New Mestiza*, the library held an event titled Honoring Gloria Anzaldúa: World Renowned Author & Icon. They invited professors Álvarez, Paccacerqua, Pérez, and Mariana Alessandri to remember the importance of Gloria Anzaldúa's writings, to raise cultural awareness about its contents, and to celebrate Anzaldúa's legacy. Suarez also led the effort to create a dynamic page on the library's website dedicated to

Anzaldúa's life, work, and legacy (McAllen). More recently, in the summer of 2019, the library hosted Gloria Anzaldúa: Poetry and Postcards, during which the public was invited to learn about Anzaldúa's life and writing. Verónica "Lady Mariposa" Sandoval, then a PhD Candidate at Washington State University, gave this presentation as part of her own return home for several weeks with an Aunt Lute-sponsored residency.[7] Following the presentation, guests had the opportunity to write postcards to Gloria and share them.

REMEMBRANCE AND CELEBRATION: *BORDERLANDS* ANNIVERSARY AT UTRGV'S CENTER FOR MEXICAN AMERICAN STUDIES

In 2017–2018, the CMAS at UTRGV chose to dedicate all of its programming to honor Anzaldúa given that it was the thirtieth anniversary of the publication of *Borderlands / La Frontera: The New Mestiza,* as per Álvarez's vision in the summer of 2017. The yearlong series of events, titled Nuestra Gloria: CMAS Celebrates the 30th Anniversary of the Publication of *Borderlands / La Frontera: The New Mestiza*, sought to put Anzaldúa front and center in all pláticas and work for the year. The Interim Director of the Center, Zulmaris Díaz, fully supported the initiative and a committee of mostly mujeres was formed to undertake the task. Álvarez, Alessandri, Paccacerqua, Saavedra, De Luna, Pérez, Amanda Tovar, and Lupe Flores led the committee. Events were taking place all over the country. For example, the Smithsonian's Latino Center event convened a panel called "Remembering Gloria Anzaldúa" on October 7, 2017, featuring ire'ne lara silva, Raquel Gutiérrez, and AnaLouise Keating. Google honored her with a Google doodle on her birthday. While many institutions engaged in a single event to honor the thirtieth anniversary of Anzaldúa's landmark publication, no others would go on to celebrate it for an entire year (Álvarez, Tovar, Alessandri 2019). On her birthday, the CMAS at UTRGV celebrated their yearlong series with cake and a plática where students, faculty, staff, and the community were invited to share the ways in which Anzaldúa's work had impacted their lives, work, attitudes, and relationships. Surprisingly, some of Anzaldúa's family came to the event and were so pleased to see young people, in particular, talk about what Anzaldúa meant to them.[8] The yearlong celebration ended with El Retorno featuring Noemi Martínez, who spoke about the GAL Project and shared her poetry, as well as other speakers.

---

7 This library event was open to the public, but Sandoval's community-based work also included poetry workshops supported by Aunt Lute and an AKR grant. Please see her essay on the Queering Cuentos project in this same volume of SSGA's *El Mundo Zurdo* conference proceedings.

8 The activities that took place that year are listed in Appendix 3.

Figure 4. Poster for Nuestra Gloria kickoff event. Artwork: Celeste de Luna, ca. 2009 Graphic design: Arnulfo Daniel Segovia.

MAKING ANZALDÚA: QUEERNESS FRONT AND CENTER IN EL VALLE

In May 2018, a Valley contingency attended El Mundo Zurdo at Trinity University. At the Esperanza Peace and Justice Center, many gathered to view the exhibit on Anzaldúa and hear a lovely concert. On this occasion, Stevie Luna, a Valley poet, was attending for the first time and upon seeing a photo of Anzaldúa holding a label that read "marimacha" over her forehead, they declared in awe, "I want to see more of that in the Valley. We don't talk about Anzaldúa's queerness enough." This coincided with another conversation at El Mundo

Figure 5. ***ANZALDÚA MARIMACHA*****, 2018**
The photograph was exhibited at the Esperanza Center in conjunction with El Mundo Zurdo, 2018.

Zurdo between de León and Pérez noting the same desire. Later that evening, Luna, Álvarez, and Poets Against Walls members Pérez, de León, and Gómez met at the locally owned and operated vegan restaurant La Botánica for dinner, a hub for cultural arts and queer space in San Antonio. There, it was agreed that they would act on the need. Poets Against Walls is a frontera collective that aims to "document and share communal stories from individual perspectives—through poetry, testimonio, and the spoken word—about life and social justice issues in the Texas borderlands and beyond" (McAllen). They had already reserved a booth, led by de León, for the Río Grande Valley Pride in the Park event that would take place in June. It was decided then that they would collaborate and take advantage of the opportunity to share their love for Anzaldúa with the queer community and its allies. This would be done in two ways. Inspired by the "marimacha" label, César L. de León, Stevie Luna, Stephanie Álvarez, Amaya Martínez Alvarez, Celina Gómez, Amanda Tovar, and Amanda Ramírez would make homemade lapel pins to give away. Descriptors like marimacha, jotx, joto, maricón, they, them, ellxs, she, and more, were combined with images in black and white, rainbow, and glitter. They used construction paper, contact paper, hot glue, a stapler, and safety pins.[9] Last, a beautiful zine titled *Pride del Valle* was created with quotes, biographic information, a beautiful print of De Luna's *Nepantla Lotería,* and illustrations by Stevie Luna and Amanda Ramírez. With additional contributions by Amanda Tovar, Stephanie Álvarez, Celina Gómez, and Emmy Pérez, the zine was distributed for free, along with the pins. Furthermore, Poets Against Walls displayed books by queer poets and writers from the Valley, encouraged event participants to contribute a line to a group poem inspired by Anzaldúa's poem "To Live in the Borderlands Means You," and raffled off free copies of Anzaldúa's books. Thousands of people attended the Pride in the Park event. The pins and zines did not last long, which demonstrated a renewed commitment to expanding awareness of Anzaldúa to a broader public in the Valley. Poets Against Walls shared more copies of the zine the following year.

Figure 6. Pins and the zine, *Pride in El Valle*, were distributed at El Mundo Zurdo, 2018. Zine artwork: Celeste De Luna, *Nepantla Lotería*, ca. 2018.

ESPERANZAS PARA EL FUTURO

In September 2018, Stephanie Álvarez applied for a Humanities Texas Community Grant to create a traveling exhibit about *Borderlands / La Frontera*

9 WAKE-UP (Womxn Artistically Kollecting Experiencias—Unidxs Prosperando) also created pins and distributed them at the same event. WAKE-UP is an all womxn poetry collective founded around 2013. They have routinely participated in various events honoring Anzaldúa.

based in large part on the class she previously taught. The inspiration came from knowing that many of the community members of the RGV still did not have access to her literature. However, we felt compelled to make her work accessible to teach them about the important contributions that the mujeres in their community have made to the world. Álvarez imagined an exhibit that could reach well over 2,000 people and let them know that one of the greatest authors of the twentieth century was a Mexican American woman from the Valley who wrote about their lives and their experiences, and graduated from Pan American College / UTRGV just like so many of them. Although noted Anzaldúa scholars such as Sonia Saldívar-Hull, Norma Elia Cantú, and Larissa Mercado-López agreed to serve as the humanities scholars for the $10,000 grant, it was not approved. A second attempt to secure grant funding was undertaken the following month, November 2017, by Emmy Pérez, Stephanie Álvarez, Mariana Alessandri, Cynthia Paccerqua, Amanda Tovar, and Arnulfo Segovia. This time, UTRGV had put out a call for proposals to fund projects that exemplified the university's strategic plan, which included becoming a B3 (bilingual, bicultural, biliterate) institution. This grant was to create

> a memorial on campus dedicated to the late scholar, writer, and artist Gloria E. Anzaldúa . . . [because] there is no better spokesperson for a bicultural, bilingual, biliterate university. Anzaldúa, a Río Grande Valley native and graduate of legacy institution Pan American College in 1968, significantly advanced these initiatives and theories, which honor the learning, knowledge, and creative worlds of Spanish, English, and Tex-Mex. She embodied the view that one's culture is an integral part of an affirming life and education (Avarez).

The grant did not seek to create a statue as, through the actions spurred by the Black Lives Matter movement to remove statues, we have come to see how problematic they can be. Instead, we collectively conceived of a memorial that "would embody the fact that Anzaldúa was a working-class, self-made scholar, and it would reflect many of her concepts, which include indigenous epistemologies, ways of healing, and writing that is highly visual: perhaps incorporating landscapes of snakes, desert flowers, and Southwest/Tejas iconography" (Pérez et al.). Nevertheless, this $10,000 grant request was not one of the ten funded projects. Yet, no perdemos las esperanzas that we will get necessary funding to make it happen. Future possibilities include full funding of the endowed scholarship in Anzaldúa's name founded by Pérez and working with the historical commission on the completion of the Gloria Anzaldúa historical marker.

Today we continue with our annual event and the graduate class has been taught another two times. Poet Amalia Ortiz, a former member of the collective WAKE-UP (see note 9) when she was an MFA student, returned to campus on

Anzaldúa's birthday in 2019 and performed her poetry. We continue to raise funds for the Anzaldúa endowed scholarship. Faculty members and graduate students have unsuccessfully applied for grants for a Gloria Anzaldúa memorial project and a traveling exhibit based on Álvarez's class. Last, we have been asked to help with the Anzaldúa historical marker as more documentation as to her importance to Texas history is needed. All the work is continued by mujeres. In 2000, around the time of Anzaldúa's last published piece, bell hooks admitted "there are not many public discussions of love in our culture right now" (xvii). With the turn of the new century, we continue to witness police brutality, mass incarcerations, unconstitutional lawmaking that prevents decent livelihoods for many, and objections to human decency—all of which have affected us as citizens of the world and have left many of us looking for discussions of love and healing. Which is why this essay, we hope, serves as a project of remembrance of the labor to honor Anzaldúa in her homeland, and of the many mujeres who have continued to keep this legacy alive. We ground this essay in love and "work that matters" with the hopes that we plant the seeds that will cultivate a more honest tomorrow.

POSTSCRIPT

More initiatives have taken place since this essay was completed, most notably a literary landmark. In late 2020, Mark Smith, director of the Texas State Library and Archives Commission and the State Librarian of Texas, contacted SSGA founder Norma E. Cantú about a possible literary landmark application opportunity, which led them to contacting Emmy Pérez at UTRGV CMAS. In early 2021, Cantú and Pérez co-wrote and applied to the Texas State Library and Archives Commission for a literary landmark to honor Anzaldúa at her alma mater. The application was selected in a competitive process for the Texas Center for the Book's 2021 Literary Landmark Roundup program. The Center for the Book then provided support for the next part of the application process to United for Libraries, a division of the American Library Association. In summer 2021, Cantú and Pérez received word that the application was selected by United for Libraries.

UTRGV CMAS, under the direction of Álvarez and Pérez, took the lead in organizing "El Retorno al Valle: Symposium on Anzaldúa and Literary Landmark Unveiling" along with a local planning committee and team. They also obtained numerous co-sponsors across campus, South Texas College, Trinity University, and Humanities Texas. It was a major event with pre-symposium activities the day before in Hargill and the Museum of South Texas History. For a complete list of presenters from El Valle and beyond, including poets, artists, scholars, and community activists, please visit https://sites.google.com/view/elretorno/home. The symposium and unveiling date changed a few times due to the pandemic, so while the landmark states Jan. 31, 2022, as the unveiling date, it was actually unveiled on March 28, 2022. It stands near the entrance to the UTRGV Library (Edinburg campus).

WORKS CITED

Álvarez, Stephanie. "El Retorno: Celebrating 30 Years of the Publication of Gloria Anzaldúa's *Borderlands / La Frontera*." Proposal to Humanities Texas. 15 Sept. 2017. Typescript.

Álvarez, Stephanie, Stephanie Brock, Janie Covarrubias, Lauren Espinoza, and Orquidea Morales, eds. "Gloria Anzaldúa, Nuestra gloria, nuestra heroína fronteriza / Our Glory(a), Our Borderlands Heroine: An Art Exhibit at Anzaldúa's alma mater, The University of Texas Pan–American." In *El Mundo Zurdo 3: Selected Works from the 2012 Meeting of the Society for the Study of Gloria Anzaldúa*. Aunt Lute Books, 2012.

Álvarez, Stephanie, Amanda Tovar, and Mariana Alessandri. "Nuestra Gloria: The Center for Mexican American Studies at the University of Texas Rio Grande Valley Celebrates the 30th Anniversary of the Publication of *Borderlands / La Frontera: The New Mestiza*." *Río Bravo: A Journal of the Borderlands* 24, Spring 2020. Archived at https://journals.tdl.org/rbj/index.php/rbj/article/view/34.

Anzaldúa, Gloria. *The Gloria Anzaldúa Reader*. Edited by Ana Louise Keating, Duke University Press, 2009.

Blackwell, Maylei. *¡Chicana Power! Contested Histories of Feminism in the Chicano Movement*. University of Texas Press, 2011.

Cotera, María. "Nuestra Autohistoria: Toward a Chicana Digital Praxis." *Toward a Critically Engaged Digital Practice: American Studies and the Digital Humanities*, a special issue of *American Quarterly* vol. 70, no. 3, Sept. 2018.

Garza-Johnson, Erika. "RGV Poet Erika Garza-Johnson on Gloria E. Anzaldúa's Influence," interview and poetry reading. Video by Emmy Pérez, recorded 14 May 2019. Poets Against Walls, Facebook.com, posted 15 May 2020.

hooks, bell. *all about love: New Visions*. Harper Perennial, 2000.

"In Memory: Gloria Evangelina Anzaldúa, 1942–2004. Web Altar for Gloria." http://gloria.chicanas.com. Last Revised 2 Oct. 2004, accessed 9 Aug. 2020.

Martínez, Noemi. Personal communication with Stephanie Álvarez. 20 Apr. 2020.

———. Personal archive. Accessed Aug. 9, 2020.

———. Presentation at El Retorno 2018. UTRGV Center for Mexican American Studies. Video by Emmy Pérez, recorded 15 May 2018. CMAS, Facebook.com, uploaded 16 May 2020.

Martínez, Noemi and Suarez, Priscilla "Lina." "This Bridge We Call Home: Finding Gloria Call for Submissions," www.caferevolucion.org; myspace.com/rememberinggloria. Accessed Jan. 13, 2020.

McAllen Public Library. LibGuide for Gloria Evangelina Anzaldúa. https://mcallen.libguides.com/anzaldua/home. Accessed 9 Aug. 2020.

Muñoz, Carlos Jr. *Youth, Identity, Power: The Chicano Movemen, Revised and Expanded Edition.* Verso. 2007.

Pérez, Emmy, Stephanie Álvarez, Mariana Alessandri, Cynthia Paccerqua, Amanda Tovar, and Arnulfo Segovia. Proposal to UTRGV "Transforming Our World Strategic Initiatives," Oct. 2017. Typescript.

"Poets Against Walls: Our Story." Poets Against Walls, Facebook.com, posted 30 June 2018; accessed Feb. 27, 2020.

Suarez, Priscilla "Lina;" "The Gloria Anzaldúa Legacy Project and the Beginnings of Honoring Anzaldúa en El Valle." El Mundo Zurdo. Trinity University, 19 May 2018, Trinity University, San Antonio, TX. Lecture.

———. Personal communication with Stephanie Álvarez, 12 Feb. 12, 2020.

———. Personal communication with Emmy Pérez, 9 Aug. 2020.

WORKS CONSULTED

Jiménez, Haydeé, and Elke Zobl. "Hermana Resist: 'Healing Communities by Writing' An Interview with Noemi Martínez," Feb. 2008. http://www.grrrlzines.net/interviews/hermanaresist.htm. Accessed 20 Feb. 2020.

Mercado-López, Larissa M., Sonia Saldívar-Hull, and Antonia Castañeda, eds. *El Mundo Zurdo 3: Selected Works from the 2012 Meeting of the Society for the Study of Gloria Anzaldúa*. Aunt Lute Books, 2013.

APPENDIX 1: EL RETORNO EVENTS

April 14, 2008
1st Annual El Retorno: El Valle Celebra Nuestra Gloria
Featured presenter: Norma E. Cantú
"Living en la Frontera: Gloria Anzaldúa and Border Theory," with a reading from *Canícula: Snapshots of a Girlhood en la Frontera*

May 15, 2009
2nd Annual El Retorno: El Valle Celebra Nuestra Gloria
Featured presenter: Norma Alarcón
Sponsored by UTPA's MAS, MFA Program, the GAL Project, and others
Held in Conjunction with SSGA El Mundo Zurdo Conference

May 26, 2010
3rd Annual El Retorno: El Valle Celebra Nuestra Gloria (not funded)
Emmy Pérez's Chican@ Poetry and Poetics Class reading from Anzaldúa's work
Including Erika Garza-Johnson, Verónica "Lady Mariposa" Sandoval, and other local poets
Valle de la Paz Cemetery in Hargill, Burial Site of Anzaldúa

March 29–April 2, 2011
4th Annual El Retorno: El Valle Celebra Nuestra Gloria
Gloria Anzaldúa: Nuestra gloria, nuestra heroína fronteriza / Our glory(a), our borderlands heroine.
Exhibit created, curated and installed by students and Professor Stephanie Álvarez as part of SPAN 6339, Special Topic: Gloria Anzaldúa. Possibly the first course focusing solely on Anzaldúa at UTPA. Taught when students petitioned for the class. Part of FESTIBA 2011.

May 16, 2012
5th Annual El Retorno: El Valle Celebra Nuestra Gloria
Featured presenter: Aída Hurtado
"Gloria Anzaldúa's Geographies of the Soul"
Held in Conjunction with SSGA El Mundo Zurdo Conference

March 8, 2013
6th Annual El Retorno: El Valle Celebra Nuestra Gloria
Featured presenter: Carmen Tafolla
"A Celebration of Gloria Anzaldúa's Essay How to Tame a Wild Tongue"

Held in conjunction with the Spanish in the US Conference

April 24, 2014
7th Annual El Retorno: El Valle Celebra Nuestra Gloria
Featured speaker: Inés Hernández-Avila
Opening by Local Poets and Artists

May 27, 2015
8th Annual El Retorno: El Valle Celebra Nuestra Gloria
Featured speaker: Sonia Saldívar-Hull
Opening performances by local poets and musicians
Symposium in collaboration with SSGA El Mundo Zurdo Conference and UT Austin Center for Mexican American Studies

March 21, 2016
9th Annual El Retorno: El Valle Celebra Nuestra Gloria
Featured speaker: ire'ne lara silva
"Grito Writing Workshop: Finding the Sources of Our Voices," with poetry reading
Opening performances by WAKE-UP and other local poets

November 1, 2016
10th Annual El Retorno: El Valle Celebra Nuestra Gloria
Held in conjunction with SSGA El Mundo Zurdo Conference
Visit to Anzaldúa's Grave at Valle de La Paz

May 5, 2017
10.5 "El Retorno: El Valle Celebra Nuestra Gloria"
Yerberia Cultura in downtown McAllen.
Release of *Imaniman : Poets Writing in the Anzaldúan Borderlands* and featuring additional books by borderlands poets whose work is influenced by Anzaldúa.
Featured readers: Noemi Martínez, Erika Garza-Johnson, Carolina Monsiváis, David Bowles, Rodney Gomez, José A. Rodríguez, César de León, McAllen Poet Laureate Priscilla Celina "Lina" Suarez, and more.
Featured artists included Celeste de Luna and Verónica Cárdenas.

May 16, 2018
11th Annual El Retorno: El Valle Celebra Nuestra Gloria
María Herrera-Sobek
Luncheon and Symposium

Conjunto Los Cardenales of La Roma High School
Visit to El Valle de la Paz Cemetery
"El Valle: 30 Years After *Borderlands / La Frontera*: Nepantlerxs Comprometidxs con el Conocimiento"
Presentations by la Comunidad, Local Poets, Artists, Activists and Scholars
Held in conjunction with the Anzaldúa Philosophy Speaker Series and in collaboration with SSGA Mundo Zurdo Conference.

April 27, 2019
12th Annual El Retorno: El Valle Celebra Nuestra Gloria
Featured speaker: Randy P. Connor
"An Anzaldúan Triptych: Presentation and Community Plática"
Cosponsored by CMAS & Río Grande Valley International Poetry Festival

May 15, 2020 and May 18, 2020
13th Annual El Retorno: El Valle Celebra Nuestra Gloria
Part I: Video Presentation by Lina Suarez
Posted on May 15, 2020, on Facebook, Center for Mexican American Studies page.
Part II: "Work that Matters: Jotería Celebration"
Roundtable, with César L. De León, Stevie Luna, Amanda Victoria Ramírez, and Victor Leo Cruz; moderated by Verónica Sandoval (recorded on May 18, 2020 and video released on CMAS Facebook page Aug/Sept. 2020)
Sponsored by the Center for Mexican American Studies

APPENDIX 2: GLORIA ANZALDÚA PHILOSOPHY SERIES PRESENTATIONS

October 9, 2009
Gregory Pappas, Texas A&M University, College Station
"Being in the Border is an Opportunity and Not a Fall from Grace"

November 19, 2009
Leigh Johnson, Rhodes College
"Heroes, Scapegoats and 'Good' Liberals: The Complicated Operations of Race in Post-Obama America"

February 4, 2010
Shannon Winnubst, Ohio State University
"Queers Have No Passports: On the Floating Borders of Nationalism"

October 7, 2010:
Jennifer Suchland, Ohio State University
"Post-Cold-War Borders: Linking the Postcolonial and Postsocialist"

February 17, 2011
Christopher Lauer, Indiana University of Pennsylvania
"Beauvoir and Nancy on Touching and Borders"

March 3, 2011
Mariana Alessandri, Cynthia Paccacerqua, and Alexander Stehn, UTPA
"The Many Borders of the Valley: First Impressions."

November 8, 2012
Robin Henderson-Espinoza, University of Denver.
"Un estilo mestizaje: Tracing Ethical Intuitions in Anzaldúa"

March 21, 2013
Jennifer McWeeny, Worcester Polytechnic Institute
"The Colonial, Catholic Body: Identity and Self-Relation in Mexican and Irish Diasporas"

November 21 & 22 2014
Pedro Di Pietri, University of California, Berkeley.
"Loving Sideways / Living Beyond Borders: Decolonizing Space in Xicana &

Latina Feminisms."
"La Jotería: Celebrating Queerness and Latinidad in the 21st Century," workshop

March 24, 2015
Aída Hurtado, University of California, Santa Barbara
"Redefining Latino Masculinities through Anzaldúa's Conocimiento and Collaborative Testimonio"

April 6, 2015
Julie Avril Minich, University of Texas, Austin
"Vulnerable Bodies and Environmental Justice in the Murals of Juana Alicia"

October 13, 2016
Omar Rivera, Southwestern University.
"Shamanic Bodies: Alcoff, Anzaldúa, Kusch, and Adean Corporalities"

April 26, 2019
Jeff Morrisey
"What's in an Image? Time, Tension, and Art's Relation to the Structure of Experience"

APPENDIX 3: NUESTRA GLORIA: CMAS CELEBRATES THE 30TH ANNIVERSARY OF THE PUBLICATION OF BORDERLANDS / LA FRONTERA: THE NEW MESTIZA

September 26, 2017
¡Feliz Cumpleaños, Gloria Anzaldúa!

October 11, 2017
Nuestra Gloria Kickoff Event, with Aída Hurtado

November 29, 2017
Ballet Nepantla

December 13, 2017
Nuestra Gloria Graduate Research Symposium

January 25, 2018
"Poetry as Conocimiento: What We Learn from the Poetics of Anzaldúan Theory," with Lauren Espinoza

January 26, 2018
Anzaldúa Plática Marathon

February 27, 2018
FOLD, with Mariana Alessandri

March 29, 2018
Women Workers at the Frontline of the Development of the Fuerza del Valle Workers Center

April 3, 2018
Anzaldúa Speaker Series in Philosophy Presents: "Gloria Anzaldúa's Radical Contributions to 21st-Century Thought," with AnaLouise Keating

April 2018
"Anzaldúa in the Elementary Schools: Reading, Trilingualism and Transculturation through Anzaldúa's Children's Literature," with Amanda Tovar and Stephanie Álvarez

May 16, 2018
11th Annual El Retorno: El Valle Celebra Nuestra Gloria, with María Herrera-Sobek

USING ANZALDÚAN THOUGHT TO DECOLONIZE THE TEACHING OF COMPOSITION, LITERATURE, AND CREATIVE WRITING AT A HISPANIC-SERVING INSTITUTION

CANDACE K. DE LEÓN-ZEPEDA

I recall the first time I heard the phrase "Hispanic-Serving Institution" (HSI) while enrolled in an English graduate program at Texas A&M University–Corpus Christi. The course was Introduction to Bibliography and Research and my White professor introduced our campus designation as an "HSI," which she explained only meant that our university enrolled a growing number of Latinx students. There was no further discussion on this topic and no effort was made to make this conversation a teachable moment (considering it was a research course). After this brief experience, I was left with too many questions: Do HSI's hire more Latinx faculty than predominantly White institutions (PWIs)? Do HSI's support existing or new culturally relevant programming or courses? As a first-generation and Chicanx student, this experience would leave a lasting effect on me and my scholarship, which continues to draw attention to HSIs and question if they are truly serving Latinx students in the classroom.

In this chapter, I introduce why and how I use Anzaldúan thought to construct/deconstruct a required English graduate course, English 7333: Teaching Composition, Literature, and Creative Writing. Before doing so, however, I contextualize the *why* and begin with a discussion focused on my campus and its designation as an Hispanic-Serving Institution. Beyond the common knowledge that HSIs are federally funded colleges and universities with at least 25 percent or more total undergraduate, full-time equivalent Latinx student enrollment, most Latinx academics are not paying attention to how fast these schools are growing. In 2002, the time I first learned of HSIs, there were only 219 designated, but in 2020, there are 523 HSIs with 328 Emerging Institutions and an average Latinx enrollment of 46 percent (HACU). This tremendous growth rate of 238 percent should surely suggest that HSIs are leading in efforts to recruit and retain faculty who are committed to culturally relevant pedagogies, programming, and curriculum designed to serve Latinx students. Evidently, this is not the case. The National Center for Education Statistics continues to reveal that Latinxs make up only 3 percent of full-time faculty at universities and colleges nationwide and of that number, Latinx females account for only 1 percent (U.S. Department of Education, 2019). Even though institutions of higher education are attempting to make recruiting faculty of color a priority, the reality is their efforts are slow to improve the underrepresentation of Latinx faculty in universities and colleges.

As a Chicanx Associate Professor who is both tenured and a department chair, I recognize both my privilege and responsibility as one among the 1 percent. I use this knowledge in all areas of my life as a scholar-activist, administrator, mentor, and professor of English in a rather small Catholic Liberal Arts and Hispanic-Serving Institution situated in the heart of Westside San Antonio, Our Lady of the Lake University (OLLU). OLLU was founded in 1895 by the Sisters of the Congregation of Divine Providence whose pursuit for social justice and bringing education to marginalized communities played a significant role in shaping OLLU's mission and is evident in our vision statement which calls attention to our "expertise in Mexican American culture." One item of pride about our campus is that 78 percent of our undergraduates and 51 percent of our graduates define themselves as Hispanic/Latino (Fall 2019 Facts). Considering our institutional culture and history, it is not surprising that OLLU is recognized as the birthplace of the Hispanic Association of Colleges and Universities (HACU), which led the effort to formally recognize and federally fund HSIs. I introduce this institutional information for two purposes. First, I am guided by principles to be mindful of our institutional legacy and HSI status to serve students who historically have been marginalized in the academy. Second, I am committed to adopting culturally relevant pedagogies and diverse curriculum for our large Latinx student population. Academic curriculum must be revisited and reconceptualized often in order to ensure that it is equitable and not a "conduit for whitestream epistemologies and values" (de los Ríos 3). Given my identity, the classroom space provides an opportunity for me to incorporate literature and voices that work to "recover and restore counterhistorical narratives as well as the epistemologies, perspectives, and cultures of those who have been historically marginalized and denied full participation within traditional discourses and institutions" (de los Ríos 3). One such voice whose work provides a theoretical perspective and dialogue for decentering Eurocentric curricula is Chicana feminist, Gloria Anzaldúa.

WHY ANZALDÚA?

In an interview with composition theorist Andrea A. Lunsford, Anzaldúa harshly criticized the field of English as reinforcing hegemonic practices of standard English and guided by Eurocentric pedagogies. When Anzaldúa was asked in the interview if her philosophies could be taught, she said yes and called on new theories that would decolonize the normative classroom. She envisioned an "alternative model" (Anzaldúa, *Interviews* 261) that would be grounded in liberatory pedagogies designed to empower student agency.

As a Chicanx rhetorician, I am called to raise consciousness and draw attention to the scholarly contributions of voices of color whose work addresses pedagogical approaches to teaching students of color. My advocacy as a Chicanx scholar can be witnessed in the theoretical design of all my curricula,[1] which attempts to emulate the spatial, cultural and racial identity of our university campus, our HSI designation, and our student demographic. When designing a course or curriculum, I often turn to Chicana feminist theory, but I find that Anzaldúan theories are the most challenging to adopt for many teachers. For instance, nepantla, nepantilism, or nepantlera might be understandable as a Náhuatl concept, a literary reference, or theoretical perspective; yet I frequently hear advocates of Anzaldúa's work question how to develop nepantla (or her other theories) in order to build a curriculum or a major assignment.

It is for this purpose that I want to make Anzaldúa's theories approachable for faculty who are teaching at HSIs and who are interested in redesigning a course. I turn to the Coyolxauhqui imperative as an accessible theory when reconstructing any class that requires a historical or Eurocentric gaze, such as English 7333: Teaching Composition, Literature, and Creative Writing, commonly known to students as Pedagogy & Theory.

The Coyolxauhqui imperative is described by Anzaldúa as a heuristic "to heal and achieve integration." It is her "symbol for the necessary process of dismemberment and fragmentation," and "for reconstruction and reframing, one that allows for putting the pieces together in a new way" (*Light* 19–20). In this process of healing,

1 Examples of other courses I teach that use Anzaldúan thought in their design include: Composition I, Composition II, Mexican American Literature, Grant Writing, Professional and Technical Writing, Visual Rhetoric, Latina Feminist Thought, and Pedagogy and Theory.

> Coyolxauhqui personifies the wish to repair and heal, as well as rewrite the stories of loss and recovery, exile and homecoming, disinheritance and recuperation, stories that lead out of passivity and into agency, out of devalued into valued lives. Coyolxauhqui represents the search for new metaphors to tell you what you need to know, how to connect and use the information gained, and, with intelligence, imagination, and grace, solve your problems and create intercultural communities (Anzaldúa, *This Bridge* 143).

Her call to construct/deconstruct in order to "create intercultural communities" is an ambitious tool to utilize when studying and historicizing any academic discipline, particularly the fields of English, literature, and writing studies. These areas of study are historically rooted in the "values and tastes of a particular social class" (Eagleton 15, 21–22). This Eurocentric and elitist ideological framework, which determined what literature was valued or what was good writing, was reinforced by academics who "treated knowledge as if it were limited to what was contained in a relatively small body of [literary texts], and the knowledge required to produce more texts of a similar (if not equal) kind" (Shumway and Dionne 5). With the shift of English departments in the 16th century from the study of Classical philosophy to literature, the need to replicate the elite canon of the academy became a common teaching practice and students were often seen as deficient in the scholastic knowledge generated by those in power. By the 1800s, writing studies (more historically recognized as Composition) grew in popularity with the first textbooks to teach standards of writing to include grammar and the modes of discourse (Connors 71–72; Pullman 17). More than two centuries later, these approaches to writing and literature continue to dominate traditional English departments as is evident by required canonical courses and the expectations of standard academic writing.

Reflecting on my own academic training in the field of composition, it included a more historical (and often homogeneous) approach to the teaching of writing. In core classes focused on pedagogy and theory, great attention was placed on male and Anglo theorists, while a small handful of multicultural theorists[2] were considered recommended readings. My professors and mentors felt it pertinent to study, for instance, the historical scholarship of Robert Scholes who historicizes English departments as existing to teach students how to achieve the wholeness of writing mobility that "models the grace, clarity, and energy that [they] admire in literary texts" (34); or, we studied David Bartholomae who studied academic-discourse assimilation in "Inventing the University" and

2 These additional theorists included a few scholars like Gloria Anzaldúa, Victor Villanueva, bell hooks, Lisa Delpit, and Mike Rose.

his belief that students must "learn to speak our language, to speak as we do . . . [in] our community" (624). Not once did my graduate seminars provide a multicultural response to these or other scholars who presented a homogeneous approach to teaching writing. Absent from "the field of study" were scholars who looked like me and wrote about the classroom space from the perspectives of either first-year students, students of color, or any marginalized student who rarely saw themselves reflected in the curriculum. And, I was not alone in these thoughts as the few students of color in my cohort would notice the absence of scholars who looked like us or shared similar experiences of feeling shamed in the writing classroom. Author of *Reclaiming Composition for Chicano/as and other Ethnic Minorities*, Iris Ruiz, shares my sentiments as she reflects on her time in a traditional English graduate program. Ruiz writes:

> Reading Composition histories and scholarship is like reading Shakespeare. I can't see myself, and, oftentimes, I can't see my friends or those who look like me. We don't look like the authors who wrote them. We are not white men. I can't see my history. It's buried in there somewhere, they tell me, but where? (1)

Like her, I also held on to the few scholars of color I could find who wrote about culturally relevant curriculum and pedagogies including bell hooks, Victor Villanueva, and Gloria E. Anzaldúa. These and other scholars of color saw me, my culture, my community, and my language and encouraged me to contribute to changes in the canonical field of writing studies, particularly since writing underscores every discipline in the university, especially all genres in English departments.

It wasn't until I was introduced to the scholarship of Gloria Anzaldúa and other Chicana feminists that I was able to find the answers I was seeking regarding the teaching of writing at HSIs. Anzaldúa's theories decenter the role of the instructor and draw attention to students' epistemologies and home-based literacies. Anzaldúa's scholarship provides a pedagogical approach for educators to reconsider traditional methods of instruction and transgress all the rigid boundaries of academic spaces including teacher–student dynamics. But, rarely is her work studied solely for its pedagogical tools when teaching writing, literature, or creative writing.

The Coyolxauhqui imperative provides a heuristic for reimagining ourselves and, I argue, bodies of thought birthed from a colonial narrative. Anzaldúa is calling attention to our own identity as broken and marginalized people, yet I interpret the Coyolxauhqui imperative as a tool to also reinterpret or reread fields of study, like English, in order to provide a new identity.

I applied the Coyolxauhqui imperative as my theoretical framework when reimagining English 7333: Teaching Composition, Literature, and Creative

Writing because it was crucial to introduce these fields through a decolonial and postmodern lens. By framing the course from this perspective, I could emphasize the significance of developing a pedagogical awareness when teaching at Hispanic-Serving Institutions with diverse student demographics. As a curricular theory, the Coyolxauhqui imperative, for me, serves three purposes. First, I confront hegemonic bodies of thought in the field of English in order to deconstruct their underlying linguistic or racial motives and instead turn to "nontraditional places" (Saldívar-Hull 46) for theories and pedagogies. Second, to identify alternative approaches to teaching writing or literature for students of different racial and ethnic racial backgrounds. Third, to reenvision or construct classrooms where students feel empowered by their cultural and linguistic identities. By deconstructing/constructing pedagogical thought for graduate students who hope to be future English teachers or professors, my desire is that they reevaluate how best to serve all students who feel disempowered in the college writing classroom or literature course.

ABOUT OUR MA-MFA PROGRAM

In 2012 our department revitalized our existing MA program and launched our MA-MFA in Literature, Creative Writing and Social Justice. Our program's mission prepares students to

> become critically engaged and socially aware scholars, writers, educators and professionals. This unique program is designed to attract and foster the growth of individuals who wish to combine creativity with practical skills and critical knowledge, all while keeping in mind the pursuit of social justice in their own work, their communities and their professional practice (MA-MFA English).

Although our program is by all standards still in its infancy, it continues to attract a majority of Latinx students who are drawn to our social justice mission and relatively diverse graduate faculty[33]. Since my appointment as the first Chicana chair of our department in 2017, my effort has been focused on decolonizing English 7333, which prepares students to teach in universities, community colleges, or high school classrooms that are situated in South Texas or at HSIs. The original graduate course included a survey of canonical approaches to teaching writing with no efforts to include diverse approaches to teaching students of color or the significance of teaching at HSIs. It is for this reason that I was inspired to disrupt students' knowledge about the body of scholarship focused on teaching writing or literature.

---

3 As of spring 2020, our graduate faculty includes three Latinxs, one African American, and two Whites.

THE SYLLABUS

I began with deconstructing/constructing the syllabus, beginning with the course description. It now explains that the course will examine nontraditional theories and pedagogical practices that can be used when teaching composition, literature, and creative writing at secondary and collegiate levels, with an emphasis on teaching at Hispanic-Serving Institutions or Latinx populations. The course is intentionally and theoretically grounded in writing studies and academic literacy from a (de)colonial and postmodern lens. This framework, I argue, invites a richer understanding and critique of the history of English, literature, and writing studies that will shape students and pedagogy in all courses and disciplines. I ask students to reflect on this question: What does it mean to decolonize the classroom? I borrow Shannon Morreira's and Kathy Luckett's assertion that the "curriculum is not just the 'stuff' that students must learn to be knowledgeable and skilled in a particular discipline. It's about more than just content. Sociologists of education argue that 'curriculum' is a highly ideological, hybrid discourse. This means that it includes implicit ways of knowing, ways of doing, and ways of being—as well as content" (Morreira and Luckett). The first page of the syllabus draws on Morreira's and Luckett's series of ten "crucial questions" to guide a richer discussion on "hidden curriculum" when building a curriculum. I adopted and modified language to pose six Arching Semester Questions that guide discussions, assignments, and lectures:

1. What do we (Composition, Literature, Creative Writing professors) value about writing?

2. How are these values reflected in the pedagogical approaches we are reviewing and who do our values serve?

3. How are these pedagogical theories and approaches developed? Who develops them?

4. How do we respond to particular historical and cultural exigencies in the construction of our classroom and with our selection of texts?

5. How are these pedagogical theories and approaches complicated or extended by new media technologies? Or, by changing notions of literacy?

6. How are these pedagogical theories and approaches complicated or mediated by institutional constraints (e.g., HSI designation, student population, etc.)? By issues of gender/race/class/sexuality/difference? By other factors?

I explain that, by the end of the semester, students should have a deeper understanding of several culturally relevant pedagogical movements. They should also begin to develop a sense of which pedagogical theories most directly influence and shape their own teaching philosophy when working with diverse student populations or at Hispanic-Serving Institutions.

REQUIRED READINGS

In order to reconstruct the identity of English, it was critical to still evaluate the history of the field, but I did so with students reading such texts alongside scholars of color and from a postcolonial and Chicana feminist gaze.[4] To explain, every text by a non-scholar of color would be framed by the following critiques: What are the limitations of this text? What voices does it exclude? Would this scholarship work for diverse student populations or be guiding principles when teaching at Minority Serving Institutions (to include HSIs and HBCUs)? A good example of how I frame this curricula design is the list of first mandatory readings students must cover. For obvious reasons, it includes Gloria Anzaldúa's "Let us Be the Healing of the Wound: The Coyolxauhqui Imperative—La Sombra y el Sueño" (Anzaldua, *Light*) but also: Lisa A. Flores, "Creating Discursive Space Through a Rhetoric of Difference: Chicana Feminists Craft a Homeland;" Yvette Dechavez's op-ed piece, "It's Time to Decolonize the Syllabus;" and Katy Waldman's "The Canon is Sexist, Racist, Colonialist, and Totally Gross. Yes, You Have to Read it Anyway."

Flores's article explains why the concept of space and crafting a home are common themes in Chicanx writing. She writes that Chicanx literature "cross[es] rhetorical borders through the construction of a discursive space or home. By employing a rhetoric of difference, [writers] construct an identity that runs counter to that created for them" (Flores 143). In a new spatial identity, they can "break down constraints imposed by other cultures and groups" (Flores 143). I recall the first time I read Flores's article (written in 1996) and how much it influenced my draw to spatial theory. Although Flores is discussing literary spaces, her attention to safe spaces, a search for home, and the notion

4 Required texts also include: *Guide to Composition Pedagogies,* 2nd edition, Gary Tate, Amy R. Taggart, et. al; *Teaching to Transgress: Education as the Practice of Freedom,* bell hooks; *Chicana/Latina Education in Everyday Life,* Bernal, et. al.; *Composition-Rhetoric: Backgrounds, Theory and Pedagogy,* Robert Connors; *Sentipensante (Sensing/Thinking) Pedagogy: Feminista Perspectives on…,* Laura Rendón; *The Rise and Fall of English: Reconstructing English as a Discipline,* Robert Scholes; *Literary Theory: An Introduction,* Terry Eagleton; *Cross-Talk in Comp Theory: Reader,* ed. Victor Villanueva; *The Courage to Teach,* Parker Palmer; *Bootstraps: From an American Academic of Color,* Victor Villanueva; *Reclaiming Composition for Chicano/as and Other Ethnic Minorities: A Critical History and Pedagogy* (recommended), Iris Ruiz.

that discursive spaces can affirm one's identity can be applied to curriculum design. Discussion questions related to this article include:

1. How do we create safe spaces in the classroom where students can feel empowered to share their own literacies, or experiences?

2. What assignments can we create that invite students to craft their own discursive spaces?

3. What kinds of assignments can we create that build bridges and invite students to cross metaphoric borders between the academy and home?

4. Why is this important when working with undergraduates, first-generation students, or Latinx populations?

The next two articles work well together in conversation as they draw attention to the more recent and ongoing conversation about decolonizing the syllabus. Dechavez's article, written in 2018, reflects on her experience as a student who encountered "the occasional person-of-color text." Eventually earning her PhD in literature, she vows to decolonize the syllabus by including only writers of color in her curriculum. She writes: "Academia, like most institutions, has long allowed White men to define the American story. Every year, students take class after class in which White writers dominate the syllabus, and students of color walk away feeling like that's all that matters, like their voices are unimportant." Her message is clear; it matters that students see themselves reflected in the curriculum. On the other hand, Katy Waldman's article responds to events at Yale where, in 2016, undergraduates aimed to decolonize their English department's curriculum. Waldman adds the counterargument that in order to "become well versed in English literature, you're going to have to hold your nose and read a lot of White male poets." She argues that English majors are responsible for reckoning with such Eurocentric or hegemonic literature to "transcend their failures." Discussion questions related to these articles include: Can a canonical course like Shakespeare be decolonized? If so, how? How can we apply Anzaldúa's notion of the Coyolxauhqui imperative to such normative literature courses without simply making them into ethnic studies?

I want to be clear that I interpret the Coyolxauhqui imperative as not only the absence of what is broken or flawed situated with the conjunction of what is new, but the balance of both existing together. Rather than eliminate all normative theories or pedagogies in the fields of English literature or writing studies, I include them in my curriculum, but situate these antiquated approaches next to scholars of color and their scholarship, which are excluded in similar courses. This reenvisioned identity of the field, dismembered and fragmented yet put together in a new way, provides a hopeful future for graduate students entering the field.

MEANS OF ASSESSMENT

Three assignments that I have crafted for English 7333—which demonstrate how I apply Anzaldúan thought—are Key Terms, Teaching Philosophy, and the Dream Class.[55] Drawing on Lisa Flores's notion of discursive spaces, it is critical that students understand terminology directly or indirectly related to the field, with the goal that they can deconstruct existing discourse in order to construct new language using their own words.

> **Key Terms:** Considering the nature of the readings this semester, you might find yourself struggling to grasp a new term, theory, or concept. Each student will adopt three key terms during the semester. You are expected to investigate each of your adopted terms before the relevant class discussion. The goal of this activity is for students to begin to familiarize themselves with new terms, theories, or concepts, and to find meaning in the text by contextualizing it with current issues or new language. In two to three pages, students will define the adopted term, theory, or concept and present them to the class. Every student is responsible for circulating their term to the class.

In the most recent semester, students selected an array of terms such as: decolonize, colonize, post-process, grammar, homogenize, feminist theory, post-colonial, language arts, cultural, canon, literacy, eco-composition, Eurocentric, hegemony, digital literacy, etc. Students share these defined/redefined terms with their classmates and we openly discuss them in class. It is often an empowering experience for students, many who identify as first-generation graduate Latinx students, when they discuss their selected term. I have heard students express some of the following sentiments of which I took note in a recent semester: "This word used to be scary to me," "I have a new perspective on the term," "I feel like I have control of this term in my own voice now." This tangible example of the Coyolxauhqui imperative can provide a long-lasting effect for students entering the field because it equips them with a sense of ownership of contentious language that they can deconstruct/construct for themselves.

The second assignment to highlight is Teaching Philosophy. The purpose of such a document is reflective and typically includes a statement about an individual's teaching beliefs or practices, including concrete examples. Although this is a necessary document for those on the job market, I deconstruct/construct this assignment to also include a strong diversity statement. Diversity statements are relatively new documents required in some job applications with the purpose of illustrating an applicant's commitment to inclusivity, equity, and diversity.

---

5 Other major assignments include Article Analysis, Job Market Analysis with formal presentation, and a Teaching portfolio.

> **Teaching Philosophy:** Your teaching philosophy should be at least a two-page statement of the theory or theories that will guide the way you teach college composition, literature, or poetry. Elaborate on how that theory would play out in practice by recognizing the student demographic you will serve, the region where the school is located, or campus designation (ex. HSI). You are expected to include your commitment to diversity and inclusion with concrete examples of the literature, scholarship, or theoretical movements you support. Each teaching philosophy is unique and should reflect on the following fundamental questions: Why do you teach? What do you teach? How do you teach? How do you measure your effectiveness? And, your focus on diversity should answer the following questions: What does diversity, equity, or inclusion mean to you? How do you work to ensure your classes are inclusive? How does your research, scholarship, or creative writing draw attention to underrepresented populations?

This assignment asks students to be intentional with how they would enact diversity by their curricular and pedagogical choices. Although most students are not employed as teachers, or have never taught, this assignment prepares them for the reality of today's job market.

THE DREAM CLASS

One of the most popular assignments is "the dream class," which requires students to put to practice the literature, theories, and class conversations. I encourage students to review a survey of syllabi in our discipline and determine how they align with their teaching philosophy or diversity statement. I draw on my own sampling of syllabi to illustrate how I deconstruct/construct courses and my efforts to always include voices of color for readings and films or through my use of intentional-language choices in my assignment handouts or activities.

> **The Dream Class:** You will develop an original syllabus for a dream class, and you must also include a sample of a Major Assignment with an associated rubric. The Major Assignment should cover approximately four weeks of instruction and include learning outcomes, a thorough description, representative assignments, any handouts, and purpose. The associated rubric should address all the major elements that will be assessed by you. The purpose of this assignment is to provide you an opportunity to apply the theories, concepts, and strategies we have discussed to a specific pedagogical context. You are strongly encouraged to develop this Assignment for a class you are teaching or would like to teach in the future.

In the most recent time I taught the class, I admired students' creative efforts with this assignment and their understanding of the Coyolxauhqui imperative.

A few astounding examples include: a) English 7xxx: A Xicanx Theopoetix: Storytelling as Survival; b) Creative Fiction: Healing Your Past through Writing, a course intended for currently incarcerated or recently released prisoners who are women of color; and c) English 4xxx: Topics in Latin American Studies: Narratives of Race, Place, and Space in Reggaeton and Latin Trap Music. It is through their sharing of work where I am quite truthfully overcome with emotion and pride that I, in a small way, am shaping the future of the professoriate with educators who are committed to decolonizing the discipline and serving a diverse student population.

SUMMARY

Anzaldúa's theories invite us, as Latinx scholars and educators, to reclaim and reinscribe ourselves (*Light*, 189) into the Euro-imagination. It is this process of making/unmaking and deconstruction/construction that becomes the *remedy* and moves us toward healing and liberation. Hartley explains in "The Curandera of Conquest: Gloria Anzaldúa's Decolonial Remedy" that

> the Chicana's process of recognizing and purging herself of this internalized alien and constantly self-damning perspective and replacing it with a positive, re-indigenized self-orientation is the primary act of decolonizing that Anzaldúa's writings make possible. In this way she provides the remedy for the root cause of the many symptoms of the colonized selfhood (136).

Due to the erasure of Latinx voices from the traditional canon or curriculum, the "symptoms" faced by so many Latinx faculty include experiences of shame, self-doubt, anxiety, depression, fear, or anger. Many of these experiences contribute to our emotional exhaustion in our pursuit to transform educational spaces, be it through our scholarship, creative writing, mentoring of Latinx students, our teaching practices, or curriculum design.

In reflecting back to my experiences as a graduate student enrolled at a Hispanic-Serving Institution, I frequently felt unwelcomed, resulting in my silence and feelings of inferiority; many times, I considered dropping out. It was not until I enrolled in a graduate English course on Chicana Feminism that I was introduced to the work of Gloria Anzaldúa and reminded that my experiences and that of my culture were valuable. I saw myself reflected in the curriculum, which inspired me to continue searching for other voices of color who shared my cultural experiences. In my time as a graduate student, it was this one graduate course that kept me from closing the door of education and ultimately inspired me to pursue a doctoral degree with the ambition to decolonize the field of English. In pursuing my PhD, it was the work of Chicana feminists and Anzaldúa that encouraged me to "transform pedagogical and institutional practices" (*Reade*r 204). Today, I find myself wanting a different experience for my graduate students than what I endured. Pedagogically, I am committed to "change how students and teachers think and read by deconstructing Euro-Anglo ways of knowing" and create classroom spaces that "reflect the needs of the world community of women and people of color" (*Reader*, 205).

Clearly, HSIs need to drastically improve their efforts for recruiting Latinx faculty who share my call to transforming educational spaces. Knowing that I am among the 1 percent of Latina faculty, I am driven to motivate my graduate students to reimagine the discipline of English and their role in higher education. Adopting Anzaldúa's Coyolxauhqui imperative when redesigning English 7392: Teaching Composition, Literature, and Creative Eriting supports my call for the fields to undergo an ideological transformation and broaden the study of language, literacy, literature, and writing to include a multicultural and postcolonial concentration on the ways students read, write, research, and respond to texts stemming from their lived experiences.

WORKS CITED

Anzaldúa, Gloria. *The Gloria Anzaldúa Reader*. Edited by AnaLouise Keating, Duke University Press, 2009.

——— *Interviews: Entrevistas*. Edited by AnaLouise Keating, Routledge, 2000.

——— *Light in the Dark: Luz En Lo Oscuro: Rewriting Identity, Spirituality, Reality*. Edited by AnaLouise Keating, Duke University Press, 2015.

Bartholomae, David. "Inventing the University." *Cross-Talk in Comp Theory: A Reader*. 2nd ed., edited by Victor Villanueva. National Council of Teachers of English, 2003, pp. 623–53. Print.

Connors, Robert J. *Composition-Rhetoric: Backgrounds, Theory, and Pedagogy*. University of Pittsburgh Press, 1997.

Dechavez, Yvette. "It's Time to Decolonize that Syllabus." *Los Angeles Times*, 8 Oct. 2018, https://www.latimes.com/books/la-et-jc-decolonize-syllabus-20181008-story.html. Accessed 17 Feb. 2020.

de los Ríos, Cati V. "A Curriculum of the Borderlands: High School Chicana/o-Latina/o Studies As Sitios y Lengua." *Urban Review*, vol. 45, no. 1, 2013, pp. 58–73, doi:10.1007/s11256-012-0224-3.

Eagleton, Terry. *Literary Theory: An Introduction*. 2nd ed., Blackwell Publishing, 1996.

"Fall 2019 Facts at a Glance." OLLU Facts and Figures, https://www.ollusa.edu/about/_resources/2019-facts-at-a-glance.pdf. Accessed 17 Feb. 2020.

Flores, Lisa A. "Creating discursive space through a rhetoric of difference." *Quarterly Journal of Speech* vol. 82.2, 1996, p. 142. *Communication & Mass Media Complete*. EBSCO. Web. 8 Feb. 2011.

HACU, Hispanic Association of Colleges and Universities. "Hispanic-Serving Institution (HSI) Fact Sheet: 2017–2018," https://www.hacu.net/hacu/HSI_Fact_Sheet.asp.

Hartley, George. "The Curandera of Conquest: Gloria Anzaldúa's Decolonial Remedy." *Aztlán: A Journal of Chicano Studies*, vol. 35, no. 1, 2010, pp. 135–161.

MA-MFA English. Our Lady of the Lake University, 17 Feb. 2020, ttps://www.ollusa.edu/cas/programs/ma-mfa-english/index.html.

Morreira, Shannon and Luckett, Kathy. "Questions academics can ask to decolonize their classrooms." *African Skies*, Nov. 2018. Retrieved from https://folukeafrica.com/questions-academics-can-ask-to-decolonise-their-classrooms/?fbclid=IwAR3cAWVuq_WRTrQJYbrvQNS0wmTxFlHEOMDKzGUDm3xDS6vXvybqy6O6p4I. Accessed 17 Feb. 2020.

Pullman, George. *Stepping Yet Again into the Same Current. Post-Process Theory: Beyond the Writing-Process Paradigm.* Edited by Thomas Kent, Southern Illinois University Press, 1999, pp. 16–29.

Ruiz, Iris D. *Reclaiming Composition for Chicano/as and Other Ethnic Minorities: A Critical History and Pedagogy.* Palgrave Macmillan, 2016. Accessed 17 Feb. 2020.

Saldívar-Hull, Sonia. *Feminism on the Border: Chicana Gender Politics and Literature.* University of California Press, 2000.

Scholes, Robert. *The Rise and Fall of English.* Yale University Press, 1998.

Shumway, David R., and Craig Dionne, eds. *Disciplining English: Alternative Histories, Critical Perspectives.* State University of New York Press, 2002.

Waldman, Katy. "The Canon is Sexist, Racist, Colonialist, and Totally Gross. Yes, You Have to Read It Anyway." *Slate*, 24 May 2016, https://slate.com/human-interest/2016/05/yale-students-want-to-remake-the-english-major-requirements-but-there-s-no-escaping-white-male-poets-in-the-canon.html. Accessed 17 Feb. 2020.

TOWARDS A NEW CONSCIOUSNESS

ON THE REVOLUTIONARY POWER OF LATINAS IN ACADEMIA

CHELSEA R. BARRON DÁVILA-CONAWAY AND JACQUELINE CANTÚ CONTRERAS

Latinas' existence in academic spaces is revolutionary. Rooted in feudal systems of power, the academy represents a mechanism of a pillar of cultural and political hegemony insofar as it perpetuates colonial capitalism and systematically excludes marginalized persons who resist academic culture (Sefa Dei and Kempf 1–24). As tools of sociopolitical dominance, academic spaces often emphasize hegemonic Euro-American narratives and epistemes that maintain power for non-racialized groups (hooks 111–118). Moreover, these spaces presuppose the universal superiority, objectivity, and scientific merit of colonial logics (Sefa Dei and Jaimungal 1–14). In doing so, academia systematically delegitimizes racialized and indigenous epistemologies and onto-epistemologies, which may contribute to a sense of hostility and alienation for Latinas at all levels of academia. The devaluation of indigenous onto-epistemologies dispossesses racialized populations of their unique intellectual assets. Further, this cognitive and cultural despotism contributes to academic inertia in which a Euro-American epistemic framework is espoused as singularly meritorious and scientific.

Despite the hostility toward racialized scholarship and identity, Latina scholars continue to flourish at the junction between Latina identity and academic culture. This essay will conceptualize first-generation Latinas' experiences in academia within the context of Anzaldúa's *borderlands theory*. The authors seek to describe the experiences and *mestizaje* power of Latina scholars by drawing connections between personal experience and existing scholarship. Moreover, in el espíritu de nuestras antepasados activistas, the authors will provide recommendations for Latina scholars and White allies to support a collective movement toward a new consciousness.

EXPERIENCES OF LATINA STUDENTS

In exasperating discussions regarding educational experiences, the authors have examined the lack of Latina representation in academia. Despite attending Hispanic-Serving Institutions exclusively, the authors have experienced disproportionate Latina representation both in the student body and among the professoriate. This underrepresentation became particularly salient as the authors moved into their graduate studies. Recent Latinx scholarship reflects these experiences. In fact, despite significant growth of the Latinx population in the United States over the past decade (Flores; United States Census Bureau), Latinas remain underrepresented at all strata of academic attainment, particularly at the graduate level (González 291–292). The dearth of Latinas in academic spaces may contribute to the perpetuation of disempowering and disaffirming educational experiences.

Classroom Experiences. In addition to a paucity of peers with similar racial and ethnic backgrounds, Latina students endure a myriad of experiences that castigate their cultural identities (González 294–297). The American academy assumes the curricular relevancy of White scholarship, while offering non-White perspectives as optional supplements to core and required coursework (hooks 111–118). Furthermore, pedagogical praxes in higher education are often geared toward White students' ways of learning, thinking, and connecting (hooks 111–118).

In her groundbreaking work on critical pedagogy, hooks argued that the lack of cultural connection with both course content and the classroom experience precipitated feelings of alienation and disconnection among racialized students (35–44). Throughout the first author's experience as a philosophy undergraduate student, not a single Latinx philosophical text was assigned, suggested, or discussed. Moreover, at the undergraduate and graduate level, both authors cherished the few Latina (and often adjunct) instructors they encountered. We longed for tenure-track Latina role models and mentors. We craved scholarship and pedagogical praxis that would awaken our transcendental and cultural subjectivities. We cringed and exchanged glances when instructors failed to acknowledge anti-Latinx microaggressions in the classroom. In addition to the covert mechanisms of disaffirmation described above, Barron Dávila-Conaway's and Cantú Contreras's academic experiences underscore the need to transform academic praxes that delegitimize expressions of Latina identity. In congruence with hooks' description of bilingual students' classroom experiences, the authors have felt peers' and instructors' unease when speaking Spanish in the classroom (35–44). Moreover, physical representations of Latina identity are often subjected to microaggressions, arousing feelings of shame, alienation, isolation, and rage in the authors. These experiences reinforce the notion that Latina and academic identities are intrinsically incongruent, obliging Latinas in the academy to consistently negotiate between expressions of identity and perceived academic legitimacy. As a result of similar experiences, many emerging Latina scholars question their place in doctoral programs and consider quitting due to the lack of support and pressure to assimilate into White academic culture (González 294–297). Unfortunately, Latina faculty encounter similar challenges.

EXPERIENCES OF LATINA FACULTY

Latinas are significantly underrepresented among the professoriate (González 291–292). Latinas held only 2.2 percent of full-time faculty positions in degree-granting colleges and universities in the United States in 2016 (National Center for Education Statistics). This lack of representation among the tenure-track professoriate may fuel the racism, White privilege, sexism, and other exploitations of power that Latina faculty encounter. Examining narratives and experiences of Latina faculty is critical insofar as it will contribute to a broader understanding of Latinas' academic experiences.

Cultural Taxation. Amado Padilla coined the term *cultural taxation* to describe the phenomenon whereby racialized faculty are tasked with additional and often non-tenure-supporting workplace responsibilities (26). These obligations frequently include serving on a disproportionate number of committees, advising a larger proportion of students compared with White peers, and serving as a de facto departmental spokesperson for diversity issues. In a qualitative study on Latinas and Black women holding full-time faculty positions, Joseph and Hirshfield found that cultural taxation persists in contemporary academic settings (125–138). Black women and Latina faculty are often expected to engage in race-related projects and research (Joseph and Hirschfield 125–138). This stereotype often provokes invitations to serve on diversity committees, teach ethnic-focused courses, and advise racialized students regardless of one's scholarly interests. Black women and Latina faculty are pressured to act as diversity experts in their departments, and Joseph and Hershfield's participants noted that little attention or merit was afforded to their non-diversity-related comments, concerns, and interests. Moreover, this group has also reported feeling burdened to point out diversity issues in their departments due to the invisibility of these concerns to their White peers (Joseph and Hirshfield 125–138).

Differential Legitimacy. Joseph and Hirshfield expanded the concept of cultural taxation to include differential legitimacy, which refers to the pressure to prove the merit of one's work and validity of one's qualifications (125–138). Latina faculty encounter challenges to their work and qualifications from both peers and students. Contemporary literature demonstrates that Latina faculty experience challenges to their merit and professionalism, assumptions of under-qualification, scholarly devaluation, and racial microaggressions (Delgado-Romero et al. 257–283; Sulé 174–178). Latinas who experience these aggressions often feel that they must work harder than White peers to receive similar respect and recognition (Laden and Hagedorn 60–61). Additionally, differential legitimization pressures Latina faculty to verbally and non-verbally communicate legitimacy in the classroom and in their departments (Joseph and Hirshfield 125–138; Sulé 174–178). In one qualitative study, several Black women and Latina faculty expressed that maintaining academic and professional legitimacy necessitates the abandonment of authentic cultural expressions in favor of conformity to Euro-American norms and expectations (Sulé 174–175).

Academic Culture. The multilevel systems of subordination and disempowerment that pollute the academy exacerbate Latinas' experiences of cultural taxation and differential legitimization. In addition to racism, sexism, classism, and other mechanisms of disempowerment, resentment of and resistance to divergent cultural praxes, accents, last names, and languages mar the experiences of Latina faculty (González 294–297). These processes impact hiring practices, tenure and promotion decisions, and the overall experiences of racialized scholars (González 291–292; Urrieta et al. 1155–1163). These experiences compounded with a lack of support, scarcity of Latina mentors, and experiences of overt racism and microaggressions have a profound impact on Latina faculty (Urrieta et al. 1155–1163). Moreover, experiences of tokenism and White peers' denial of race and diversity issues can provoke feelings of isolation and second-class membership in academic departments (Joseph and Hirschfield 125–138; Urrieta et al. 1155 1153). The hostility described above demonstrates the need to conceptualize Latinas' academic experiences from a theoretical framework grounded in Latinx epistemologies and cultural values. The authors assert that borderlands theory provides a framework for understanding and processing these experiences.

BORDERLANDS THEORY

Latinas' experiences in academia can be conceptualized within the framework of Anzaldúa's borderlands theory. Anzaldúa described a borderland as a physical and psychosocial space that exists at the junction between two cultures (42–44). These hostile, ambiguous spaces are occupied by a dominant group whose members wield power and control as tools of subjugation and disempowerment. Pushed away by both dominant and mother culture, the delegitimized (those who are 'othered') experience rejection, alienation, isolation, and insecurity, resulting in social and cultural insecurity (Anzaldúa 23–45). Within the borderlands, only members of the dominant culture and those who align with them are granted political and sociocultural legitimacy (Anzaldúa 42–44).

Border dwellers live in a constant state of fear and transition. They are hybridized such that they belong to neither the oppressors nor the oppressed. They exist in dualistic cultural contexts and receive contradictory messages and rejection from the worlds they straddle. Those who have been delegitimized must identify mechanisms for coping with life in this hostile and unwelcoming territory (Anzaldúa 42–45). The contemporary Latina copes with life in the borderlands by embracing flexibility and ambiguity. She is tolerant of uncertainty and contradictions. Her pluralistic personality enables her to flourish in the sordid dichotomy of her environment (Anzaldúa 99–113). She has developed *mestiza* consciousness, or "an identity that is fluid, resilient, and oppositional" (Delgado Bernal et al. 126).

THE BORDERLANDS OF ACADEMIA

The experiences of Latina scholars can be conceptualized as a borderland between Latina and academic identities. Too academic for *la raza,* she is accused of being uppity, acting White, and thinking she is all that. Too Latina for academia, she is told to dress more professionally, stop speaking Spanglish, and manage her sensitivity to racialized issues. She is not fully embraced by either culture. She may perceive her only chance for success in academic culture as assimilation and alignment with Whiteness. Her existence in this borderland is wrought with transitions, contradictions, and fear. However, Anzaldúa described contemporary Latinas as resilient catalysts for change (99–113). She asserted that Latinas in the borderlands possess knowledge as the *outsider within*, and draw on expertise and experience from both cultures as a source of strength. *Mestiza consciousness* enables Latina scholars to adapt to contradictory, ambiguous, and changing environments, remain resilient in the face of rejection and delegitimization, and remain steadfast in opposition to threats to their power and legitimacy.

TOWARDS A NEW CONSCIOUSNESS

Despite challenges at every level of the academy, Latina students and faculty, in true *chingona* fashion, consistently demonstrate persistence and resilience (Gloria and Castellanos 87–92; Urrieta et al. 1163–1166).

Contemporary Latina scholars are moving beyond the cultural shame and self-doubt that White-normative academic culture works tirelessly to instill. Instead, they are using their strength as border dwellers to disrupt the systems that seek to disempower them.

Sulé noted that Latina faculty are employing critical pedagogies and integrating critical race theory into their work to meet the needs of diverse students (177–178). Moreover, Latina scholars are increasingly rejecting paradigms of mentorship created by and for White academics. Latina mentors are replacing traditional modes of mentorship with novel, Latina-created models that are congruent with Latinx epistemes and identity (Brunsma et al. 6–10; Ek et al. 543–549; Figueroa and Rodríguez 25–27; Murakami and Nuñes 289–297; Villaseñor et al. 54–60). For example, recognizing the unique challenges Latina faculty encounter in the tenure process, a group of Chicana scholars developed *muxerista* mentoring, which leverages Latinas' social capital while acknowledging cultural and institutional barriers (Ek, et al. 344–349).

Additionally, Latina scholars are utilizing nontraditional modes of scholarship, such as counter stories—from critical race theory—to challenge dominant narratives (García 261–262). Recent Latinx scholarship supports the notion that Latinas are diverging from the dominant culture and acting as catalysts for academic change. These acts of resistance and disobedience are demonstrative of Latina scholars' recognition of the strength in their status as outsiders within the academy. In the following section, the authors provide recommendations for Latina scholars to progress toward a new and empowered consciousness.

RECOMMENDATIONS FOR LATINA SCHOLARS

Show up and show out. Engaging in verbal and nonverbal proclamations of Latina identity sends an affirming message to Latinx and non-Latinx peers alike. Moreover, doing so asserts our right to take up academic space and express ourselves authentically in professional environments. Put on your gold hoops. Draw on your eyebrows. Speak Spanish in classrooms and faculty meetings. Rock your huaraches. These subtle acts of resistance normalize Latina presence and challenge the White-normative standards of professionalism and academic legitimacy. It is time to let the academic world know: *aquí estamos y no nos vamos; nosotras estamos aquí.*

Mentorship is another avenue for Latina resistance in the academy. Villaseñor and colleagues contend that Latina-to-Latina mentorship is imperative for academic success (54–60). Mentorship can have a positive impact on the educational and professional attainment of Latina undergraduates (Ek et al. 543–549), graduate students (Brunsma et al. 6–7), and faculty members (Murakami and Nuñes 289–297). Recent Latinx scholarship suggests exploring and utilizing mentorship models that emphasize Latina epistemologies and experiences and de-emphasize mentees' assimilation with Whiteness. In addition to mentors, the authors advise Latina scholars to utilize familial support (Villaseñor et al. 56–62).

Family is a central component of Latinx culture. Although many Latinx parents are ill-equipped to provide guidance on specific academic challenges, the authors encourage Latina scholars to use family as a source of support. Cavazos, Johnson, and Sparrow found that familial support and encouragement is a significant strength for Latina scholars (312). Additionally, evidence indicates a strong correlation between Latinas' academic achievement and parental support (Gandara 175–178). The authors suggest that Latina scholars maintain positive familial connections and reach out to these individuals during times of stress, doubt, and isolation.

Finally, as a means of successfully navigating borderlands, Anzaldúa recommends transcending dualistic modes of thinking. She rejects thinking that reinforces an us/them mentality (99–113). From this perspective, Latinas in the academy can reflect on their own conceptualizations of academia and address dualities in their thoughts. Resist the notion that Latina and academic identities are mutually exclusive. One can exist wholly and comfortably in each culture without the need to reject the other.

RECOMMENDATIONS FOR WHITE ALLIES

Latinas possess the power to disrupt and enact change in the academy. Furthermore, as persons in power, White allies can use their privilege to assist Latinas in this process. The authors recommend that White scholars reflect on and examine feelings of defensiveness, resentment, and resistance that Latina narratives arouse. Acknowledge these responses and explore the ways that they may impact your allyship and interactions.

As members of a collectivist culture, Latinas thrive in environments that allow the expression of cultural identity and meaningful connection with others. Therefore, it is imperative that academic departments cultivate a culture of inclusion. An inclusive campus culture enables Latinas to effectively navigate postsecondary institutions (Tovar et al. 173–174). The authors encourage White allies to organize events that celebrate Latinx culture on campus. Hosting these celebrations will demonstrate acceptance of Latina students and foster Latina-to-Latina connections. This inclusive approach will establish on-campus Latina networks and assist Latina scholars in normalizing their experiences in academia.

As discussed above, Latinas frequently encounter barriers to academic and professional attainment (Holloway-Friesen 123–127). Latinas are more likely than other groups to experience microaggressions (Yosso et al. 667–673) and oppression (Hurtado and Ponjuan 243–248), which can have an adverse impact on the mental health of this population (Sue et al. 355–359). The authors recommend that White allies work to prevent the perpetration of anti-Latinx microaggressions and oppression by discussing power, privilege, and cultural differences within institutions. Creating a safe space for students and faculty to reflect on their beliefs, stereotypes, and biases may contribute to a culture of awareness and self-reflection. If a Latina encounters these adverse experiences in the academy, the authors recommend that White allies cultivate a welcoming and safe space for these women to share their experiences.

Finally, the authors recommend that White allies honor divergent ways of thinking, learning, and existing. To do so, the authors recommend that White allies examine dominant beliefs about how students learn and how academics communicate professionalism. Remain open to the idea that there are different ways to exist in and navigate academia. Further, maintain a critical perspective on the culture and expectations in classrooms and academic departments. Inspect the scholarship assigned in classes and the cultural diversity of the professoriate. Consider how these experiences may impact Latina students and faculty.

CONCLUSION

The academy is an imperialist system that employs various mechanisms of subordination and exploitation that delegitimize Latina identity. These power structures impact academia at all levels, from pedagogical approaches in the classroom to professorial hiring practices (Coleman 764–765; hooks 111–118). White-normative academic culture has an adverse impact on Latina students and faculty and obliges them to endure additional burdens and barriers that White scholars do not encounter (Joseph and Hirschfield 125–138; Padilla 26).

These experiences can be understood within the framework of Anzaldúa's borderlands theory. From this perspective, Latinas inhabit the borders of Latina identity and academia. They maintain plural, hybridized personalities and encounter resistance and rejection from both the dominant and mother culture. However, existence in multiple cultural contexts empowers Latinas with dual insight and the power to define their existence. Further, residence in this borderland fosters the development of the *mestiza consciousness*, which engenders resilience and tolerance for change.

It is imperative that Latinas in the academy draw on the work of contemporary Latina scholars working to challenge existing systems of domination. Engaging in acts of solidarity with Latina scholars and resistance against White-normative culture will empower Latinas to disrupt the systems of subordination that disempower them. Latinas, therefore, maintain the power to effect change in the academy and pave the way for a new Latina scholar.

WORKS CITED

Anzaldúa, Gloria. *Borderlands: The New Mestiza.* 4th ed., Aunt Lute Books, 2012.

Brunsma, David L., David G. Embrick, and Jean H. Shin. "Graduate Students of Color: Race, Racism, and Mentoring in the White Waters of Academia." *Sociology of Race and Ethnicity,* vol. 3, no. 1, 2017, pp. 1–13.

Cavazos, Javier, Michael B. Johnson, and Gregory S. Sparrow. "Overcoming Personal and Academic Challenges: Perspectives from Latina/o College Students." *Journal of Hispanic Higher Education,* vol. 9, no. 4, 2010, 304–316.

Coleman, Major G. "Racism in Academia: The White Superiority Supposition in the 'Unbiased' Search for Knowledge." *European Journal of Political Economy,* vol. 21, 2004, pp. 762–774.

Delgado, Bernal, Dolores C. Alejandra Elenes, Francisca E. Godinez, and Sofia Villenas. *Chicana/Latina Education in Everyday Life: Feminista Perspectives on Pedagogy and Epistemology.* SUNY Press, 2006.

Delgado-Romero, Edward A., Lisa Y. Flores, Alberta M. Gloria, Patricia Arredondo, and Jeanett Castellanos. *The Majority in the Minority: Expanding the Representation of Latina/o Faculty, Administrators and Students in Higher Education.* Stylus, 2003.

Ek, Lucila D., Patricia D. Quijada Cerecer, Iliana Alanís, and Mariela A. Rodríguez. "'I Don't Belong Here': Chicanas/Latinas at a Hispanic-Serving Institution Creating a Community Through *Muxerista* Mentoring." *Equity & Excellence in Education,* vol. 43, no. 4, 2010, pp. 539–553.

Figueroa, Julie L., and Gloria M. Rodriguez. "Critical Mentoring Practices to Support Diverse Students in Higher Education: Chicana/Latina Faculty Perspectives." *New Directions for Higher Education,* vol. 171, 2015, pp. 23–32.

Flores, Antonio. "How the US Hispanic Population is Changing." Pew Research Center, https://www.pewresearch.org/fact-tank/2017/09/18/how-the-u-s-hispanic-population-is-changing/. Accessed on 13 Sept. 2019.

Gandara, Patricia. "Passing Through the Eye of the Needle: High-Achieving Chicanas." *Latina Journal of Behavioral Sciences,* vol. 4, no. 2, 1982, pp. 167–179.

García, Alyssa. "Counter Stories of Race and Gender: Situating Experiences of Latinas in the Academy." *Latino Studies,* vol. 3, no. 2, 2005, pp. 261–273.

Gloria, Alberta M., and Jeanett Castellanos. "Desafíos y Bendiciones: A Multiperspective Examination of the Educational Experiences and Coping Responses of First-Generation College Latina Students." *Journal of Hispanic Higher Education,* vol. 11, no. 1, 2011, pp. 82–99.

González, Juan C. "Surviving the Doctorate and Thriving as Faculty: Latina Junior Faculty Reflecting on Their Doctoral Studies Experiences." *Equity & Excellence in Education,* vol. 40, no. 4, 2007, pp. 291–300.

Holloway-Friesen, Holly. "Acculturation, Enculturation, Gender, and College Environment on Perceived Career Barriers Among Latino/a College Students." *Journal of Career Development,* vol. 45, no. 2, 2018, pp. 117–131.

hooks, bell. *Teaching to Transgress: Education as the Practice of Freedom.* Routledge, 1994.

Hurtado, Sylvia, and Luis Ponjuan. "Latino Educational Outcomes and Campus Climate." *Journal of Hispanic Higher Education,* vol. 4, no. 3, 2005, pp. 235–251.

Joseph, Tiffany D., and Laura E. Hirschfield. "'Why Don't You Get Somebody New to Do It?': Race and Cultural Taxation in the Academy." *Ethnic and Racial Studies,* vol. 34, no. 1, 2011, pp. 121–141.

Laden, Berta V., and Linda S. Hagedorn. "Job Satisfaction Among Faculty of Color in Academe: Individual Survivors or Institutional Transformers?" *New Directions for Institutional Research,* vol. 2000, no. 1, 2000, pp. 57–66.

Murakami, Elizabeth T., and Anne-Marie Nuñez. "Latina Faculty Transcending Barriers: Peer Mentoring in a Hispanic-Serving Institution." *Mentoring & Tutoring: Partnership in Learning,* vol. 22, no. 4, 2014, pp. 284–301.

National Center for Education Statistics. "Full-Time Faculty in Degree-Granting Post-secondary Institutions, By Race/Ethnicity, Sex, and Academic Rank: Fall 2013, Fall 2015, and Fall 2016." https://nces.ed.gov/programs/digest/d17/tables/dt17_315.20.asp. Accessed on 10 Sept. 2019.

Padilla, Armando M. "Ethnic Minority Scholars, Research, and Mentoring: Current and Future Issues." *Educational Researcher,* vol. 23, no. 4, 1994, pp. 24–27.

Sefa Dei, George J., and Cristina Jaimungal. *Indigeneity and Decolonial Resistance.* Myers Education Press, 2018.

Sefa Dei, George J., and Arlo Kempf. *Anti-Colonialism and Education.* Sense Publishers, 2006.

Sue, Derald W., David Sue, Helen A. Neville, and Laura Smith. *Counseling the Culturally Diverse: Theory and Practice.* John Wiley & Sons, 2019.

Sulé, Venice T. "Restructuring the Master's Tools: Black Female and Latina Faculty Navigating and Contributing in Classrooms Through Oppositional Positions." *Equity & Excellence in Education,* vol. 44, no. 2, 2011, pp. 169–187.

Tovar, Esau, Merrill A. Simon, and Howard B. Lee. "Development and Validation of the College Mattering Inventory with Diverse Urban College Students." *Measurement and Evaluation in Counseling and Development*, 42, 2009, pp. 154–178.

United States Bureau of the Census. "Hispanic Heritage Month 2018." https://www.census.gov/newsroom/facts-for-features/2018/hispanic-heritage-month.html. Accessed on 18 September 2019.

Urrieta, Luis, Lina Méndez, and Esmerelda Rodríguez. "'A Moving Target': A Critical Race Analysis of Latina/o Faculty Experiences, Perspectives, and Reflections on the Tenure and Promotion Process." *International Journal of Qualitative Studies in Education,* vol. 28, no. 10, 2015, pp. 1149–1168.

Villaseñor, María J., María E.Reyes, and Imelda Muñoz. "*Mujerista* Mentoring for Chicanas/Latinas in Higher Education." *Journal of College Student Retention,* vol. 15, no. 1, 2013, pp. 49–64.

Yosso, Tara J., William A. Smith, Miguel Ceja, and Daniel G. Solorzano. "Critical Race Theory, Racial Microaggressions, and Campus Racial Climate for Latina/o Undergraduates." *Harvard Educational Review,* vol. 79, no. 4, 2009, pp. 659–691.

THE TROJAN BURRA MULA OF GLORIA ANZALDÚA

CHARACTERIZING THE OTHER AND FACING CHALLENGES IN EDUCATION

ERIKA ZAVALA

While scholars discuss interdisciplinarity in a variety of ways, this work attempts to integrate the concept as a philosophy that intersects multiple disciplines and students' interests and constructs knowledge existing beyond disciplinarity. In this essay, I explore the work of Gloria Anzaldúa as it encompasses vast categories related to art, literature, and education. Her work identifies her as a Chicana writer, poet, theorist, feminist, and more. However, this essay refers to her as Latinx/Chicanx in nonbinary ways and as a part of the inclusion of all Hispanics, Latinos(as), and those considered Chicanos(as) in the United States. As such, her artistic and literary vocation is a direct example of a Latinx who managed to surpass significant social obstacles and, at the same time, overcome challenges in higher education.

In this platform, the Gloria Evangelina Anzaldúa Papers, housed in the Benson Latin American Collection archives at the University of Texas at Austin, hold interesting artifacts of her life, such as ID cards, medical records, and poems, songs, and blueprints. And in so doing, create an exhibit of cultural and literary Latinx heritage. Anzaldúa's litero-artistic phase offers a significant contribution to academic scholarship because art and writing are tools for others to witness the world we live in. Likewise, Anzaldúa's writings underscore their importance as a knowledge-making source. Thus, among her art and as part of a social transformation and responsibility to Latinx knowledge and education, Anzaldúa makes a call to knowledge, to reading/writing, and to education; further, she advises that acquiring these fundamentals are examples that offer authority/power in the social world.

Therefore, this paper explores feminist perspectives based on Anzaldúa's *Borderlands / La Frontera* and the subaltern theory in Gayatri Spivak's writing that underscores the need for visibility for people in third world countries who are often viewed as the *Other*. Similarly, this essay reconceptualizes and interprets the metaphor of the *Trojan Burra Mula* in which Anzaldúa offers a blueprint for transparency and the exposure of the subaltern woman and her challenges during her journey as a student in a hegemonic world.

LATINX CHALLENGES IN US EDUCATION

For many Latinx, the importance of completing a degree in a higher-education institution is more than a personal goal, obtaining a university diploma *es un sueño familiar*, a family dream. Those that come from the working class believe, and rightly so, that education can solve financial challenges and related issues in life. In the same manner, the authors of "Locked Doors, Closed Opportunities: Who Holds the Magic Key" express that "[h]igher education is a principal pathway of access to the economic and opportunity structure, and of ensuring the right to claim one's benefit as a valuable citizen of US society" (Zambrana and Hurtado 14).

Unfortunately, an inappropriately low number of Latinx students are pursuing doctoral degrees in the United States, which explains the lack of representation of Latinx faculty in institutions of higher education. In the 2020 article "Values, Acceptance, and Belongingness in Graduate School: Perspectives from Underrepresented Minority Students" (197), Alexandria Miller and Susan Orsillo present national data showing that 16 percent of the US adult population identifies as Hispanic or Latino, and only 7 percent of those completed a doctoral degree compared to Whites, who earned 70 percent of total completed doctorates (197). Nevertheless, the continuing gap between enrollment, persistence, and attainment in the doctoral education of Latinx students is evident. In the same manner, there is an abundance of research that has explored factors that affect Latinx in education. Hence, this paper emphasizes that for many Latinx students, earning a higher-level degree is a big challenge, and it can be synonymous with survival in the White world.

Deficit Thinking. For some time, Mexicans in the United States have been ascribed with deficit thinking. In "The Evolution of Deficit Thinking: Educational Thought and Practice," Richard Valencia describes deficit thinking as being applied to those with "limited intellectual abilities, linguistic shortcomings, lack of motivation to learn and immoral behavior" (2). Certainly, this concept remains alive and continues in stereotyping Latinx students. Consequently, it could be why many Latinxs pursue education not only for survival. It is also an act of resistance to prove and advocate that Latinx students are not all afflicted with deficit thinking. This essay, therefore, advocates increasing our capacity to generate collective consciousness in the culture of Latinxs in education and to show that we are just as capable as others of contributing meaningful material support to the culture as a whole.

Unfortunately, the constant challenging of intelligence is ironic in Latinx culture; in fact, the ideology of 'deficit thinking' is also very persistent within our community. For example, it is common to use the Spanish word for a donkey, *burro,* for those who are not good at school. Hence, the expression "*¡ay cómo eres, burro!*" which means "you are so stupid," is especially used when someone does not understand an idea quickly enough. In the same manner, if we fail at school, people may say it is because we are "burros." On the opposite, *los listos* are those who are considered intelligent and those who earn good grades in school. Likewise, listos are those that became doctors, lawyers, and engineers, *se convierten en el orgullo de la familia*, the pride of their family. Latinx students that dislike school are likely to drop out and never finish a degree. Consequently, they usually obtain jobs requiring much physical effort and low wages. Therefore, they are considered burros for quitting school and subsequently, *seguimos en las mismas*, with no political power. We remain silent with no voice, as the *Others*, as *los invisibles*.

However, many other factors could increase Latinxs' capacity to earn a degree. For instance, Miller and Orsillo stated that "Although the nature of the challenges and stressors students face may vary across fields of study, personal characteristics, and program environments, one likely universal stressor is the increased academic responsibilities associated with doctoral study" (198). Similarly, Anzaldúa manifested all of these factors in her blueprints of the Trojan Burra Mula. Hence, in illustrating Anzaldúa's art, this essay concurs that "the culture of doctoral education needs to be examined further, and such examinations need to account for power, resistance, and agency within and along racialized demarcations" (Gildersleeve et al. 94).

AN APPROACH TO RECONCEPTUALIZE THE *OTHER*

This conceptual framework incorporates postcolonial theory by feminist scholar Gayatri Spivak in her essay "Can the subaltern speak?" Simultaneously, this work integrates border feminism, which recognizes the lack of representation and visibility of women of color in academia and integrates factors of dual consciousness. Comparing both, this study explores the *Other* that Anzaldúa theorizes in *or* through her work with fundamental aspects of neocolonialism, where she posits herself as a woman, as inferior of ethnicity and skin color, and as a working classmate seeking to surpass the hegemonic world.

Subaltern Theory. In "Can the Subaltern Speak?," Gayatri Spivak assigns the term *subaltern* to the oppressed, voiceless groups, such as peasants, proletariat, women, and indigenous people, and explains how hegemonic ideology influences the silence and invisibility of identities, especially those belonging to a third world country.

Borderlands. As formulated by Anzaldúa, Borderlands theory has found that there is a duality inside us. She introduced the term *Nepantilism* to mean to be in a stage of *Nepantla,* a Náhuatl word that means living in the in-between space (*Borderlands*). Therefore, "Living in nepantla is a survival strategy, but transitional, transcultural *nepantlera/os* possess the power to effect political change" (Black 243).

The Other. The vision of this research is to contribute to a feminist interdisciplinary project to expand artistic and literary canon to include marginalized Latinx voices in education. After introspection, it can be concluded that the subaltern and borderlands theories suggest the oppressed subject can increase the visibility of such matters, bucking a denial made by capitalism either through discrimination or exploitation and that it takes great courage to do so. Likewise, this paper presents Gloria Anzaldúa's work as a witness of the subaltern. *It fills* a need for political representation/authority for the *Other,* the marginalized people in the hegemonic world. Thus, characterizing the *Other* as being in search of visualization, like subaltern theory, Gloria Anzaldúa in *Borderlands* theorizes the importance of valuing our cultural beliefs, analyzing our emotions, and creating conscious courage while engaged in the effort to obtain a degree in higher education.

THE TROJAN BURRA MULA AS A METAPHORICAL INTERPRETATION

Connecting art, literature, and education in a metaphorical interpretation, this work presents Anzaldúa as one who contributes to the inter/transdisciplinary research initiative since her work takes part in the academy beyond a single field and even extends into the nonacademic community. Hence, this essay interprets some of her blueprints, the objective of which is to continue promoting the Anzaldúa heritage while simultaneously delving into research to examine the culture of doctoral education being understood as "the social-cultural and institutional contexts in which students live and work" (Lovitts 150). Therefore, exploring how educational culture is reflected for Latinx students could help to understand the challenges that Gloria Anzaldúa has overcome and what she shared through her art while trying to inspire better futures for her audience.

BRIEF DEFINITIONS OF *TROJAN*, *BURRO(A)*, AND *MULA*

Historically, the *Trojan horse* is the name given to a large wooden horse that the Greeks used to gain access to Troy, according to Greek author Homer. The story begins during the Trojan War. After being unable to conquer the besieged Trojans, the occupying Greeks built a massive wooden horse and left it at the gates of Troy. No sign of the Greek warships or warriors remained in view of the Trojans as they wheeled the horse inside. After dark had fallen, Greek soldiers burst out of the wooden horse and ransacked the city. This was how the Greeks won the war, and the legend of the Trojan horse was born. In present times, the Trojan horse can represent maliciousness, a virus, or terrorists of the internet and technology. Ironically, these two viewpoints of the term *Trojan*—the historical and the contemporary—could open bilateral interpretations of the Trojan Burra of Anzaldúa's teachings. The *burro(a)* or donkey is known as the animal that carries all, and many consider it less intelligent. Colloquially, in the Latinx culture, it is a word used for someone strong, and perhaps not bright. When a donkey is interbred with a female horse, the result is a *mula* (mule). A *mula* is defined as an animal with much resistance to work, and who is commonly infertile. This animal is known for its *terquedad* (stubbornness) toward any challenges. However, the *mula* is often recognized as more intelligent and resilient than the *burro*.

Utilizing four images that depict the Trojan Burra Mula in blueprints, this interdisciplinary analysis explores Anzaldúa's litero-artistic attributes and presents the connection between her writing and drawings, offering insights into the metaphor. The following illustration (see next page) by Anzaldúa is titled *The Trojan Mula at the University Gate* and presents *the silence, the seduction*, and *the tolerance*.

In an interview with Linda Smuckler, Anzaldúa stated, "My subconscious was communicating through my painting, but I wanted to articulate the ideas" ("Spirituality" 91). Clearly, her words have defined that the drawing was initially part of her subconscious and helped develop her ideas. In the same way, this study concurs that "Anzaldúa's artwork plays an integral part in her theory-making process" (Ishii 2). It is the position of this essay that Anzaldúa theorized in her art a call to better understand the culture of Latinx students inside higher education by analyzing her own subconscious art as it relates to our experiences.

El Silencio (The Silence). In her illustration, *The Trojan Mula at the University Gate*, a packhorse—the Trojan Burra Mula—appears inside a locked University Gate. Indicating a connection with the story of the Trojan war, the "burra or burro" in quotes is not only the animal loaded with responsibilities; she remarks that the burra presents the many challenges in catching academic overload work and facing these challenges as an activist, educator, and student. Along with carrying all those tasks, inside the burra's stomach is written "Trojan mula," and it represents "the students of color, the working class, the *Other(s)*" (*The Trojan Mula at the University Gate*, Figure 1). Thus, metaphorically, the Trojan Burra Mula, as the *Other* and the student of color, imparts the image of a silenced warrior.

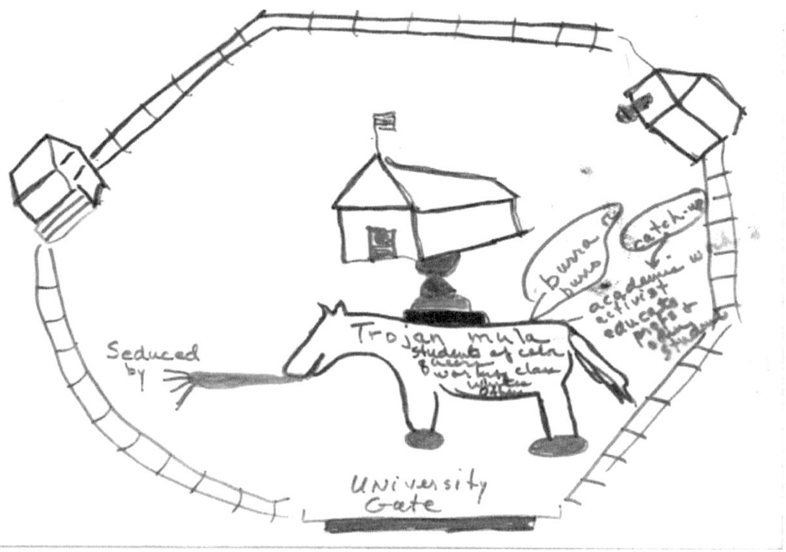

Figure 1. Gloria Anzaldúa, Blueprint: *The Trojan Mula at the University Gate*, n.d.; Nettie Lee Benson Latin American Collection, University of Texas Libraries, the University of Texas at Austin.

Silence is a topic that Anzaldúa reflects on in much of her work. For instance, in *Borderlands*, she wrote, "The dark-skinned woman has been silenced... for 300 years she was invisible... Many times she wished to speak, ... She remains faceless and voiceless, but a light shone on her veil of silence" (23). As a result of this world of silence, Anzaldúa demonstrates the effects of colonization and the continuing adversity of silence for students of color in doctoral programs.

La Tolerancia (The Tolerance). Allegorically, Anzaldúa's artwork represents the subaltern as a packhorse, symbolizing the student of color. And as part of the subordinates, she had to learn to accept impositions and ideologies that were inherently part of the system. Equally, she had to learn to adapt and resist while shouldering injustice and working through a stacked system. Like the mula adopting any resistance, Anzaldúa also learned to struggle through a mindset of forced confusion in the process of acculturation. For example, she talks about this world of contradictions of the *nueva mestiza*, who is "developing a tolerance for contradictions, a tolerance of ambiguity. She learns to be an Indian in Mexican culture, to be Mexican from an Anglo point of view" (79). Ergo, we could say literally that she silently lived and challenged the normal sense of belonging, of authority, and of being accepted. Therefore, characterizing the *Other* represents many of the challenges within herself that identify with the need to become visible in the representation of the subaltern. Similarly, in "Toward a Mestiza Rhetoric: Gloria Anzaldúa on Composition and Postcoloniality," Lunsford describes the university's symbol as this great walled city, and then someone takes the Trojan Burra into the city gates. Anzaldúa claims, "At night the belly of the *burra* opens, and out comes the 'other' trying to make changes from inside. Furthermore, I have a visual for that… There's your Trojan *Burra*" (13).

La Seducción (The Seduction). In the same image, Anzaldúa illustrated a carrot and then wrote "seduced by" (*The Trojan Mula at the University Gate*, Figure 1). We know that when we see food, it stimulates the appetite, and when we eat it, we feel empowered. Similarly, we can explain that the burro is an herbivore, seduced by the carrot and is open to the desire to eat it. It is the dangling carrot that lures. Then subjectively, we can manifest that the carrot symbolizes knowledge, which metaphorically converts knowledge into the desire for power. Lunsford states, "There is something very seductive about fitting in, and being part of the preexisting culture, forgetting differences, and going with the way of the norm. The western theory is very seductive, and pretty soon, instead of subverting and challenging and making marks on the wall, you get taken in" (13). Respectably, we can say that the carrot is the seduction from which we must be strong and resist in order to earn a degree in higher education. Similarly, bringing change is challenging because the university wall or city pulls you into its waiting arms. The following image (see next page) represents *the responsibilities*, *the isolation*, and *the sacrifice*.

Las Responsabilidades (The Responsibilities). "Epistemologies of the Wound: Anzaldúan Theories and Sociological Research on Incest in Mexican Society" is another interview conducted by Gloria González-López where Anzaldúa mentions burros as the metaphor for obtaining a degree. When the interviewer asked her,

> "Do you think I am a vendida?" She replied, "No mujer, you are a burra! You are a Mexican burra who has been trying to survive." She explained that while many White heterosexual men in academia may enjoy a feeling of pride in being the Trojan horses of knowledge and intelligence, "Latinas who survive academia are burras in pain, female donkeys who go through the cracks of institutions while having to carry a heavy load on their backs" (19).

Thereby, this essay manifests the conviction of the narrative and artwork of Gloria Anzaldúa. In so doing, this essay demonstrates that in her drawing, the responsibilities of the subordinates are part of the increased workload and, by extension, they are indicative of oppression by the hegemonic world. In the same category, Anzaldúa's artwork involves consciousness on many levels and works to secure links between personal and political resistance for Latinx regarding obstacles in higher education. Anzaldúa tried to denounce the continued practice in the academic world to exploit the graduate working class and students of color: paying low salaries while imposing responsibilities in teaching that require disproportionate time and work; overburdening students, creating a continued challenge to becoming knowledgeable; reading and writing effectively and academically; fulfilling responsibilities and dealing with complex emotions fueled by cultural differences. All of this may be overwhelming and take time away from the ability to focus on what is essential: learning and preparation to obtain a degree.

La Isolación (The Isolation). Another concept to interpret metaphorically is *isolation.* Isolation is defined as separating an individual from all social contact, shunning social activities, and avoiding contact with others. Equally, isolation is a mental state of being alone, not necessarily being without social connection. Further, isolation, as informed by Anzaldúa in her *Nepantilism* is the stage where "*la mestiza* is a product of the transfer of the cultural and spiritual values of one group to another" (*Borderlands,* 78). Therefore, in living as a student of the working class, "[t]he ambivalence from the clash of voices results in a mental and emotional state of perplexity, internal strife results in insecurity and indecisiveness" (78). In the same manner, her isolation during school affected her education, further representing the Trojan Burra Mula as the characterization of the *Other,* facing educational challenges yet learning to adopt ideologies of colonization. Nonetheless, while the Trojan Burra Mula lives in isolation, simultaneously, this isolation helps grow consciousness and power by obtaining knowledge. In *Borderlands,* Anzaldúa wrote, "En la soledad Ella prospera. Rebellion grows" (Here in solitude she grows, rebellion grows; 23), further supporting the Trojan Burra Mula theory.

El Sacrificio (The Sacrifice). As seen in the blueprint, Anzaldúa included at the end a phrase that dictates, "Race before gender, race before sexuality" (*The Trojan Burra Mula*, Figure 2). Here we can conclude that she tries to make us understand that old nationalisms consider race the initiation to cause awareness and recognize us as the *Other*, and argue that we need to stand together by race before our sexuality.

Figure 2. Gloria Anzaldúa, Blueprint: *The Trojan Burra Mula, n.d.*; Nettie Lee Benson Latin American Collection, University of Texas Libraries, The University of Texas at Austin.

El Colonizado (The Colonized). The image, *The Colonized Consciousness*, demonstrates a process of transformation [Figure 3]. Here the characterization of the *Other* is erotized by a desire ("Colonized Consciousness"). The figure shows that the Trojan Burra Mula is already colonized; however, it is out of the academic gate. In this image, the animal represented is not a burra. Therefore, it seems to mean that the animal is free and obtains power and authority. It speaks and writes for/to/about the *Other* in its representation.

Nevertheless, the illustration also includes an embodiment that looks like a giant bird flying or a ghost hanging around. Fed by the desire of the *Other*, this illustration is characterized by a living stage of transformation that empowers with discernment and authority through knowledge. It can be theorized that neo-colonization helped her understand the social construction and impositions of the western world. Thus, Anzaldúa questioned in the picture, "who/what constructs?: language, ethnic cult., dom., pop, sexual pref., profession." (*The Colonized Consciousness*, Figure 3) Hereafter, Anzaldúa not only manifested the desire to achieve visibility in the representation of the subalterns, it appears that she began to understand the cause of oppression created by cultural and social impositions. Consequently, this work manifests and "posits resistance into Anzaldúa's creativity that can serve as a survival tactic for those who experience various oppressions, including racism, sexism, heterosexism, and/or classism" (Isihii 1).

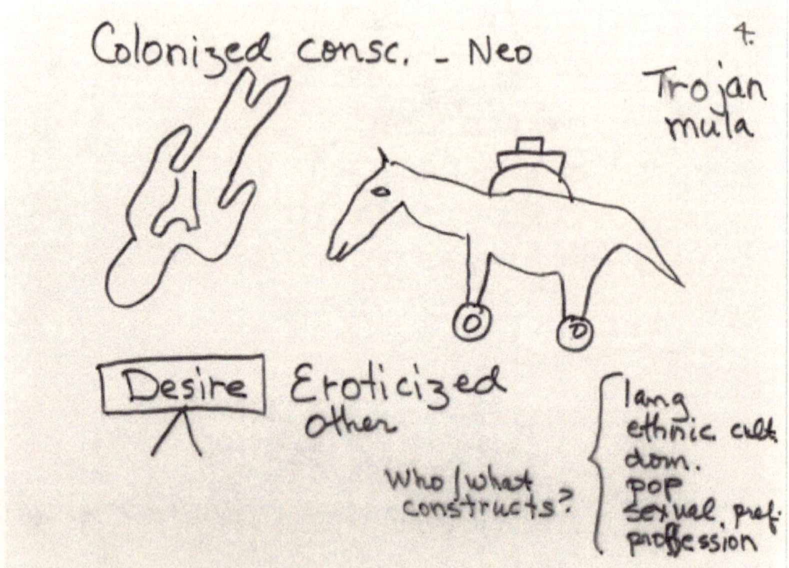

Figure 3. Gloria Anzaldúa, Blueprint, *The Colonized Consciousness*, n.d.; Nettie Lee Benson Latin American Collection, University of Texas Libraries, The University of Texas at Austin.

La Mensajera (The Messenger). The last illustration is titled "La activista/artista" and characterizes the Trojan Burra Mula, converted now into the form of a horse [Figure 4]. We can then say, given the material already discussed, among other things, this image represents a transformation of herself. Similarly, in *Borderlands,* Anzaldúa talked about a transformation. She wrote, "The female being is angry, sad, joyful, is *Coatlicue*, dove, horse, serpent, cactus" (67). Hence, trying to decolonize those impositions, she declared, "She learns to transform the small 'I' into the total Self" (83). Lunsford stated, "We were over here, we were the 'other' with other lives, and the '*nos*' was the subject, the White man" (8). Thus, it became the activist/artist and the messenger. Subsequently, a symbolic interpretation of this sketch seems to warn future generations of students about the sacrifice of taking the educational path. Although education will require sacrifice, this essay demonstrates allegorically that it could be the key that opens visibility in representation to the *Other*(*s*) and is a highly recommended path to achieve such goal(s).

Anzaldúa stated, "This step is a conscious rupture of all oppressive traditions of all cultures and religions. She communicates that rupture, documents the struggle, reinterprets history and, using new symbols, shapes new myths" (*Borderlands* 82). Parabolically, this study uses the image of "The Activist/Artist" in [Figure 4] to make an association to the "Trojan Burra Mula" in [Figure 2]. Therefore, this drawing represents a woman who has lived through many challenges in academia. And cataloged as the *Other* in a White world, the picture shows an interpretation that by sacrifice to education, the outcome can result in a transformation that wholly synchronizes author(ity), liberty, and power. Equally, as represented in the drawing, an empowered woman is leaving the past struggles behind, and the messenger is showing others how history can be made, despite their positions as subaltern.

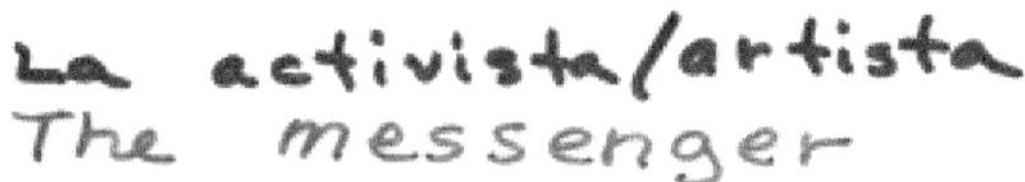

Figure 4. Gloria Anzaldúa, Blueprint: *La activista/artista*, n.d.; Nettie Lee Benson Latin American Collection, University of Texas Libraries, The University of Texas at Austin.

CONCLUSION

In the tradition of silence, Anzaldúa represents her ability to imagine, enact, and inhabit space that goes beyond challenges in education. Hence, it is essential to continue promoting Anzaldúa's legacy to magnify the state of our current conditions and inspire more extraordinary efforts in academia. Endeavors in the field of higher education mentioned in this study attempt to contribute to a future investigation by suggesting the continued incorporation of blueprint art into inter/transdisciplinary studies as ways to conduct literary and artistic research studies. I concur with Ishii: "Indeed, Anzaldúa's sketches offer a significant contribution to academic scholarship, especially for scholars who hope to obtain a deeper, more sophisticated understanding of her theories" (3). The journey of doctoral education should be examined, whereby insight into understanding potential graduate students leads to increased enlightenment and time invested in a diverse multicultural and inter/transdisciplinary educational workforce. Attention to similar kinds of creativity may assist fields invested in social change. Furthermore, this work concludes that Anzaldúa's blueprint images can easily initiate conversations between disciplines about her art and provide an educational impetus for future generations.

WORKS CITED

Anzaldúa, Gloria. Blueprint of *La activista / artista*. Date unknown. Nettie Lee Benson Latin American Collection, University of Texas Libraries, University of Texas at Austin. Austin, TX.

———. Blueprint of *The Colonized Consciousness*, n.d.; Nettie Lee Benson Latin American Collection, University of Texas Libraries, University of Texas at Austin.

———. Blueprint of *The Trojan Burra Mula*. Date unknown. Nettie Lee Benson Latin American Collection, University of Texas Libraries, The University of Texas at Austin, Austin, TX.

———. Blueprint of *The Trojan Mula at the University Gate*. Date unknown. Nettie Lee Benson Latin American Collection, University of Texas Libraries, The University of Texas at Austin, Austin, TX.

———. *Borderlands / La Frontera: The New Mestiza*. Aunt Lute Books, 1987.

———. *Light in the Dark / Luz en lo Oscuro: Rewriting Identity, Spirituality, Reality*. Duke University Press, 2015.

———. "Spirituality, Sexuality, and the Body: An Interview with Linda Smuckler." *The Gloria Anzaldúa Reader*. Duke University Press, 2009, pp. 74–94.

Black, Charlene. "Introduction to Part III: The Intersection of Contemporary Latin American Art and Religion." *Religion and the Arts*, vol.18, no.1–2, 2014, pp. 239–244.

Gildersleeve, Ryan Evely, Natasha N. Croom, and Philip L. Vasquez. "'Am I Going Crazy?!': A Critical Race Analysis of Doctoral Education." *Equity & Excellence in Education,* vol. 44, no. 1, 2011, pp. 93–114.

González-López, Gloria. "Epistemologies of the Wound: Anzaldúan Theories and Sociological Research on Incest in Mexican Society." *Human Architecture: Journal of the Sociology of Self-Knowledge*, vol. 4, no. 3, 2006, pp. 17–24.

Ishii, Sara. *Gloria E. Anzaldúa's "Art as a Mode of Research": Applications in Feminist Research Methods and Feminist Rhetoric*. 2018, Texas Woman's University, Ph.D. dissertation.

Lovitts, Barbara E. "Being a Good Course-Taker is Not Enough: A Theoretical Perspective on the Transition to Independent Research." *Studies in Higher Education*, vol. 30, no. 2, 2005, pp. 137–154.

Lunsford, Andrea A. "Toward a Mestiza Rhetoric: Gloria Anzaldúa on Composition and Postcoloniality." *JAC*, vol. 18, no. 1, 1998, pp. 1–27.

Spivak, Gayatri C. "Can the subaltern speak?" *Die Philosophin*, vol. 14, no. 27, 2003, pp. 42–58.

Miller, Alexandria N., and Susan M. Orsillo. “”Values, Acceptance, and Belongingess in Graduate School: Perspectives from Underrepresented Minority Students.” *Journal of Contextual Behavioral Science*, vol. 15, 2020, pp. 197–206.

Valencia, Richard R. *The Evolution of Deficit Thinking: Educational Thought and Practice.* Routledge, 2012.

Zambrana, Ruth E., and Sylvia Hurtado. *The Magic Key: The Educational Journey of Mexican Americans from K–12 to College and Beyond.* University of Texas Press, 2015.

LA FACULTAD AND DECOLONIAL PEDAGOGY

TEACHING VALERIE MARTÍNEZ'S EACH AND HER

CECILIA AMANDA MACIAS

Valerie Martínez's book-length poem, *Each and Her*, published in 2010 by Arizona University Press, sets a sharp focus on the traumatic violence in Ciudad Juárez and the persistent femicide that occurs there, perpetuated by drug culture, capitalism, and the dehumanizing victimization of women. As is the case with many contemporary injustices, it is alarming that such travesties continue as daily life goes on seemingly unaffected. Works such as *Each and Her* are effective tools for enacting *decolonial pedagogies* in the writing classroom. Teachers and students are asked to place themselves intimately close to texts and concepts that contend with violence. Simultaneously, members of the classroom negotiate with covert institutional violence characteristic of academic spaces. Although scholarship points to an awareness of the inherent violence in the teaching of writing, pedagogies that deal specifically with the violence related to the decolonization of academia, course content, and the mind, and how these are enacted in the classroom, are an ongoing project.

The line of inquiry pursued in this paper was prompted by a teaching experience I had when I was invited to guest lecture in Dr. Adrianna M. Santos's undergraduate Latinx Literature class at Texas A&M University–San Antonio. I chose to instruct the students on Martínez's book, *Each and Her*, written in the tradition of social justice literature. In this essay, I recount a lesson I taught in which I experienced an emotional response to discussing violence against women and subsequently self-censored the expression of that emotion.

By analyzing this incident, I will investigate how the experience of teaching texts on violent subject matter are served by decolonial pedagogies and Anzaldúan concepts like *la facultad*. Decolonial pedagogies can help reframe epistemologies, and prior experiences of both teachers and students, so that violences of both the text and the classroom are openly acknowledged, discussed, and critically negotiated. I argue that unpacking affect in teaching is essential to this reframing as emotions are necessary to the critical conversations related to content that confronts violence. The speaker demands the reader follow closely on the path of painful discovery; "sígame," Martínez writes (50). In order to follow, teachers and students must bring their whole selves. This includes the emotional self.

Throughout the poem are long sections naming the many victims of femicide in Ciudad Juárez and depicting in vivid detail the violence committed against the bodies of these women. The text critiques the culture of violence against women as a negative effect of capitalism. The author centers women who work in maquiladoras on the border, indicating the dehumanization of women, their bodies, and their labor.

The nature of the content called for a definition of *femicide* and other terminology in order to facilitate discussion in the classroom related to the work. The terms were defined as a group, with clarification and context offered by me. One term I chose to define is *femicide*, as many of the students were not familiar with the term and could not offer or conjecture definition based on context clues. As I began to define the term for the class, I became emotional and paused my instruction, turning my gaze from the students. This moment, coupled with the challenges of teaching a text that discusses violence against women, led me to question the epistemologies and pedagogies I enacted in the delivery of my lesson.

The self-censoring I performed is, in fact, a behavior reflective of a type of violence. Decolonial pedagogies and theory of la facultad serve to address this type of covert violence by placing critical conversations related to this type of violence into open discussion, acknowledging the necessity of emotion for the production of knowledge. By naming the experience and unpacking the role affect plays in teaching, I am resisting an erasure of this part of myself and recuperating what was lost in the moment of delivering the lesson in the classroom.

Gloria Anzaldúa introduces the concept of la facultad in her work *Borderlands / La Frontera.* La facultad draws on indigenous epistemologies and pushes back against Western colonial thought, especially as it relates to emotional sensibilities. Anzaldúa describes la facultad as a heightened sensibility developed in individuals who must navigate covert structural violence in order to exist and survive. In her description, la facultad can be understood as a type of sixth sense:

> It is anything that breaks into one's everyday mode of perception, that causes a break in one's defenses and resistance, anything that takes one from one's habitual grounding, causes the depths to open up, causes a shift in perception. This shift in perception deepens the way we see concrete objects and people; the senses become so acute and piercing that we can see through things, view events in depth, a piercing that reaches the underworld (the realm of the soul). (Anzaldúa 61).

In order to decolonize the mind, we must decolonize our emotional sensibilities. Emotions are a social construction, and, as Anzaldúa points out, developed through experience. They can be a site for an intimate iteration of social control but may also serve as a site of political resistance (Boler 112). I choose to use the term *la facultad* instead of similar terminology, like *emotional intelligence*, for example, because the latter maintains connectivity to Western colonial philosophies. La facultad allows the subject to ascertain "the meaning of deeper realities, to see the deep structure below the surface," beyond closed off and cold rationality, and is absolutely necessary to the decolonial project (Anzaldúa 60). In entering into conversation on decolonial pedagogies by way of la facultad, we are empowering teachers to utilize their emotional sensibilities as a tool for critical instruction in the classroom, reframing emotion as a necessary and valuable labor rather than an impediment to instructional delivery.

Decolonial pedagogies serve as an extension of the broader decolonial project into the classroom. According to Monzó, "Decoloniality frames the issues related to class struggle, patriarchy, racism and other antagonisms through the perspectives of the indigenous groups" (516). Decolonial pedagogies and thought are essential to dismantling the structural violence that outlines acceptable behavior, including when, where, and how it is acceptable to express emotion and by whom. When discussing content in the classroom through a critical decolonial lens, students are being asked to empathize with indigenous populations that suffered colonization, and bring into question the contemporary iterations and the legacy of colonization within the social structure.

Related to la facultad and affect, decolonial thought allows for the acknowledgment of experiences and realities below the surface, especially in subjugated groups. Decolonial theory supports an investigation of the dialogic relationship between overt and covert violence. The colonized subject is at once experiencing the covert and often internal violence of colonization, while suffering the real physical traumas and overt violence of the ongoing colonial project. It is important that the connections between the two be critically engaged in order to address the violence colonization perpetuates and to understand how this perpetuation is achieved both within and without the self.

Employing decolonial pedagogies also invites criticism of hegemonic ways of thinking and knowledge production. To enact decolonial theory "requires that we commit 'epistemic disobedience,' that we interrogate the 'naturalness' and 'superiority' of a Western, objective and individualistic approach to knowing and being in the world, and its claim to possessing an 'advanced' and 'civilized' people and society" (Monzó 519). Enacting decolonial pedagogies in the classroom communicates a clear political standpoint, purposefully addressing the hegemonic norm, and allowing the instructor to draw on nontraditional ways of knowing, teaching, and producing new knowledge. However, decolonial pedagogy is, of course, imperfect. According to Fanon, "decolonization is always a violent phenomenon" (35). If this is accepted as truth, then enacting decolonial pedagogies invites a type of violence into the classroom by breaking down familiar and comfortable structures.

When being faced with a disruption of the overarching power structure, a lack of social stability can occur, but for whom? If stability is the potentiality being impeded, then decolonial pedagogies certainly enable this type of violence. However, it is not the goal of decolonial pedagogy to ameliorate all forms of violence. As Fanon asserts, violence is always necessary for change. The risk is, however, that a certain hierarchy of violence can be suggested by decolonial projects. This does not mean that efforts to decolonize society and the classroom should be abandoned, but that the labor of critically considering the impact of enacting such theories, analyzing the ramifications of violence related to social instability, and making carefully considered choices is absolutely necessary. In the decolonial classroom, violence takes the form of "a different kind of learning, a different kind of teaching, and the decolonization of normative pedagogical structures" (Fujino et. al. 71). It requires the full participation of teachers and students, which includes full intellectual and emotional participation. How do you create these conditions?

In large part, the expression of emotion involves the aesthetics of performativity. An individual's enactment of self-censoring related to emotion supports a "respect for the established order" (Fanon 38), and effectively transfers the responsibility of policing behavior from the hegemonic power structure to the individual. I consider this type of internalized violence to be a form of *susto*, or trauma that requires mindful healing and the careful recovery of the spirit within teaching and the classroom. There is also a cultural censoring that occurs, specifically in Latinx communities, related to trauma known as *susto*. Susto is the belief that the soul, an essential facet of la facultad and its functionality, retracts into the body in response to trauma.

Decolonial pedagogies allow for the unpacking of cultural susto, the repression of emotion and sensibility across a population, in order to heal and address social injustice. Emotion, though often considered individual and private, is in fact collective as it is socially constructed. As noted earlier, social structures determine how, when, and where emotion is expressed and by whom. Decolonial pedagogies aimed at critically considering affect are not meant to destroy the social ordering of emotions but to disrupt the potentially violent ordering of them. These pedagogies allow room for discussion around why teachers and students feel certain emotions related to content, or, conversely, do not feel them. It allows for inquiry and critical considerations to be made about the degree to which emotions are being influenced by the dominant social order, or not. The ideal result is that students and teachers will be able to have explicit discussions about emotion, its role in knowledge production, and a "meta-discourse about the significance of different emotional expressions, silences, and rules in relation to the power relations that define cultural injustices" (Boler 83).

The aim here is not to categorize emotion, or label certain emotions as political resistance and others as collusion with the hegemonic norm, but to support the inclusion of emotion and la facultad in critical discussion and the understanding that they are a necessary aspect of the process of learning. In understanding emotional response as socially constructed and conditioned behavior, we invite critical engagement and investigation of affect related to the study of violent subject matter. According to Boler, "emotions have been consistently educated, whether explicitly or inexplicitly, in every classroom" (32). Locating the social construct that guides our behavior and pushing back against the structures that are repressive can allow for clarity in how our emotions work within the process of learning and producing new knowledge.

Historically, emotional labor may not have been readily recognized because it does not lend itself to commodification that supports the capitalist structure that Martínez criticizes in her poem. Therefore, the self-imposed repression of emotion can be viewed as an extension of colonial violence and an example of the restriction of physical mobility. It has been established that emotions are socially influenced, conditioned, and structured, and may not be as individual or private as previously thought, but the experiencing of them is inarguably embodied by individual subjects. By allowing the full physical experience of emotion, and its subsequent expression, a form of content is being provided to further facilitate critical discussion, and the prioritizing of emotional labor in both teaching and learning. These ideas push against violent structures that call for the solely rational or intellectual engagement free from emotion, centralizing la facultad as a critical aspect of intellectual understanding. Pedagogically speaking, the work of centralizing la facultad and emotional sensibilities involves critical self-reflection, analysis of differences in the experience of emotions, analysis of emotional conduct, and rigorous contextualizing of emotional experience (Boler 82). This model gives students the opportunity to develop a keen sense of their emotional selves and critically consider how they operate beyond the classroom.

Building on decolonial pedagogies, recent scholarship articulates a transformative pedagogy. Although both projects have similar goals, transformative pedagogy seeks "to develop ways of knowing and ways of being that do not only augment individual and collective understanding of social structures and social relations, but also transform them through collective analysis and action" (Fujino et al. 69). This emphasis on action is an opportunity for teachers and students to further disrupt violence within the classroom and in spaces beyond academia. Transformative pedagogies enable "participants to develop the theoretical and intellectual tools needed for understanding the affective and cultural violence that higher education can cause and condone, and to transform disempowerment and disenfranchisement into gaining a voice and taking action" (Fujino et al. 72).

The efforts transcend critical discussion by rooting discussion and teaching in the goal of making change and actively working against injustice. Within transformative pedagogy, there is still room for la facultad, deeper senses and sensibility, but the inclusion of a call to action gives developed emotional sensibility a greater purpose. Passive empathy does little to ameliorate the violence discussed in class. It is critical that these discussions lead to collective and motivated efforts for change. This can be achieved by the inclusion of service-learning pedagogies and, indeed, by continuing to confront overt violence in teaching texts like Martínez's *Each and Her*.

WORKS CITED

Anzaldúa, Gloria. "La Facultad." *Borderlands / La Frontera: The New Mestiza*. Aunt Lute, 2012, pp. 60–61.

Boler, Megan. *Feeling Power: Emotions and Education*. Routledge, 1999. EBSCO*host*, https://search.ebscohost.com/login.aspx?direct=true&db=nlebk&AN=122655&site=eds-live&scope=site.

Fanon, Frantz. "Concerning Violence." In Frantz Fanon, *The Wretched of the Earth*. Translated by Richard Philcox, with essays by Jean-Paul Sartre and Homi K. Bhabha, Grove Atlantic, 2004, pp. 35–106.

Fujino, Diane C., Jonathan D. Gomez, Esther Lezra, George Lipsitz, Jordan Mitchell, and James Fonseca. "A Transformative Pedagogy for a Decolonial World." *Review of Education, Pedagogy, and Cultural Studies*, vol. 40, no. 2, 2018, pp. 69–95.

Galtung, Johan. "Violence, Peace, and Peace Research." *Journal of Peace Research*, vol. 6, no. 3, 2016, pp. 167–191.

Martínez, Valerie. *Each and Her*. University of Arizona Press, 2010.

Monzó, Lilia D., and Peter McLaren. "Critical Pedagogy and the Decolonial Option: Challenges to the Inevitability of Capitalism." *Policy Futures in Education*, vol. 12, no. 4, 2014, pp. 513–525.

"QUEERING CUENTOS: BORDERLAND INTERGENERATIONAL NARRATIVES THROUGH ANZALDÚAN SCHOLARSHIP"

ANZALDÚAN HISTORY, REFLECTIONS AND RESOURCES FROM THE 2019 AUNT LUTE SUMMER PROGRAMMING IN THE RGV

VERÓNICA "LADY MARIPOSA" SANDOVAL

During the summer of 2019, Joan Pinkvoss, cofounder, executive director, and editor of Aunt Lute Books, invited me to create a three-week public poetry workshop as part of their community outreach programming to the Río Grande Valley (RGV). My workshop titled "Queering Cuentos: Borderland Intergenerational Narratives through Anzaldúan Scholarship" featured public community gatherings, public poetry readings and discussions, community crafting and postcard writing sessions, writing prompts and poetry workshops, material collection for publication, traditional lectures, and an analysis of border politics through Gloria Anzaldúa's *Borderlands / La Frontera: The New Mestiza.* This essay documents the rich experiences of that summer and outlines the lesson plans and discourse that developed from this summer residency. It also incorporates my presentation as part of the opening plenary session entitled, "*Borderlands / La Frontera* in the Río Grande Valley: Poetry & Art Workshops Beyond University Walls" at El Mundo Zurdo 2019: Planetary Citizenship: Anzaldúan Thought Across Communities, Histories, Culture.

DOING WORK THAT MATTERS: ANZALDÚA'S HISTORY IN THE RÍO GRANDE VALLEY BORDERLANDS

The 2019 Aunt Lute summer programming in the Río Grande Valley grew from a need identified by Emmy Pérez and her students. Pérez's inclination toward the creation of this program stemmed from her extensive experience in teaching community-based creative writing workshops as a political framework.[1] This programming was also an extension of Anzaldúan stewardship and care work by borderland artists, poets, scholars, and educators whose labor helped to establish and highlight her influential work in the RGV. The Gloria Anzaldúa Legacy Project (GAL Project) was founded in 2007 by RGV activists and poets Noemi Ixchel Martínez, Priscilla Celina Suárez, and Daniel García Ordaz. Through their mission "to enhance the community by means of local arts and humanities ventures, particularly cultural awareness" (Suárez and Martínez 10), GAL paid tribute, promoted, and educated the local community about the work of Gloria Anzaldúa (3). Members of the GAL Project spoke at public events, area schools and libraries, and produced free zines as informational literature. Their labor and participation were sought after for many years by community members looking to produce Anzaldúan projects and events valley-wide. The community-based work by the Gloria Anzaldúa Legacy Project is seen by many as foundational in helping to bridge Anzaldúa's work to the RGV community outside of university spaces.

Helping to expand Anzaldúa's work and discourse within the University of Texas–Pan American (UTPA), now University of Texas Río Grande Valley (UTRGV), was Dr. Robert Johnson, whose area of expertise is the Beat Generation. Dr. Johnson began teaching Anzaldúa in 1997 after the appearance of her work in the *Heath Anthology*. He would eventually begin teaching *Borderlands / La Frontera* in its entirety in 2001 in his South Texas Literature course.[2] In 2006, the following professors are known to have taught Anzaldúa's work at UTPA[3]: Dr. Stephanie Álvarez, Dr. Guadalupe Cortina, Dr. Sonia

---

1 Emmy Pérez, email to author, August 4, 2020. Prior to her arrival in the Río Grande Valley, Pérez taught detained youth and adults in El Paso and New Mexico. In 2007, she created ENGL 4357: Creative Writing and Social Action, a course for graduate and undergraduate students at UTPA. ENGL 4357 facilitated writing workshops and opportunities for students to aid Pérez in teaching RGV youth and adults at local juvenile and adult detention centers. Pérez's course framework has also facilitated the teaching of creative writing workshops at La Union Del Pueblo (LUPE), and the Life Center at El Milagro Clinic (The Lower RGV Community Health Management Corp.).

2 Dr. Robert Johnson, phone interview with author, February 15, 2020.

3 This list of professors is not meant to be a comprehensive list of those who have taught Anzaldua's work at UTPA/UTRGV. Professors listed are based on courses that I took as a

Hernández, Dr. Glenn Martínez, Dr. Edna Ochoa, Emmy Pérez, Dr. Kamala Platt, Dr. Corey Wimberly,[4] and Dr. Marci McMahon (beginning in 2008 when she arrived at UTPA).[5]In the spring of 2011, Dr. Stephanie Álvarez taught the first-ever course dedicated to Anzaldúa at the petition of graduate students in the Modern Languages department (Álvarez et al. 123). After this initial class, other faculty members taught courses that were dedicated to the work of Anzaldúa, including Marci McMahon, Cynthia Paccacerqua, and Cinthya Saavedra. In 2019, Álvarez formalized the course by proposing it and having it added to the course catalog in the Mexican American Studies Program, MASC 6355: Gloria Anzaldúa.[6]

As we moved into the twenty-first century, Anzaldúan thought and scholarship continued to flourish in the RGV. In the mid-2000s, discussions by junior faculty across disciplines at UTPA began to crystallize the idea of a speaker series. In 2007, Dr. Cory Wimberly hosted the first guest philosopher to present on Anzaldúa's legacy ("Honoring Gloria"). In 2008, through the effort and leadership of Dr. Adriel Trott, UTPA officially established the Gloria Anzaldúa Speaker Series in Philosophy ("Nuestra Gloria: Speaker Series"). Founded by Wimberly, this series honors "Gloria Evangelina Anzaldúa's life and work by highlighting its unique philosophical significance. The Department of Philosophy together with the ongoing support of the Center for Mexican American Studies . . . invites intellectuals to share their current research, projects and/or to lead workshops with students, faculty, staff and the local and diverse communities" ("Nuestra Gloria: Speaker Series").

After a 2007 invitation to participate in a GAL community poetry reading, Pérez, through a continued relationship with Suárez and Martínez, recognized the need to be supported in their efforts on the UTPA campus.[7] In 2008, Pérez would establish a yearly Anzaldúan campus event which began as "Living en La Frontera: Gloria Anzaldúa and Border Theory with a Reading from *Canícula: Snapshots of a Girlhood en la Frontera* (2008)." During the Q&A portion of "Living en La Frontera," Pérez publicly asked author Norma Cantú what she and her students could do to promote Anzaldúa's work on campus. Cantú suggested a yearly campus event like "Living en La Frontera,"

---

student at UTRGV. Names were also collected via phone calls and texts to professors that continue to teach at this institution.

4 Emmy Pérez, text messages to author, February 15, 2020.

5 Dr. Marci McMahon, Facebook message to author, February 17, 2020.

6 Emmy Pérez, email to author, August 7, 2020.

7 Emmy Pérez, email to author, August 5, 2020.

which was dedicated to highlighting the work of Anzaldúa.[8] El Retorno: El Valle Celebra Nuestra Gloria, would officially begin in May of 2009 with the help of GAL members, poets, artists, students, and faculty. This free annual public event sponsored by UTPA[9] features a graveside ceremony, catered lunch, art display, poetry presentation, and keynote speakers such as Dr. Norma Alarcón, Dr. Aída Hurtado, Dr. Inés Hernández-Avila, Dr. Carmen Tafolla, Dr. Sonia Saldívar-Hull, ire'ne lara silva, Randy Conner, and Dr. María Herrera-Sobek ("Nuestra Gloria: El Retorno").[10] Another community project that helped to incorporate Anzaldúa's legacy outside of the university is the Valley International Poetry Festival (VIPF). Sponsored by Art That Heals and founded in 2008 by Daniel García Ordaz and Brenda Riojas, this four-day festival brings together poets and participants from across the world. The festival features community poetry readings, workshops, a slam competition, and the VIPF Poetry Pachanga and Dinner. ("Río Grande Valley"). Consistent with García Ordaz's political labor as a founding member of the GAL Project, VIPF was dedicated to the memory of Anzaldúa (García Ordaz). In 2008, the VIPF closing event consisted of a spiritual poetry reading in San Juan. Participants read Anzaldúa's work, as well as original work inspired by Anzaldúa, Greek mythology, and more.[11] In 2009, VIPF began to include a site visit to Anzaldúa's grave as a closing to the festival. The first was facilitated by Priscilla Celina Suárez of the GAL Project, who for many years has served as a liaison between the Anzaldúa family and the community. Participants of VIPF who attend the closing

---

8 Dr. Norma Cantú, per my attendance as a poetry presenter at the event.

9 Emmy Pérez, per emails with author, August 5, 2020. In 2008, funding came from departments within the College of Arts and Humanities. After 2008, most of the funding would come from the Mexican American Studies (MAS) Program at UTPA. When the Center for Mexican American Studies was established in 2011, the event was funded by CMAS, and continues to this day at UTRGV.

10 It is important to note that although Anzaldúan events may have found campus sponsors throughout the years to provide monetary support, these sponsorships are not indicative of an institutional endorsement of Anzaldúa's work, nor of the support for the labor that these events entail. In its foundation, El Retorno relied on the labor and creative insight from local artists, poets, community members, and students at UTPA/UTRGV. Emmy Pérez's work towards the establishment, coordination, and successful execution of El Retorno was for many years unrecognized and uncompensated. The continuation of the work would not have been possible without MAS's and, later, CMAS's administrative support of the event and compensation for invited speakers' travel and honoraria.

11 Daniel García Ordaz, educator and poet, per Facebook message to author, August 5, 2020.

ceremony pay homage to Anzaldúa, they read poetry in her honor, pray, and discuss her impact in their lives.[12]

Through scholarship, creative work, celebrations, and community outreach, the Río Grande Valley has for many years established itself as a space for the continued engagement of Anzaldúa's work. The ability of her discourse and theories to connect with borderland students and community members throughout various disciplines continues to encourage opportunities for the unpacking and creation of "work that matters."[13] As a daughter of the RGV and, like Anzaldúa, of Coatlicue, I too have built upon this legacy, with my poetry and in my pedagogy.[14] "The 2019 Valley Poetry Workshop Project" became an ideal space for continuing this work.

THE 2019 VALLEY POETRY WORKSHOP PROJECT: BRAINSTORMING AT EL MUNDO ZURDO

The 2019 Valley Poetry Workshop Project (VPWP) emerged from talks between participants and organizers during the 2017 meeting of the Society for the Study of Gloria Anzaldúa. Emmy Pérez and Joan Pinkvoss contemplated ways to strengthen and extend the work that Pérez and her UTRGV students were already doing within alternative Río Grande Valley high schools. Pérez's project held during the summer of 2017 had produced meaningful discourse among the participants, helping to facilitate the creation of new poetry from young writers.[15] Witnessing the students' enthusiastic responses, Pérez recognized the

---

12 Per my attendance of the first VIPF gravesite visit, and the multiple VIPFs that I have participated in.

13 To learn more about the labor of women in the RGV helping to establish the importance of Anzaldua's work, please see Chapter 1 of this volume, "Honor a Nuestra Gloria: Remembering Gloria Anzaldúa in the Río Grande Valley" by Stephanie Álvarez, Emmy Pérez, and Sergio G. Barrera.

14 For more on Anzaldúa as a daughter of Coatlicue, see Irene Lara's "Daughter of Coatlicue: An Interview with Gloria Anzaldúa." *Entre Mundos/Among Worlds: New Perspectives on Gloria Anzaldúa,* edited by AnaLouise Keating, pp. 41–56, Palgrave Macmillan, 2005.

15 Emmy Pérez, per email with author, August 4, 2020. In the Summer of 2017, Emmy Pérez collaborated with former PSJA librarian Carolina Castillo in organizing a weeklong creative writing workshop for students from three alternative high schools in the PSJA school district. One of the schools serviced during the 2017 project included Sonia Sotomayor, an alternative high school for young mothers. To facilitate the workshop, Pérez collaborated with community poet and activist Odilia Galván Rodríguez and MAS graduate students Mónica Álvarez and Valerie Cerda. The 2017 workshop focused on bilingual creative writing and was an affiliate program of *Barrio Writers.*

potential benefit to participants if these workshops could be extended beyond a week. In their discussion at the Anzaldúa Conference, Pérez and Pinkvoss identified a need for financial support to create an extended summer workshop project. It was then that Pinkvoss of Aunt Lute Books, in consultation with Pérez, decided to write a grant proposal that would support the 2019 summer programming.

Ultimately it would be Aunt Lute's Joan Pinkvoss and Maya Sisneros who crafted a winning proposal funded by The Alice Kleberg Reynolds Foundation.[16] This funding allowed for the extension of Pérez's poetry project into a three-week summer program at Sonia Sotomayor and Buell Central alternative high schools. Supplementary components to Pérez's Poetry Project included a three-week printmaking workshop. In addition to working within alternative public schools, the VPWP offered a three-week writing workshop open to the public at the McAllen Public Library for LGBTQIA+ members and allies.

The Valley Poetry Workshop Project ultimately involved public poetry readings, printmaking, poetry production, undergraduate and graduate student co-teaching, and outreach programming with alternative high schools. The project included the collection of the produced community work for a forthcoming limited-run publication by Aunt Lute Books. The primary workshop facilitators in the community project were borderland artist, educator, and nepantlera Celeste De Luna; professor of creative writing, activist, and Texas Poet Laureate 2020 Emmy Pérez; and me, poet, sCHOLAr, and Río Grande Valley native, Lady Mariposa. The central organizer, logistics coordinator, and community liaison for facilitating the project as a whole was Emmy Pérez. Additional class facilitators included poet and borderland historian Dr. Carolina Monsiváis, plus co-teaching assistants and poets María García and Amanda Victoria Ramírez. All participants who led and helped to organize workshops were compensated through grants. Grant funds were also used to facilitate additional components for the project including the invitation of local poets to participate in workshop proceedings, workshop materials, food, and crafting supplies for community events. All workshop participants were provided with a complimentary copy of *Borderlands / La Frontera*, the foundational text of our programming project.

The Valley Poetry Workshop Project, then, built on the legacy of Gloria E. Anzaldúa and the multiple legacies of Anzaldúan discourse produced in the RGV. It built on traditions of poetry as philosophy and for healing—of writing as "the path of the red and the black ink" (Anzaldúa, *Borderlands*

16 *The Alice Kleberg Reynolds Foundation* makes grants to nonprofit organizations serving specific south and central Texas counties. AKR grants fund charitable works, education, medical, literacy, and scientific purposes (Guidelines).

87–97). It acknowledged the borderlands as a place of struggle and a generative space, and through Aunt Lute, it connected university resources to community.

QUEERING CUENTOS: BORDERLAND INTERGENERATIONAL NARRATIVES

Workshop Objective: My workshop objective was to produce intergenerational Anzaldúan discourse through contemporary narratives of borderland LGBTQIA+ lives. Through Anzaldúa's poetry and theories, workshop participants worked towards unpacking the complicated tapestry of todos los cuentos that define them, composing poetry that encapsulated their movimientos de rebeldía, their politicization, their resistance, their survival, and their own naming. Helping me to envision the parameters for my workshop objective and coordinating the venue locations for our workshop and poetry reading, was Emmy Pérez.

Demographics: Initially, the grant was written with program participants envisioned to be LGBTQIA+ community members between the ages of 15 and 25. These parameters correlated with the initial grant proposal for community programming that created the workshops in alternative Valley high schools. Ultimately, only one person under the age of 18 signed up to participate in the public portion of the Valley Poetry Workshop Project. Therefore, the parameters for the public workshop were widened to include LGBTQIA+ participants of all ages and allies.

Class Schedule and Location: Queering Cuentos (QC) featured three lesson plans. The weekly lesson plan was presented twice a week; once on Tuesday to accommodate Group 1 participants, and then again on Thursday to accommodate different participants in Group 2. This arrangement also allowed the predominantly working-class group members an opportunity to switch between Tuesday or Thursday workshops to accommodate any changes in work schedules. QC was held in a reserved conference room at the McAllen Public Library on Tuesdays and Thursdays between 5:00 p.m. and 8:00 p.m. Saturdays were reserved for poetry workshops where students also listened to and visited with invited LGBTQIA+ community poets. At QC Poetry Workshops, students shared their work, heard commentary on their writing, and worked towards implementing critiques and comments into their work. Corresponding with the Tuesday and Thursday group framework, poetry workshops occurred twice on Saturday. This arrangement allowed participants to workshop with group members who read their poems prior to attending class through posts on private QC Facebook groups.

Lesson Plans and Writing Prompts

Lesson Plan Week 1: Contando Cuentos: Theory in the Flesh

- Anzaldúa Biography
- Outline Anzaldúa's Publications, Overview of Anzaldúan Theory and the El Mundo Zurdo Conference ("Gloria Anzaldúa: Reflections from the Borderlands")
- Popcorn Read chapter 1, "The Homeland, Aztlán/El otro México"
    - Discuss Borderland Narratives: Political Landscape, Militarized Borders, Material Conditions
- Intergenerational Narratives through Video:
    - Watch "History of McAllen 1961–1970" & "History of McAllen 1971–1980"
    - Watch "In Luv with the Valle: Coco Valle Mix," by Big Rene
- Read to "To live in the Borderlands means you" and discuss

> *Writing Prompt 1:* Construct your own "To live in the Borderlands means you," piece. However, construct your poem with the sounds of your Valley experience. Select one quintessential song that reminds you of the Valley.
> - Piece does not need to be a litany poem.
> - Song does not have to be your favorite song, or a reflection of your eclectic taste in music. The song should instead remind you of life in the RGV.
> - Piece will be presented by students during Saturday workshop after playing a portion of their selected song.

For Next Week:

- Read chapter 2, "Movimientos de rebeldía y las culturas que traicionan."
- Read Anzaldúa's "La Prieta"

Week 2: Movimientos de Rebeldía en Un Mundo Zurdo

Part One: Group Discussion of Assigned Readings

- Discuss "Movimientos de rebeldía y las culturas que traicionan" by dividing the class into groups. Groups should:
    - Present a summary of the material
    - Discuss significant themes, definitions, or ideas
    - Identify and discuss:
        - Conflicts arising for your own naming.
        - How are your ideas and identities a rebellion, and why?

How is your understanding of culture a rebellion?
How is your spirituality a rebellion?
How is your form of community a rebellion, and why?

- Discuss Anzaldúa's "La Prieta" as a class

Part Two: To Queer the World: En Un Mundo Zurdo

- Towards El Mundo Zurdo
- Radical Queer Politics
- Queer Subjectivity
- Discuss Homonormativity & Pinkwashing by Viewing the Videos "Equal," and "Top 10 Best Pride Festivals" (Clinton, MsMojo).
    - Critical analysis of Gay Pride and Marriage through the videos "*Gay Pride & Capitalism" and "How Marriage Will Never Set Us Free"* (Novara Media, Spade and Dector).

Writing Prompt 2: Construct a rebeldía poem. After reading Anzaldúa's "Movimientos de rebeldía y las culturas que traicionan," and "La Prieta," think about what you would say if you could speak to your cultura. What narratives would you tell those keepers of traditions, those proprietors of properness? Unraveling your understanding of self vs. the you that is expected, what would you tell your own memories? What would you tell your mother, your friends, and your loved ones of your rebeldía, your embrace of the queer? How could an understanding of your rebeldía help change the world? How would it change those you love, and change the way you love? How has your rebeldía changed your spirituality, changed the way you see God?

For Next Week:

- Read chapter 5, "How to Tame a Wild Tongue"
- Read chapter 7, "La conciencia de la mestiza / Towards a New Consciousness"

<u>Week 3: Wild Tongues Toward a New Mestiza Consciousness</u>

- Discuss "How to Tame a Wild Tongue"
- Discuss "La conciencia de la mestiza / Towards a New Consciousness"

Writing Prompt 3: How do you live your mestizaje? Gloria states en "La conciencia de la mestiza / Towards a New Consciousness," "Soy un amasamiento. I am an act of kneading, or uniting and joining that not only has produced both a creature of darkness and a creature of light, but also a creature that questions the definitions of light and dark and gives them new meanings." (*Borderlands* 103) The new Mestiza:

> puts history through a sieve, winnows out the lies, looks at the forces that we as a race, as women have been a part of. Luego bota lo que no vale, los desmientos, los desencuentos, el embrutecimiento. . . . This step is a conscious rupture with all oppressive traditions of all cultures and religions. She communicates that rupture, documents the struggle. She reinterprets history and using new symbols she shapes new myths. She adopts new perspectives. (104)

Your poetry prompt for this final week is to tell us about your amasamiento, your multiplicity, your coexistence with the complicated understandings of yourself. How do you embrace the complications of your culture? How do you hold multiple degrees of beliefs, ideals and hopes, even when some of these beliefs seem to be counterproductive to each other? How do you live your multiplicity?

Workshop Reflections and Anzaldúan Frameworks

Week 1 Reflection: June 1, 2019: Proclaiming Narratives and Space

My intention for week one was to impart to the participants the importance of their own narratives, of speaking, creating, and insisting on these narratives. Through class discussions of readings, film, and their own experiences, I wanted students to recognize that there are others telling their stories for them, and that these foreign reflections lack nuance and are not the narrative that people living within the borderlands would tell. We noted how outsider narratives become valid in the national imaginary, and are often featured prominently in academic and mainstream forums. As a native of the Río Grande Valley, I asked them, as well as myself, "How do we talk about ourselves? How do we create borderland narratives?"

After reading "The Homeland Aztlán / El Otro México," we watched two videos produced by the City of McAllen discussing the city's history and growth. Students recognized the McAllen narrative through Anzaldúa's observations of the border, where "the only 'legitimate' inhabitants are those in power, the whites and those who align themselves with whites" (*Borderlands* 25–26). The two McAllen videos outlined a twenty-year time span in the Río Grande Valley without showing or discussing the local community or culture. Community members mentioned by the City of McAllen were "winter Texans," temporary white visitors to the RGV that large sections of the local economy financially depend on ("History of McAllen: 1961–1970"). The 1970s video ends with a devastating flood that negatively impacted parts of McAllen. It was only then that students were able to see their community members wading among flood waters ("History of McAllen: 1971–1980"). Group members noted the distortion of McAllen's foundation and its erasure of the actual people that helped make it.

Students juxtaposed the two city videos with "In Luv with the Valle" by Big Rene. Big Rene is a Río Grande Valley independent TexMex–Valley hip-hop artist who records with the help of rapper and local producer HustleMinds of HustleMinds Entertainment (Big Rene, "Bio"). "In Luv with the Valle," features video collage of RGV cities, with Big Rene conducting a Valley-wide roll call, and discussing Valley socioeconomic conditions while proclaiming his love for life en el Valle.

> I'm in love con el Valle . . . my heart cannot deny it. Old school, I thought you knew, been repping the valley since I was two. . . . Puro respect, I'll never forget my roots are from the RGV. 83 will always be the artery to connect us all . . . Unemployment ranks high. Poorest places, ranked high. Lowest pay but we still survive, got to keep on living that valley life.

Students reviewed the visual power of showing everyday images of borderland spaces. They noted the function of naming and laying claim to these borderland cities, especially the smaller ones that tend to be forgotten as part of the RGV landscape. Unpacked through class discourse was the importance of including within their narratives not only what is happening within the RGV, but also proclaiming the Río Grande Valley by name as borderland people.

The histories that participants shared were rich, diverse, disruptive, challenging, and more. Topics included homelessness, misgendering by family and friends, the insistence on institutions to misgender, flooding in the valley, traffic, construction, and post-Trump aggressions in the borderlands. On the border that Reagan called a frontline and war zone, Trump's border policies have continued to create "a shock culture, a border culture, a third country, a closed country" (Anzaldúa, *Borderlands*, 33). A month before the start of our workshop, Trump's immigrant deterrence measures included "separating migrant families, deploying American troops to the border and returning asylum seekers to Mexico as they await immigrant court hearings" (*New York Times*). In our workshop students commented that Anzaldúa's work was relevant to contemporary borderland conditions, and that *Borderlands / La Frontera* felt as if it was written specifically from conditions in 2019, and not in the 1980s.

Week 2 Reflection: June 9, 2019: Queering the World in Lots of Different Ways

This week's focus centered on radical queer politics. The lecture revolved around Anzaldúa's quote in a 1999 interview in *Colorlines*. Anzaldúa stated:

> It's not enough to be queer sexually, but we have to be queer in the way we think and the way we see the world. We have to be queer because

> queer is always at odds with the status quo. Instead of buying in as lesbians that we're just like all the other guys, we're just folks, the only difference we have is our sexual preference, we have to say that we are not normal. Who wants to be normal? Normal is those fuckers that are polluting the world, the oppressors. We have to "queer" the world in a lot of different ways. (Hernández, 1999)

I asked the class to think of how they queer the world. How do they challenge culture, traditions, the status quo, and themselves? As discussed in "La Prieta," how do they critique those they love and what we love without completely destroying or dismissing the lived realities and conditions of those lives (Anzaldúa, *This Bridge*)? By unpacking the material in "Moviementos de rebeldía" and "La Prieta," questions we examined of our rebellion as a class were: 1) How are our ideas and identities queer? 2) How is our challenge and modification of culture queer? 3) How are our kinship formations queer?

This section on radical queer politics sought to unpack homonormativity by critiquing the capitalization of Pride through Pinkwashing. Using Dean Spade and Craig Willse's "Marriage Will Never Set Us Free," I highlighted how centering gay marriage in LGBTQ rights agendas is removed from the needs of those within marginalized sectors of the LGBTQIA+ community. Through this discussion on gay marriage the class recognized how focusing on marriage rights more often benefits middle-class queers who use marriage as a way to secure property rights and other benefits that are not afforded to disenfranchised members of queer communities. Instead, influenced by Anzaldúa's challenge to queer the world, I outlined a queer theory framework that extends queer from subjectivity into coalitions through socioeconomic and queer existences. Queerness, as understood beyond identity / in addition to identity, can challenge and oppose the status quo and institutions of power, allowing us to form and to become un Mundo Zurdo.

<u>Week 3 Reflection: June 13, 2019: Language and Coalitional Politics</u>

Week three allowed us to brainstorm about coalitional politics. Part of our conversation focused on language and its importance as tied to the punishment that many in our community experienced for speaking Spanish. An item of interest in our readings was Anzaldúa's discourse on masculinity. Students reflected on Anzaldúa's invitation to bring men into the conversation by stating "que no se nos olviden los hombres" (Anzaldúa, *Borderlands* 105). We discussed tenderness seen as vulnerability, and regional examples of toxic masculinity. The class also unpacked Anzaldúa's call for coalitional politics, and noted that for some of us this is difficult as we insist on the importance of creating third spaces and continuing to focus on the needs of our specific communities. Together we discussed Anzaldúa's new mestiza consciousness as her call for us to understand how these coalitions could be possible en un Mundo Zurdo, ultimately encouraging us to engage them.

QUEERING CUENTOS AND COMMUNITY GATHERINGS

Creating poetry and workshopping poems with students while unpacking Anzaldúan discourse was the foundation of my three-week summer program. However, also important to my framework as an educator—and native of the Río Grande Valley—was highlighting the RGV literary community to newer writers. Several of the writers in QC had been writing for many years; however, they had established no formal connection with the vibrant community of poets who are creating and sharing work along the border. Saturday workshops therefore featured special guest poets from the RGV, all LGBTQIA+ identified. The Río Grande Valley poets Stevie Luna, César L. De León and Esther Martínez came to QC and shared their work, discussed their process, listened to and commented on the poetry of workshop participants. Their inclusion in the Saturday workshops helped participants build writing networks, thereby helping to ensure that participants continued creating and sharing their work in the community.

Additional events that I facilitated through the Queering Cuentos workshop included the "Postcards to Gloria" event. This community event was held at the McAllen Public Library on June 8, 2019, at 3:00 p.m. The event featured a presentation on Anzaldúa's legacy in the Río Grande Valley and included a community crafting session. Attendees had the opportunity to make and share postcards dedicated to Anzaldúa. The final component of the programming event for QC was the "Queering Cuentos Community Poetry Reading." The event took place on June 14, 2019, at Luna Coffee House in McAllen, Texas. This reading featured the participants of the QC workshop presenting the poetry they had created through class prompts.

CONCLUSION: RADICAL QUEER POLITICS EN UN MUNDO ZURDO

As a sCHOLAr, I often feel like an outsider being invited into spaces that I will have to fight to make my own. However, being asked to create poetry and unpack discourse in my home community felt different. Centering *Borderlands / La Frontera* in a political poetry workshop did not feel like a scholastic fight, but a cyclical return home. This summer residency allowed me to bridge the worlds I had been straddling since moving to eastern Washington State, trying to live and work in a predominantly white institution on the Washington-Idaho border. Combining material learned at Washington State University with Anzaldúan theory, I was able to articulate a course framework that implemented elements of my chola research with the creation of a poetry workshop. My use of El Mundo Zurdo through theory in the flesh and radical queer politics allowed me to articulate a critical foundation that challenged participants to consider commonalities with untraditional queer subjects. As per my dissertation research on queer subjectivity: In *This Bridge Called My Back*, Cherríe Moraga describes the understanding of our political self as a "theory in the flesh," "one where the physical realities of our lives—our skin color, the land or concrete we grew up on, our sexual longings—all fuse to create a politic[s] born out of necessity. [It's how] we attempt to bridge the contradictions in our experience, . . . by naming ourselves and telling our own stories in our own words" (19). It is this politic born out of necessity, moving specifically towards what Anzaldúa called El Mundo Zurdo, that can allow for discourse about queer subjectivity, separate from identity politics. Anzaldúa states:

> [In] the pull between what is and what should be . . . [the] Mundo Zurdo path is the path of a two-way movement—a going deep in to the self and an expanding out into the world, a simultaneous recreation of the self and a reconstruction of society. . . . Between them and among others, I build my own universe, El Mundo Zurdo. . . . The rational, the patriarchal, and the heterosexual have held sway and legal tender for too long. . . . Only together can we be a force, . . . a network of kindred spirits, a kind of family (Anzaldúa, "La Prieta" 208–209).

It is through la facultad of creating this Mundo Zurdo that I connect this queer imagining to subjects like cholas, undocumented immigrants, los atravesados (Anzaldúa, *Borderlands* 25), the working poor, the homeless, those dying of HIV, those with mental health issues, and those who are differently abled. As a theory in the flesh en un Mundo Zurdo, one that we are trying to build, these different subjects are queer through their political embodiment as feared and dismissed subjects in the nation state.[17]

Anzaldúa's Mundo Zurdo and her calls for queering the world continue to fuel new schools of thought such as those of Cathy Cohen, whose work builds on her theory through a discourse of radical queer politics. The poetry and dialogues the flowed from these three weeks joined this larger discourse and work of radical queer politics—and it also brings to light troubling realities. En Un Mundo Zurdo, we recreate ourselves and recreate society, when we do as Cathy Cohen suggests, and embrace the deviant in our imaginings of a better world. In

17 Political embodiments are unpacked within my dissertation as cholas and material cholas whose working-class subjectivity and survival strategies challenge nation state discursive formations of lives with value. For more see Welfare Gangster frameworks in Chapter 2 of my dissertation project.

her "Remarks Upon Receiving the Kessler Award," Cohen describes how queer scholars in writing about death, race, violence and queerness should marshal a different Black body to mark these intersections. She notes that although there are more traditional subjects for analysis, such as CeCe McDonald, a Black trans woman who was imprisoned for second-degree manslaughter when she defended herself from a transphobic and racist attacker, Cohen proposes that we should also embrace Michael Brown as part of a radical queer politic. She states:

> For me, Michael Brown's death is deeply connected to the killing of Sakia Gunn and the attack on and incarceration of CeCe McDonald, not because of his sexual practice or his identity, or his performance, but instead because Michael Brown, CeCe McDonald and Sakia Gunn, as well as other young folks of color, operate in the world as queer subjects. The targets of normalizing racializing projects intent on pathologizing them across the dimensions of race, class, gender, and sexuality while normalizing their degradation and marginalization until it becomes what we expect, the norm, until it becomes something we no longer see, or pay attention to. (12)

Cohen advocates for building on the traditions of those who challenged the police at moments like the Stonewall riots, AIDS activists who challenged the government that had denied them the right to live, and trans activists who are helping to transform language, laws, and how we understand ourselves. It is the resilience and resistance of what Cohen calls "less traditional queer bodies" that we should embrace as models (14; Sandoval 7–9).

Using theories, histories, narratives, and critiques of the political and social economic conditions of the Río Grande Valley, queers and allies unpacked queer subjectivity and radical queer political presences. Through the breakdown of El Mundo Zurdo, theory in the flesh, and radical queer politics, Queering Cuentos outlined for participants how queering the world is a challenge to power rather than a rainbow celebration of "we are just like you." By highlighting how their rebeldía challenges traditions, culture, gender, and notions of family, participants were able to recognize that their lives, already lived through El Mundo Zurdo, had taught them the skills they need to queer the world. We need more summers like the summers of 2019—summers where community and university can come together in the community to build expansively queer spaces.

The ability to produce community projects with frameworks that are central to your political praxis is rare, and rarer still is the funding to engage in this work. Therefore, it is essential to acknowledge Aunt Lute and Emmy Pérez for the labor they invested in bringing this workshop to fruition. Their vision helped to bridge elements of my own understanding, and left a lasting impact on the community members who participated. Through the space that Anzaldúa's work created, the members of "Queering Cuentos" would go on to meet several times after the closing of our workshop. They gathered at each other's homes, shared food, and continued to unpack *Borderlands / La Frontera*. The QC poets continue to keep communication and friendships with each other through an informal group known as *Los Queers*. The poetry that many of the participants created, along with the postcards from our community crafting event, are currently with Aunt Lute as they work towards the publication of texts from this community project. As of July 2020, Aunt Lute is committed to reapplying for grant funding from the AKR Foundation to facilitate another Anzaldúan summer project in the future.

WORKS CITED

Álvarez, Stephanie, Stephanie Brock, Janie Covarrubias, Lauren Espinoza, and Orquidea Morales. "Gloria Anzaldúa, Nuestra Gloria, Nuestra heroína fronteriza / Our Glory(a), Our Borderlands Heroine: An Art exhibit at Anzaldúa's Alma Mater, The University of Texas–Pan American." *El Mundo Zurdo 3: Selected Works from the 2012 Meeting of the Society for the Study of Gloria Anzaldúa*. Aunt Lute Press, 2014, 123–139.

Anzaldúa, Gloria. *Borderlands / La Frontera: The New Mestiza*. Aunt Lute, 2007.

———. "La Prieta." *This Bridge Called My Back: Writings by Radical Women of Color*, edited by Cherríe Moraga and Gloria Anzaldúa, SUNY Press, 2015, 198–209.

Big Rene. "In Luv With the Valle (CoCo RGV Remix)." *YouTube*, uploaded by Big Rene, 2 Dec. 2016, https://youtu.be/e-clsBrJPmQ.

———. "Bio." Valle Brand, https://bigrene.com/bio. Accessed 11 February 2020.

Cantú, Norma E. Keynote address. "Living en la Frontera: Gloria Anzaldúa and Border Theory, with a Reading from *Canícula: Snapshots of a Girlhood En La Frontera*," 14 April 2008, University of Texas–Pan American, Edinburg.

Clinton, Hillary. "Equal." *YouTube*, uploaded by Hillary Clinton, 24 June 2015, https://youtu.be/g2Y9abmNuRw.

Cohen, Cathy. "#DoBlackLivesMatter? From Michael Brown to CeCe McDonald on Black Death and LGBTQ Politics." Remarks upon receiving the Kessler Award from the Center for Lesbian and Gay Studies, 12 Dec. 2014, Elebash Auditorium, Graduate Center, City University of New York.

"Gay Pride & Capitalism: What is Pinkwashing?" *YouTube*, uploaded by Novara Media, 19 June, 2016, https://youtu.be/J4LP0z493oY.

"Gloria Anzaldúa: Reflections from the Borderlands." *YouTube*, uploaded by upta0, 16 Sept. 2016, https://youtu.be/rI6AGsbHMFc.

Guidelines. *The Alice Kleberg Reynolds Foundation* (AKR Foundation). https://akrfoundation.org/guidelines/. Accessed 19 July 2020.

Hernández, Monica. "With Heart in Hand / Con Corazón En la Mano: An Interview with Gloria Anzaldúa," *Colorlines*, Race Forward, 20 Oct. 1999. https://www.colorlines.com/articles/heart-handcon-corazon-en-la-mano.

"History of McAllen: 1961–1970." *YouTube*, uploaded by exploremcallen, 30 Sept. 2011, .https://youtu.be/SEr_hZsfZ7c.

"History of McAllen: 1971–1980." *YouTube*, uploaded by exploremcallen, 30 Sept. 2011, https://youtu.be/je2kOu7mJ0s.

"Honoring Gloria E. Anzaldúa's Philosophical Legacy at UTRGV." Anzaldua Speaker Series in Philosophy, 14 February 2020, wordpress.com. https://anzalduaspeakerseriesphilosophy.wordpress.com/.

Lara, Irene. "Daughter of Coatlicue: An Interview with Gloria Anzaldúa." *Entre Mundos/Among Worlds: New Perspectives on Gloria Anzaldúa*, edited by AnaLouise Keating, Palgrave MacMillan, 2005, 41–55.

Marriage Will Never Set Us Free. YouTube. Video interviews conducted by Dean Spade and Hope Dector at Queer Dreams and Nonprofit Blues Conference, convened Center for Gender and Sexuality Law, Columbia Law School, and Barnard Center for Research on Women (BCRW), Barnard College, 4–5 Oct. 2013. Uploaded by BCRW, 29 Sept. 2016, https://youtu.be/rZjb5zynkB4.

Moraga, Cherríe. "Entering the Lives of Others: Theory in the Flesh." *This Bridge Called My Back: Writings by Radical Women of Color*, edited by Cherríe Moraga and Gloria Anzaldúa, SUNY Press, 2015, 19.

New York Times. "As Immigrants Are Packed into Encampments, Border Patrol Struggles with Overcrowding." Crossing the Border Newsletter, 16 May 2019, https://www.nytimes.com/2019/05/16/us/immigrants-mexico-tents.html

"Nuestra Gloria: El Retorno." *UTRGV Center for Mexican American Studies*, 15 Feb. 2020, https://www.utrgv.edu/cmas/nuestra-gloria/retorno/index.htm.

"Nuestra Gloria: Speaker Series in Philosophy." UTRGV Center for Mexican American Studies, 15 Feb. 2020, https://www.utrgv.edu/cmas/nuestra-gloria/speaker-series/index.htm.

García Ordaz, Daniel. SSGA Public Group. *Facebook*, 9 Mar. 2020. https://www.facebook.com/groups/gloria.anzaldua.society/permalink/10157413977619086/.

"Río Grande Valley International Poetry Festival." *ValleyPoetryFest.Org*, 15 Feb. 2020, http://www.valleypoetryfest.org/

Sandoval, Verónica. Introduction. "Chola Work: A Genealogy of Homegirl Legacies of Resistance," Washington State University, PhD dissertation, 2022.

Suárez, Priscilla Celina, and Noemi Martínez. *Gloria Anzaldúa Legacy Project Zine*. Café Revolución Productions. 2007.

Spade, Dean, and Craig Willse. "Marriage will Never set us Free." *Organizing Upgrade*, https://archive.organizingupgrade.com/index.php/modules-menu/beyond-capitalism/item/1002-marriage-will-never-set-us-free.

"Top 10 Best Pride Festivals." *YouTube*, uploaded by MsMojo, 24 June 2017, https://youtu.be/1un0Q2zuE_M.

PART II

TELLING LIVES: TESTIMONIOS, AUTOHISTORIA, ORAL HISTORY, AND AUTOETHNOGRAPHY

THE GENDERED CONSTRUCTION OF BORDER-CROSSING INTO CANADA: IMMIGRANT AND INDIGENOUS WOMEN'S LIFE HISTORIES

ALIA HAZINEH, THERESA JBEILI, AND KATHLEEN THOMAS-MCNEILL

INTRODUCTION

To be a border-crosser in Canada is to belong everywhere and nowhere, to exist in a space where one is simultaneously "of Canada" and "of somewhere else." The act of crossing borders is more than passing over geographical lines. When a woman moves from the Global South to Canada, she brings her homeland and life experiences inscribed on her body, spirit, and mind. Ethnic markers, language, and accent are visible, embodied experiences. However, there are imperceptible borders such as spirituality, education, and violence that, in addition, create emotional borders. Thus, the woman herself is a "*borderzone*"; she cannot be understood simply through her phenotype or cultural context. What happens when women of color cross geographical lines and their original framework of reality clashes and melds with others? Our paper is an attempt to reify this in-between space, or *nepantla*, of a border-crossing woman's identity. We provide a contextual, comparative analysis of border-crossing narratives where the influence of race and gender is ubiquitous and where the guiding principles of spirituality and religion are intertwined.

Based on the narratives of six women border-crossers, we argue that Canada objectifies "belonging" with the bureaucratic hurdles of citizenship. Yet, in accordance with Gloria Anzaldúa's symbolic system of *conocimiento*, our data shows that truly belonging to a homeland is embodied in the interplay between a woman's imaginative capacity, *la facultad*, and her internal conflicts, *the shadowbeast*.[1] Thus, we argue that the bureaucratic notion of citizenship does not authentically constitute *belonging*, but instead, works to categorize, dehumanize, and alienate. Our research participants crossed into Canada, and, as a result, the entire nation of Canada became a *borderzone* within which they negotiated their notions of *self*, in their own *nepantla*. By looking through the lens of *conocimiento*, we dismantle preglobalization perceptions of identity and belonging as homologous, static, and exclusionary bureaucratic entities in Canada.

METHODOLOGY

This paper is the work of a two-term, undergraduate, independent study project conducted at Dalhousie University in Halifax, Nova Scotia, Canada. Our research consisted of six open-ended interviews between three and five hours in length with border-crossing women. In this context, Indigenous women venturing from reserves into their colonized homeland are border-crossers as well. Our approach deliberately breaks with traditional anthropological models whose structure often denies the "coevalness" of its informants (Lavie and Swedenburg 1). Instead, we embarked on a feminist-collectivist approach, collaborating with our participants in order to bring in multiple perspectives that cross disciplines as well as geographical boundaries. This is a condensed version of the full research paper.

BORDER-CROSSERS

> Kira:
>
> When people ask me where my home is, I feel like they are asking me where I belong and I don't know. . . Ask me where I'm from, it's an easier question.

Kira is from Venezuela. She is passionate, optimistic, and quick to laugh. Even though she struggles to define *home* and find a sense of belonging in Canada, Kira maintains an impressive balance between being headstrong and open-minded. "What do I see when I look in the mirror?" She laughed at Kathleen's seemingly rhetorical question, "I'm super small, I'm Black, and I have super curly hair!" In her response about traveling to Canada at nineteen, Kira shared that it was "the first time I'd moved to a place. I mean, in that moment I wasn't escaping from anything. Things were bad but not *as* bad as now in

---

1 The terms *conocimiento, la facultad,* and *shadowbeast* originate from Gloria Anzaldúa's works *Borderlands / La Frontera* and *Light in the Dark / Luz en lo oscuro.*

Venezuela." Imitating her younger self, she exuded, "I was like, 'Oh my God I'm moving! Yeah!' . . . I was, like, hanging out all the time with Mexican people, Koreans, and Japanese. . . . It was very different to *anything* I had lived in my life before." Kira's family was economically privileged in Venezuela, and they enjoyed regular vacations. "I'm really grateful that I went to Disneyland so many fucking times because I was kinda familiar with the culture. It wasn't a shock for me when I first came."

> Ella:
>
> Sometimes I feel worried to tell [Canadians] I'm Palestinian. But, I'm still Palestinian.
>
> Yeah, . . . that's tough. I don't know what [else] to say.

Meet Ella, a twenty-seven-year-old singer, chef, and border-crosser from Gaza. Sitting in a coffee shop, behind soft dark curls that frame her almond eyes and tentative smile, she shared with Alia her story of navigating a turbulent, years-long border-crossing experience. Ella continues to work on reconciling the dramatic changes her new Canadian life brings after living in Gaza for twenty-four years. "I feel like I'm in the process of, like, finding my identity, . . . like, who am I? Am I gonna be still thinking the same? . . . Or, am I gonna be developing my skills and my thinking?" Ella moves through the world with anxiety that stems from no longer being in Gaza. She told Alia, "The question of home is very hard. . . Home's still home, where I was born in Gaza Strip, Palestine. But for me now, being away from home and all the difficult situations there, I am trying to make my home here in Canada."

> Raissa:
>
> My religion, for sure, has the right of way over anything else. My 'Lebanese-ness' also . . . If you told me to . . . give [myself] two top identities, it would be my religion and my . . . background. These are two things I don't think I could compromise.

These are the sentiments of Raissa, a twenty-five-year-old Lebanese border-crosser. "[We] came here in 2006," she began her story. "My dad is a surgeon and he got his degree from Laval University, Quebec. . . In 2006, . . . he got a locum[2] in Antigonish and that was the summer when Israel was bombing us [Lebanon]. Because of the . . . the situation [July War, 2006] that was going on, all Canadian citizens were asked to leave [Lebanon]. So we'll just . . . go on long 'vacation.'" Due to the war, this "vacation" became permanent for Raissa and her family. Although facing few bureaucratic struggles immigrating to Canada,

2 A temporary position.

Raissa grapples with the fractured familial connections in Lebanon. She told Theresa that it is difficult "missing things that happen over there and feeling like you wanna be over there but you can't . . . and same for my family [in Lebanon]. They feel like they're missing us and they're missing watching us grow up and living with us day to day." Her smile dissolved as she continued, "When we were living there . . . we were part of each other's lives directly. Whereas, when you don't live close to each other, you still love them . . . but . . . they're not really part of your life . . . so you don't know what they're like."

> Ariel:
>
> At sixteen, I was told that I will be getting married to an older man and will be going to Canada as his bride. . . . Canada was not my choice, it just, like, happened.

Comfortably ensconced on Kathleen's living room sofa, thirty-six-year-old Ariel took a deep breath, pushed her long, auburn-dyed hair from her face and launched into her story. "I was pretty much pressured into a marriage. . . . A year later I arrived here [from Pakistan] in my new home and it was miserable. Then, I became a teenage mom." She paused, sipping her peppermint tea. "But I think there's a much deeper and more powerful emotional migration story, because even though I was physically here, I had never thought of Canada as my home. I wanted to leave because I was being abused in my marriage." She grinned at Kathleen and said, "I fantasized about climbing down the house that I lived in, out of the window like Rapunzel, and running away with my daughter." Today, Ariel is a public speaker and a women's rights activist who shares her story wherever she can, from living rooms to international conferences. "When I look back and think, '*Why* did I go through all of that abuse . . .'" She trailed off, staring into the middle distance for a moment. "But the work that I'm doing now to help thousands, if not millions, of people around the world . . . I love it. It gives me meaning and purpose and wakes me up every morning."

> Lila:
>
> Going back home, my African friends [say], "Oh, you're so Canadian." I'm like, "No! I'm in the middle!" I feel offended… 'cause I want [them] to know that yes, I grew up here [Canada], but I'm still Zambian, right?

Lila is a twenty-two-year-old Zambian border-crosser and university student. On a chilly Thursday afternoon, she met with Alia outside a campus study room. Lila wore bright colors that mirrored her playful humor and vibrant smile. She laughed often throughout the three-hour interview as she described the struggle of finding a space where cross-cultural expression between Zambian and Canadian traditions and values was comfortable. "Home," she explained, "is a little bit of both places. I'd probably start off by saying home is where I'm from, Zambia. But, I would also include Nova Scotia because this is where I was raised." For Lila, negotiating the concept of home is an intricate dance between two cultures that continue to complicate and antagonize each other. She confessed her deep love for her Zambian homeland and the essential role that family, "the most important thing," plays in her life.

> Willard:
>
> I was taught that being Mi'kmaw wasn't about how you looked. It was about the way you acted throughout society and the way you viewed the world. It wasn't your skin. . . . Since I knew that from such a young age, for [other children] to try and say I wasn't Mi'kmaw just because of the color of my skin was so weird because . . . everything I do is Mi'kmaw, every day.

Unlike our other research participants, Willard, a nineteen-year-old woman from Indian Brook, Nova Scotia, has been a border-crosser from childhood. She met with Theresa in the kitchen of her Victorian-style townhouse. Willard currently lives in Halifax while attending university, but has to cross "colonial borders" when she goes to the reserve to visit family. As an Indigenous woman, Willard often collides with labels like "status" and "borders," terms she refers to as "colonial expressions." She explained, "It sucks that I have to say 'full status'[3] 'cause like, that's a colonial thing. But . . . it's literally a daily part of our life, so the only way I can talk about that is if I literally use a colonial term." Willard associates home with her life on the reserve where her entire community is her family. "Canadian culture is more . . . capitalist based. Everyone's just trying to get their own nuclear family into the best it can be. . . . They only care about themselves and their family."

THE LACUNA: CANADA'S NEGLECT OF SPIRITUALITY AND RELIGION IN DISCUSSIONS OF IMMIGRATION

As we reviewed the literature, we discovered a lacuna in Canadian border-crossing research. The bureaucratic process of Canadian citizenship is secular; thus, many assume that border-crossing and integration are also secular experiences. Canadian immigration literature is a classic example of confirmation bias, favoring information that confirms society's preexisting beliefs. That

3 Maintaining Native identity based on legal criteria.

is to say, Canadian secularism tends to demote spirituality and religion to a somewhat ambivalently respected and even inconsequential aspect of identity.[4] Our findings, contrarily, conclude that the experience of border-crossing is anything but an exclusively secular endeavor.

In Canadian literature, the border is defined almost exclusively in geographical terms and refers to the border-crossing woman bureaucratically as "immigrant." This approach treats a woman's challenges as speed bumps along a linear path—from point A, the initial act of crossing the border, to point B, cultural integration and citizenship. This linear framework is adverse to Anzaldúa's nonlinear, multifaceted definition of borderzones. For her, a borderzone is physical, emotional, and spiritual; it is "where the Third World grates against the first and bleeds, . . . a vague and undetermined place created by the emotional residue of an unnatural boundary, . . . a constant state of transition" (*Borderlands* 25). Popular literature's neglect of border-crossing women's spirituality is partly a result of the research parameters used by Western scholars. According to Smadar Lavie, "colonial idealism is still at the very heart of scholarship, because funding for research and publications are mostly situated in North American and Western European institutions that set the research agenda" (29). Our data follows Anzaldúa's approach and breaks with this popular neglect, as it incorporates the entirety of a woman border-crosser's experience, *especially* the interwoven thread of spirituality.

EL ARREBATO, THE RUPTURE: AN ENDING, A BEGINNING

You are no longer who you used to be, . . . abandoned by all that's familiar. . . . Exposed, naked, disoriented, wounded, uncertain, confused, and conflicted, you're forced to live en la orilla—a razor-sharp edge that fragments you.

(Anzaldúa, Light 125)

When the French and British colonized Turtle Island and renamed it North America, they brought their religion-state traditions with them (Wallace 15). By the end of the seventeenth century, the Church of England controlled Upper Canada and the Roman Catholic Church, Lower Canada (15). Due to such colonial roots, *Christianocentrism*, the centering or overemphasis of Christianity, is ubiquitous in Canadian culture. Today, Canadian society's continued

4 For example, in Madine VanderPlaat's comprehensive review of Canadian literature on immigrant women's integration, "Integration Outcomes for Immigrant Women in Canada," religion is referenced only once, in the context of Muslim women's experiences job hunting while wearing hijabs. We argue that spirituality and religion are, to varying degrees, principal facets of culture.

subconscious allegiance to colonial, White, European Christianity is evident. Canadian religion-based statutory holidays—Good Friday, Easter Monday, and Christmas Day—all operate around a Christian calendar. Likewise, the secularism that arose with enlightenment in Europe, by equating itself with rationalism, pushed a homogeneous colonial agenda in Canada. Multiculturalist policy maintains that within one unified Canadian culture, multiple *other* cultures coexist. This Canadian culture, however, is influenced by what Dolores Chew calls "secular fundamentalism,"[5] whereby the secularist majority see one reality "in black and white, devoid of nuance and subjectivity" (87). In other words, the negative aspects of secularism (or secular fundamentalism), omnipotent rationalism and homogeneity, support colonial and Christiano-centric Canadian culture. These unconscious biases poison the good that is inherent in multiculturalism. Multiculturalist policy can, in many ways, serve as a smoke screen for secularist exclusionary material practices. In reality, what "diversity" permits, specifically in terms of spirituality and religion, turns out to be entirely limited. Next, we outline discursive power structures inherent in most Canadian life. The "rupture" that a border-crossing woman confronts when she enters Canada is entangled in this hegemonic landscape of "systematic racism, and marginalization" (Anzaldúa, *Light* 125). As she becomes "Canadian," the country's social structures work to delegitimize the spirituality inherent in her border-crossing, consequently fragmenting her understanding of the world and of herself.

Canadian Christian Multiculturalism

Today, Canada's "diversity model" is exceptional on the global stage. According to Irene Bloemraad, "Canadians who most strongly identify themselves as patriotic are also the most supportive of immigration and multiculturalism" (1). Political discourse around multiculturalism emerged during the Trudeau era in the 1960s. Eve Haque discusses how this multiculturalism emerged in tandem with bilingualism.[6] The duality of this grouping, while it sought to challenge the existing hierarchy of Anglo-Celtic dominance (most visibly from French Canadians), also served to "erase the founding status of Indigenous peoples and render the '*Other* ethnic groups'[7] as mere cultural communities peripheral to

5 In the context of our paper, secular fundamentalism is distinguished from secularism. Where secularism is a positive force (e.g. the 'separation of church and state'), secular fundamentalism is the extreme sect that calls for policies such as the prohibition of religious paraphernalia in public.

6 The 1963 Royal Commission on Bilingualism and Biculturalism.

7 "Other ethnic groups" was how all non-French and non-English immigrant groups were defined legally during the commissions.

the now-acknowledged 'two founding races,' the French and English" (81). From these roots, Canada developed its Christianocentrism by invisiblizing its settlers' Christian values. As Willard pointed out to Theresa in her interview, "The Western culture, that's the main culture, . . . that's what everything revolves around." Canada's liberal objective of a unified, inclusive world through secular assimilation is a paradox. For example, during instances of civil disobedience, Indigenous protectors are often posited negatively; their demands are perceived as "inherently divisive and reactionary" (Coulthard and Simpson 252). In Canada, when Indigenous communities protest state-led construction on stolen land, we may hear settlers remark, "It is just a pipeline, right?" The vision of a world unified under the "one, true, reality" of secularism and capitalist modernity demands Indigenous populations dispossess and erase themselves by breaking their connection to the land. Since Indigenous activists reject Canada's secular segregation of land from identity, they often find themselves crossing the border of secularist multiculturalism's "acceptable difference" into the category of a state "problem." The state, with its transcendent power and authority, thus decides not only *who* deserves religious and spiritual "tolerance" but also *what* constitutes religion and spirituality in the first place.

Secular Fundamentalism

Canadian multiculturalism insists on tolerance for religious diversity; however, multiculturalist rhetoric camouflages Western secularist and Christian prejudices, specifically when it pertains to the right to practice any religion. Dominant culture equates secularism with rationality and then binarily positions it *against* religio-cultural particularities (Haque 87). Raissa, for instance, is a Maronite.[8] When asked how she believes Canadian people view her religion, she said, "They think it's silly . . . They have a different perspective and they don't prioritize it like I do. It's not relevant [to them]." Since Canadians minimize Raissa's religious experience, she avoids discussing her beliefs. Many Canadians operate under the pretense that multiculturalism, being our national identity, precludes intolerance for religious difference. Canada's secular fundamentalism, however, invalidates religious truth claims, while its Christianocentrism compels such invalidations to focus on non-Christian religious expression. Multiculturalist policy *on paper* seems to serve as an exemption, for privileged (and Christian) Canadians, from taking responsibility or accountability for the structural racism, discrimination, and invalidation of *Other* religious truth claims that still exist in our system today.

---

8 A sect of non-European Christianity that originates in Syria but is now firmly rooted in Lebanon.

Today, we can see tensions arise as Canadian demographics become increasingly heterogeneous with the influx of non-Judeo-Christian cultures, religions, and races. This changing new demographic challenges not only the current secular attitude, but White, European privilege. Lila acknowledged this phenomenon when she noted, "Canada has been accommodating [to my family's religious practices], but only because Christianity is . . . the dominant religion in the Western world."

NEPANTLA, THE IN-BETWEEN: TORN BETWEEN CONFLICTING REALITIES

After leaving the home culture's familiar cocoon, you occupy other ideological spaces, begin seeing reality in new ways, questioning both the native culture's and the new culture's descriptions of reality.

(Anzaldúa, Light 71)

Canada's secular model pits homogenized, White/European Canadian identity against particular *non-Western* cultural expressions. This social configuration creates a *rupture*, or an us-against-them dichotomy that border-crossing women must constantly negotiate. All the women in this study felt pulled between conflicting realities, the norms of Canada's White majority and the familiar norms of their homeland.

Nice and Polite: Canadian Racism

There is a ubiquitous boundary that exists between secular subjects and non-liberal, fundamentalist cultures. As Roxana Ng notes, in this atmosphere, the boundary between what, to the hegemonic universal, is tolerable and what is not becomes a practice of demarcation (84). Ng argues that the point at which ethnicity becomes significant for border-crossing women is when they do not perform "adequately" (103). Willard spoke to this when she described Canadians' confusion as she explained that her mother was an Indigenous Mi'kmaq woman and a lawyer. Willard said, "it's almost like they don't even realize they're being racist . . . because it's just been such a societal norm that if you're a marginalized person you usually don't achieve things like that." The association of Indigenous identity with poverty runs so deep that (White? Christian?) Canadians often struggle with associating prestige with a racialized identity. In social situations, Canadians have the tendency to put visible minorities into a singular obscure group, that of the cultural Other: this category includes everybody else, but no one in particular.

Ella worked in the service industry as a barista and cook, and, while no longer an observant Muslim, she has experienced judgment and discrimination. People made assumptions and judgments about her upbringing, religious practices, and worldview simply based on her appearance. "Customers," Ella puzzled, "really judge you . . . from the face. Like they just look at me and they assume. . . . [They say,] 'You look like a Muslim' or 'You look like you're from Iran.' You can't just look at someone and assume. . . . I don't go and ask people, . . . 'Do you believe in something?' . . . They don't really ask [about your religion] but they really judge you." These simplistic assumptions illustrate yet another inadequacy in arbitrary demarcation policy. Not only does it contribute to the us-versus-them discourse, it assumes that *Others* (minority cultures) are ahistorical and static and subscribe to changeless cultural norms.

These women most frequently encountered racism under the guise of ignorance. There is a racist continuum that starts with benign ignorance at one end and has terrorism at the other. An example of benign ignorance was shared by Kira. She found that Nova Scotians frequently sought her out to talk about her race when "they don't actually know anything about Latin America. . . . There is no worse way to be racist than not knowing anything. . . . Like, you don't care!" However, ignorance can quickly cross into racism and take on more ominous qualities when people make overt assumptions about abilities based on skin color. Ella was closing her café when "a guy came and said I just realized that you're not White, not Canadian. [Then] he kept asking me about drinks and telling me to make them in certain ways, like I didn't know. He was being really rude to me." In this case, Ella found herself being perceived as Other and her competence and authority were subsequently dismissed.

The Shadow: A Case of Mistaken Identity Politics

Anzaldúa describes these rigid, seemingly incompatible belief systems as the *shadowbeast,* "the psyches of . . . culture and nation, . . . the past problems of family, community, and nation, . . . made up of the destructive aspects, psychic wounds, and splits" (*Borderlands* 49, 57). The shadowbeast works on both a collective and personal scale. In Canada, both Ariel and Ella's shadowbeast manifest almost identically in their mutual disdain for Arab men. Ariel's marriage was full of emotional, physical, and financial abuse. It has been many years since Ariel left her marriage; however, she makes it clear: "I don't mingle with Pakistanis and South Asians too much. I feel like there's always going to be judgment there . . . I faced a lot of backlash when I left my marriage. . . It was ugly, and all from that community. So I just stay away." Ella shared this sentiment and was adamant that she would not marry an Arab man. She stated categorically, "I hate Arab men." With this universalized disdain for all Arab/Pakistani men, these women find themselves in the shadow of Anglo culture, where Muslim-presenting phenotypes are frequently categorically evaluated. They have internalized a belief system (and in Ariel's case, based on actual experience), whereby minority cultures, specifically Arab men, are viewed as ahistorical and controlled by immutable customs. This common categorization is extremely pertinent in the current climate of the Global North where we are witnessing increasing surges of Islamophobia. While one must guard against the ease with which *Arab men* and *violence* slide easily into a common category, there are real patriarchal manifestations of violence within Muslim countries that exist in varying degrees in all cultures (Christian patriarchy for instance). These issues are layered and complex, and informed by a multitude of factors, including these women's personal experiences both in Canada and in their homeland.

According to Anzaldúa, race is "an experience of reality from a particular perspective and a specific time and place (history)," and Canada's secular fundamentalism works to validate White settler culture while placing visible minorities into a singular group of threatening cultural Others (Anzaldúa *Light*, 127). This tenuous structure continues to perpetuate social ruptures and serves to cement Canada's racialized Christianocentric hierarchy. It also distorts what fluidity exists between majority White and minority non-White cultures by overlooking their interconnectedness.

COYOLXAUHQUI, A COMMUNITY: A NEW PERSONAL NARRATIVE

> *Your resistance to identity boxes . . . calls you to retribalize your identity to a more inclusive one, redefining what it means to be . . . a citizen of the world, classifications reflecting an emerging planetary culture. In this narrative, national boundaries dividing us from the "others" (nos/otras) are porous, and the cracks between worlds serve as gateways.*
>
> *(Anzaldúa, Light 141)*

Canada is a space where multiple cultures coexist and thrive. Yet, for too long, Canada's colonial, secularist, bureaucratic imperatives have mandated that women border-crossers deny their mestiza identities and assimilate into predetermined identity categories to become "true" Canadians. We explore some methods that these women use to refuse the suffocating limitations of Canadian identification practices. Through the lens of Anzaldúa's *conocimiento* stage of Coyolxauhqui, where new personal and collective narratives emerge, we can see how Canada can provide mestizas with a unique space to explore the cracks between culturally defined identity borders. In this stage, one "owns [their] shadow, allowing the breath of healing to come into [their] lives" (Anzaldúa, *Light* 123). As this process unfolds, Canada becomes the borderzone where these women dismantle rigid perceptions of identity and belonging. Willard articulated this effect beautifully when she asserted her Mi'kmaw identity's boundlessness that is neither singular nor determined in advance. She told Theresa, "Everything I do is Mi'kmaw, every day." For her, being Mi'kmaw does not mean anything other than being exactly who she is every day—on and off the reserve. In every moment of Willard's multidimensional identity, she is Mi'kmaw.

Bucking the System: What is a Woman?

When we asked these women to define what "being a woman" meant to them, their initial answers paralleled the traditional patriarchal definition. They referenced the adversities as members of an inequitable, gendered society. Kira shared that being a woman meant "being scared of dressing in a certain way, or being scared of what people are going to think if I dress a certain way." Ella expressed, "Sometimes I felt like why wasn't I a man—who had control of things, could do things?" These looming patriarchal perceptions of being a woman exemplify a manifestation of a collective shadowbeast—mainstream Anglo culture's implicit categorization of womanhood.

However, as these women pondered the question, their answers shifted. Their narrow definition of womanhood evolved to one that reached beyond rigid stereotypes. Kira noted, "Those are *imposed* things. . . . They are not real!" They eventually began to articulate "womanhood" in their own terms, bridging incongruent realities. When Lila described her identity she proudly told Alia:

> I'm a Black woman . . . and the idea of . . . the femme is a powerful thing, even if society may not see it that way. Women . . . have a lot of power in that . . . we raise people, we're like the main social support systems. . . . That's really powerful whether or not you're a mother. . . . You're always going to be supporting others. . . . That's something that every woman should carry.

Ella commented, "Understanding yourself as a woman *everyday* makes you feel like, no I don't want to be a man. . . . I *can* be responsible for things. I *can* carry heavy things." Ariel concurred, wrapping everything up with, "I think because I was told that because I am a girl I couldn't do this or that, it has just kind of made me more rebellious. Like . . . I'll show you, watch me!"

Because Anglo secular norms or the familiar norms of their homeland did not adequately serve their personal definitions of womanhood, these women challenged their inner *facultad* and nourished their "ability to accommodate mutually exclusive, discontinuous, and inconsistent worlds" to create a new narrative for themselves (Anzaldúa, *Light* 79, 81). Each of these women channel their *facultad* by turning inward to engage the soul and their inner resilience.

Back to the Drawing Board: Overriding the Colonial Binary

When I write . . . [it] feels like I'm creating my own face, my own heart—a Nahuatl concept. My soul makes itself through the creative act. It is constantly remaking and giving birth to itself through my body. It is this learning to live with la Coatlicue that transforms living in the Borderlands from a nightmare into a numinous experience.

(Anzaldúa, Borderlands 95)

Ariel embodies *Coyolxauhqui* in her active renegotiation of her personal narrative. After leaving her abusive marriage, she created a new, independent life for herself and her children. In essence, there now exists a kind of internal split: before and after, Pakistani culture and Canadian culture, old self and new self. Internalizing this dichotomy, Ariel's younger self was subsumed into a *shadowbeast,* through shame, humiliation, and anger.

In March, 2019, Ariel published her autobiography. The cover is her wedding photo: a seventeen-year-old girl in traditional Pakistani wedding garb. She told Kathleen, "When my book cover was being designed, . . . I was having fights with my publisher. . . . I don't identify with that scared mouse on the cover anymore. I don't like her. . . The woman in the red heels and the western dress, the strong power figure, that's me." A few months later, Ariel was a keynote speaker at a graduation in Ottawa. As she was handing students their degrees, she had an epiphany. "[I]t just struck me that I was on stage at that age to get married. . . . That's how old I was in that picture on the cover. And these *kids*, they were coming on stage to get the degrees." For the rest of the ceremony, Ariel sat on the stage and thought about her seventeen-year-old self. She marveled at how "she was the one who did not give up on her education, who did all the chores during the day, served her in-laws, cooked the food, and still went into her room in the middle of the night and studied and completed her high school . . . without any support." Today, Ariel has a very different feeling towards that young woman. "I'm like, holy fuck! . . . [I]f I hadn't fought all those hard battles then, I wouldn't even be who I am today. . . . I just felt so much compassion for this little girl that was me. . . . If there's anyone who's the hero of the story, it's her, and if there's anyone who deserves to be on the cover, it's her." After the graduation, Ariel went back to her hotel, pulled the book cover up on her phone, and "sat there for an hour crying and saying thank you to that girl." She called her publisher the next day and said: "The cover's fantastic!" Reconciling her past and present, Ariel was able to reclaim foundational moments of her past that are integral to her identity as a border-crossing woman. She overrode the *shadowbeast* that deemed her identities incompatible and reified the fluidity that exists between. The graduating students inspired Ariel to walk through a spiritual gateway and she put herself back together on her own terms.

LAUGH AND THE WHOLE WORLD LAUGHS WITH YOU: CONCLUSION

This paper is a platform for the narratives of border-crossing women in Canada; their narratives are given space, influence, and power, both within their own contexts and within Canadian immigration literature. Canada's multicultural landscape is no utopia, but we consider it to be a place rich with potential. As the stories of these women attest, Canada can provide a space for various types of positive self-discovery. For Ariel, Canada is quintessentially diverse. She explained, "If you choose not to take part in a set of cultural values that you do not agree with, then you will find another community and another set of values that you will align yourself with."

Anzaldúa describes *conocimiento* as a cycle of spiritual activism wherein border-crossers discover the ambiguous space between and among socially determined identities (Anzaldúa *Light,* 119). As these women evolved through *conocimiento,* they discovered the fiction of a superior White monoculture and created for themselves an identity that hybridized all their border-crossing experiences. For them, the entire nation of Canada became a borderzone within which they negotiated living in *nepantla*, reconciling between their *facultad*—the agency of spirituality, and their *shadowbeasts*—the vagaries of political subjectivity. These women also became their own borderland of sorts, where colonial and patriarchal perceptions of Canadian identity began to unravel through reflective and creative dialogues.

The experiences of these six women, a microcosm of a far greater population, demonstrate the need for a broader immigration lens, one that acknowledges and addresses the folly of predetermined, one-dimensional social identities. As Arturo Escobar argues, the problems we face in a globalized world lack modern solutions. To progress, our understanding of the world must be "broader than the Western understanding of the world" (16). One way forward is to understand how Canada's secular fundamentalism inhibits nuance, a critical aspect of understanding people and their cultures. Negotiating diverse and often seemingly contradictory perspectives has never been more crucial. When we legitimize multiple perceptions of what exists, we create spaces where new and stronger cultural narratives can grow. This approach can go some distance in counterbalancing lingering worldviews that promote violence and prejudice with the hope to minimize the us-versus-them mentality. One example is the dire need to decolonize our understanding of Indigeneity as subaltern, and support Indigenous activists in their attempt to break the West's monopoly on "legitimate forms of knowledge." Using Anzaldúa's model, we conclude that the stories of border-crossing women offer Canada a unique opportunity. Understanding and integrating the more nuanced aspect of spirituality in these women's lives is an important conduit toward achieving authentic and inclusive multiculturalism.

WORKS CITED

Anzaldúa, Gloria. *Borderlands / La Frontera: The New Mestiza*, 4th ed., Aunt Lute Books, 2012.

———. *Light in the Dark / Luz en lo Oscuro: Rewriting Identity, Spirituality, Reality.* Duke University Press, 2015.

Bloemraad, Irene. "Theorizing and Analyzing Citizenship in Multicultural Societies." *The Sociological Quarterly*, vol. 56, no. 4, 2015, pp. 591–606.

———. *Understanding "Canadian Exceptionalism" in Immigration and Pluralism Policy.* Migration Policy Institute, July 2012, https://www.migrationpolicy.org/pubs/CanadianExceptionalism.pdf.

Chew, Dolores. "Feminism and Multiculturalism in Quebec: An / Other Perspective." *Canadian Woman Studies*, vol. 27, no. 2/3, Spring 2009, pp. 84–92.

Coulthard, Glenn, and Leanne Simpson. (2016). "Grounded Normativity / Place-Based Solidarity." *American Quarterly*, vol. 68, no. 2, 2016, pp. 249–255.

Escobar, Arturo. "Power and Visibility: Development and the Invention and Management of the Third World." *Cultural Anthropology*, vol. 3, no. 4, 1988, pp. 428–443.

Haque, Eve. "Homegrown, Muslim and Other: Tolerance, Secularism and the Limits of Multiculturalism." *Social Identities*, vol. 16, no. 1, 2010, pp. 79–101.

Lavie, Smadar. *Wrapped in the Flag of Israel.* University of Nebraska Press, 2018.

Lavie, Smadar, and Ted Swedenburg. *Displacement, Diaspora, and Geographies of Identity*. Duke University Press, 1996.

Ng, Roxana. "Constituting Ethnic Phenomenon: An Account from the Perspective of Immigrant Women." *Canadian Ethnic Studies: Études Ethniques Au Canada*, vol. 13, no. 1, 1981, pp. 97–108.

VanderPlaat, Madine. *Integration outcomes for immigrant women in Canada: A review of the literature, 2000-2007.* Atlantic Metropolis Centre, 2007.

Wallace, James. "Misunderstood and Mischaracterized: Canada's Four Models of Religion–State Relations." *David Anderson*, 25 May 2014, http://www.davidanderson.ca/canadas-four-models-of-religion-state-relations/. Accessed 19 Apr. 2010.

TRAUMA AS NONORDINARY REALITY

USING ANZALDÚAN THOUGHT IN RECUPERATING PAINFUL MEMORIES

YVETTE CHAIREZ

In the tradition of Gloria Anzaldúa I am attempting an autohistoria-teoría to examine a shared memory my cousin Maricela and I have of our late abuelo appearing as an apparition at our abuelita's front door one summer day in 1987. Our Lita's husband was a domestic abuser and child sexual predator—he was also staunchly protected by the women in our family. I am interested in reevaluating this "memory" as a moment of "nonordinary reality" while using Anzaldúa's concepts of *nepantla* and *ensueños* to further aid in making sense of its occurrence. Throughout, I will use Anzaldúa's spelling of *nonordinary* as it most commonly appears in *Light in the Dark / Luz en lo Oscuro*, sans hyphen. I will also be using a pseudonym in place of my cousin's name and will not refer to my Lita's husband as my "abuelo" again.

In my experience (both lived and academic), I have come to understand that nonordinary realities are too often begotten by traumatic events. In Cathy Caruth's foundational work *Trauma: Explorations in Memory*, she writes: "Central to the very immediacy of this experience . . . is a gap that carries the force of the event and does so precisely at the expense of simple knowledge and memory. The force of this experience would seem to arrive precisely, in other words, in the collapse of its understanding" (7). The "gap that carries the force of the event" and the "collapse of its understanding" suggests an entire blockage of the event in the victim's mind, but Anzaldúa's theorizations of the workings of the psyche suggest the force and the collapse function as the formations of gateways to other levels of consciousness: nonphysical worlds or nonordinary realities—spaces that offer *alternate* realities where the trauma does not exist. Because of this established tie with trauma, I am using Anzaldúa's theories of nonordinary reality, ensueños, and nepantla as they might relate to coping with life's traumatic events. By intersecting Anzaldúa's theories with trauma studies, I am hoping to navigate the multifariousness of a particularly haunting memory I share with my cousin Maricela.

UNINVITED AND UNWELCOME: THE MEMORY OF MY LITA'S HUSBAND

He showed up at the front door that afternoon attempting to hand each of us a nickel. Maricela and I had been jumping on our Lita's bed like we weren't supposed to when we heard the knock at the front door.

Maricela, who was six at the time and is two years older than I, was the one who opened the door. I remember her looking way up at him like he was incredibly tall and incredibly revered. I cannot remember his features now, or what the look was like in his eye. I just remember a shadowy silhouette shaped like the man from the old pictures my Lita would show us. The silhouette was illuminated from behind by a soft yellow light framed by rays that were prickly and white. Maricela, after staring in awe for a moment, was rewarded with a coin. He reached toward her and she instinctively turned up her palm, where he placed the nickel. She ran off to show our Lita, leaving me there. I watched her go, and when I turned back to face him, hoping he had vanished, he was reaching his arm toward me too, as though trying to hand me something. But I did not reach back. I distinctly remember thinking: why the hell would I want a nickel?

He bent at the waist so his wobbling face could gaze oddly at me beneath the sharp spikes of light surrounding him. I backed away, looked over my shoulder, and my Lita was hurrying into the room. Because I thought it was what she would want me to do, I turned to take his "gift." He was no longer there when I did. After directly poking her head out onto the front porch and looking in every which direction for the dead husband who Maricela said had been there just moments before, my Lita scolded me in Spanish for having the front door open, asking in all seriousness if I wanted strangers to come in and get us. I told her sincerely that I did not. After ensuring the door was securely locked, my Lita made a big show of taking a seat in her favorite red paisley armchair. *¿Por qué no lo invitaste?* she shouted, going on to explain that spirits can only enter a home if they are invited. My cousin and I exchanged glances, realizing with shame that it had never occurred to us to ask him in.

TRAUMA, THAT INTERGENERATIONAL GHOST

The way I have always rationalized this occurrence is that Maricela and I must have been playing pretend, which was common for us; and our Lita, touched that we were incorporating her late husband, played along by admonishing us for failing to let him in and by forever keeping the nickel he "gave" to Maricela. I cannot explain why Maricela and I opened the door alone back then, or why we would have pretended that the grandfather we barely even knew and had no recollection of was giving us money. Indeed we were raised to believe it was men with money who would bless us girls with a life worth living if we behaved. I seriously doubt he was there to reward us for behaving, though. The most vivid memories I have of Maricela are of us pinning one another to the floor, hitting each other in the face.

Thinking back on this with the gift of hindsight thirty-five years later, I see in this memory indications of generational trauma that has been passed on to all the women on my mom's side of my family. I see in this memory foretellings of what was to come and forewarnings of manipulations of power by men. But I do not believe Lita's husband would have been the one to warn us. If I were to believe my Lita's claim that he wanted to be let in, then I'd have to assume it would be to gain access to his daughters' little girls. Death came for him before he'd had time to properly groom us for sexual abuse. Where did my instinct to not let him in come from if I had heard nothing but glowing reviews of his ability to take care of and provide for his family?

Why my Lita wanted him back in her house, I will never understand. When my tía, in her never-ending attempt at performing Christian sanctimony, visited me at my home in Las Vegas after my first miscarriage, *my* never-ending attempt to get her to turn my cousins' father in for child molestation finally broke something in her. She confided in me, visibly shaking, that her father had "approached" her and my mom (her older sister) for sex when they were teenagers. My therapist at the time told me "approached" is a code word victims use that means he actually tried or succeeded in forcing himself on them. I did not press my tía about it. I knew very well that speaking any further on the matter, or using words that clarified what really happened, made the trauma all too real. In fact, in the next breath, she wondered whether she and my mom just had the same nightmare of him coming into their room those nights. She said, in all seriousness, that what she thinks she remembers certainly cannot be true—it must be the devil testing her. This plays into her theory that the women of our family are cursed.

His presence that afternoon was threatening and, without having been explicitly told this yet, I knew it. I have always thought that, in taking the nickel (which my Lita kept in an old ring box in a chest of drawers in her blue bathroom), Maricela's silence had been bought. Because everyone who believed that Maricela and I experienced a true visit from the true spirit of our Lita's husband is a victim of sexual abuse, I will begin linking Anzaldúa's concepts with theories from trauma studies, particularly those dealing with generational trauma.

Cathy Caruth's idea that trauma isn't trauma until it comes back to haunt you (Cavalli 364) actually positions this memory as a site of trauma for me. I do not have any tangible traumatic experiences with my mom's father, or any other actual memories of him at all, but my mom, my aunt, my Lita, and, I suspect, Maricela's older sister did; therefore, I theorize that I have been traumatized by him through my relationships with them.

For as long as I remember, every time our Lita would tell us a story about what a good man he was, I always got the nagging feeling she was lying. And I have always traced the origins or rationale of that feeling back to the front door of her house that afternoon. So although linguistically I could not find a way to represent what actually happened to form this memory, and also did not have the language skills (nor the agency within my family) to work out what it meant, the memory has served as a type of guiding consciousness, as Caruth suggests, of the intergenerational trauma that the women in my family have suffered. This specific consciousness became a cautiousness that I embodied in my interactions with all men, and today it informs my work as both a writer and scholar drawn always to the treatment of women and mothers in literature and society, and men's roles in our suffering. Thus, in Anzaldúan terms, this cautiousness has become an embodied gesture manifest in my writing (Keating xxiii). Though theories of trauma's effects on one's psyche pay close attention to the role of the dream world, any mention of an affected person's encounters with ghostly characters or hauntings is explained away by this dream world and its relation to our imaginations (Dragojlovic). This is where I see Anzaldúa's work with the spirit world informing trauma studies: Rather than explaining away such hauntings with psychoanalysis, reconsidering them as *nonordinary realities* offers trauma victims more agency and control over their afflictions.

ENTERING NONORDINARY REALITIES

In *Light in the Dark*, Anzaldúa pays particular attention to "the imagination's role in journeying to 'nonordinary realities'" and the imagination's role in our "identity construction and reconstructions" (7). As a writer creating nonordinary realities each time I sit down to pen fiction, I am well aware that identity construction can take place even from something that is occurring apart from one's physical world. Though I would embody these occurrences, I had never before considered these "imaginative flights" (7) as existing on the same plane as my physical reality. It has been life changing, life affirming really, to read Anzaldúa's pronouncement that our imaginations are empowering and transformative, and that other people's versions of our reality *disempower* us.

I have been treating this memory (and, by extension, all that it implies) as a "phobic object," something Cavalli explains as a thing to be avoided at all costs (372). Looking at it as a moment of nonordinary reality instead helps me face what the memory signifies and helps determine how I can possibly use it to serve me moving forward (Cavalli 366)—keeping Anzaldúa's reasoning in mind as I do:

> Judging stories of nonliteral realities . . . as "made up," our western society invalidates the meanings and healing they offer. . . . Do we make dreams, or does something outside us originate and orchestrate them? Is imagination's nonordinary reality real? . . . Who cares, as long as the information (whether metaphorical or literal) gained from a shamanic journey makes positive changes in a person's life . . . Are spirits literally present or are they imaginally present? They are both. Fantasy is not just a way to cope with, correct, or supplement reality. . . . [A]ccording to Jung, neither the conscious world's literal reality nor the unconscious world's nonliteral reality is absolutely real (37).

NEPANTLA: WHO IS STUCK BETWEEN WHAT?

Switching from regarding this memory as a phobic object to a nonordinary reality puts me in an in-between space, nepantla. Anzaldúa's theory of nepantla is multifaceted. At its core the theory proposes "the point of contact . . . between worlds—between imagination and physical existence, between ordinary and nonordinary (spirit) realities" (2), a borderland where "reality" and nonordinary reality intersect and interact.

Though I have settled on explaining this memory as a product of playing pretend, it took nearly twenty years of wrestling with it to try and discern where the actions of it might have taken place: in a dream? in my mind? in a story my cousin may have invented for us to tell? in a story our Lita may have told us both? So now I must ask: did it take place in the actual threshold between this world and the spirit world, like my Lita believes? The theory of nepantla (coupled with nonordinary reality) allows me to finally stop worrying about that—stop worrying about where the memory came from or whether it is true. The fact that the images of it exist means it is real.

In this way, then, even children playing pretend create parallel realities in which they play, explore, and engage. In doing so, in "tuning in to the 'other' mind or 'other' self," they may discover "an inner, underground river of information"—a well of knowledge that may not have been accessed had it not been for their journeying into the imaginal (Anzaldúa 28). Playing pretend, then, is a nepantleric activity that creates nonordinary realities for us to explore. And in this case, the nonordinary nature of this memory served as a formative lesson in identifying and denouncing misogynistic behaviors. This memory does not need to be "real" nor does it (thankfully) need to be physical or tangible to have been impactful.

ENSUEÑOS AND HEIGHTENED CONSCIOUSNESS

When I look at ensueños as stories "created for me by something outside of myself (soul, spirit, the universe's unconscious)" to initiate a response in me, a heightened consciousness, then a new world of possibilities as to what the function and legacy of this memory is supposed to be opens up and, in fact, aligns with Cavalli's theory that intergenerational trauma seamlessly threads through the lives of a family's third generation in a way that ensures they feel the oppression of the trauma (are conscious of it) without knowing explicitly what it is or where the heightened consciousness comes from.

Thinking about Anzaldúa's claim, then, that mestizas develop special senses to protect ourselves, to sense the rapist behind us before he gets us, and Cavalli's contention that I may have been acting on anxieties passed on to me from my mother or aunt (363) that I did not yet understand, I can see my Lita's husband's figure in this memory as a preemptive attempt by my own mind to banish him, knowing no one else did and no one else in my lifetime would. An unexpected takeaway from this project is the idea that "imaginal flights of reality" (Anzaldúa 26) are important modes of identity construction: Whether Maricela and I were playing pretend or not, the outcome of that imagined reality has, no matter how minutely, shaped in some way the identities of everyone who indulged in the moment of reality we may have fashioned. After this process, I am still left knowing that my family's reality remains occupied by this horrible man who I have always wished I had no memory of at all. My Lita and my aunt died without ever coming out from under his oppressive influence, and my cousins, due to his sick actions, were taught to love and forgive child abusers. My mother, who has also passed on, is the only one who may have exhibited some signs of subversion, or aversion, towards him, and I am grateful she seemingly passed that on to me. Perhaps this resistance was already at work in my subconscious when her father appeared at the door that day.

MOVING FORWARD

While I was initially worried going into this that reliving this memory and reexamining it would be retraumatizing, remembering it through the framework of nonordinary reality has actually brought peace and even taken away its patriarchal power. Every way I came at it produced the same calming thought: the fact that this memory exists and has impacted my life, has influenced how my family thinks of me and how I think of them individually, means that it is *real*. It does not matter if it was make believe, or if it was a lie Maricela involved me in, or if it was really a case of my world crossing with the spirit world; it is real. Even the naming of the concept—"nonordinary reality"—serves to remove the stigma of memories like this one. *Nonordinary* indicates we cannot control it like we would an ordinary course of strictly earthly events, while *reality* indicates it is nonetheless a qualitative occurrence worthy of attention. Linguistically, the term also suggests *distance*, as in, we may never be able to come close enough to fully grasp it. Hearing that a past experience is nonordinary can certainly cause one to take a step back and reexamine it, as I did. For me, understanding that trauma memories are essentially out of the ordinary made it easier for me let this memory simply be. Once I was able to make it stay still in my mind, I was able to overtake it. Because instances of trauma often cannot be accurately recalled by victims, I end this exploration proposing that studying the effects of trauma with the aid of Anzaldúa's theories of nonordinary reality, nepantla, and ensueños stands to offer the victim more agency over the experience and their feelings.

WORKS CITED

Anzaldúa, Gloria. *Light in the Dark / Luz en lo Oscuro: Rewriting Identity, Spirituality, Reality.* Duke University Press, 2015.

Caruth, Cathy. *Trauma: Explorations in Memory.* Johns Hopkins University Press, 1995.

Cavalli, Alessandra. "Transgenerational Transmission of Indigestible Facts: From Trauma, Deadly Ghosts and Mental Voids to Meaning-Making Interpretations." *Journal of Analytical Psychology*, vol. 57, no. 5, 2012.

Keating, AnaLouise. "Editor's Introduction: Re-envisioning Coyolxauhqui, Decolonizing Reality: Anzaldúa's Twenty-First-Century Imperative." *Light in the Dark / Luz en lo Oscuro*, Duke University Press, 2015.

Dragojlovic, Ana. "Affective Geographies: Intergenerational Hauntings, Bodily Affectivity and Multiracial Subjectivities." *Subjectivity*, vol. 8, no. 4, 2015.

THE GENERATIONAL DISCONNECT

BEING MY PARENTS' NAVIGATOR

ANGIE CONTRERAS

While being a first-generation American is defined in different ways and holds a different weight for each person, when I apply it to myself, it simply means the first: the first to be born in the United States, the first to go to school. I have encountered many firsts in my short lifetime. Because I was the first child to be born on the "right" side of the border, I have always served as my parents' navigator through life in the United States. In many ways, my being an interpreter has made me a bridge between their new culture and the one I was born into, and, at the same time, it has highlighted the divisions between us. While the US-Mexico border is a physical separation between the two nations, my borderlands are a symbol of divided identity and culture between me and my immigrant parents. In this essay, I explore the generational disconnect between people who are first-generation US Latinx of Central American descent and their Latin American-born immigrant parents, using Gloria Anzaldúa's concept of Nepantla to illuminate the complexities of living in the in-between. Being born in this country has been an enormous challenge, but even with the seemingly endless responsibilities that my parents have placed on me, living in the borderlands has allowed me to flourish. As Anzaldúa reminds us, there cannot be growth and creation if there are no challenges.

MY NEPANTLERA ORIGIN

My identity is a shapeshifter—with every situation came a different version of self. It was not something I did consciously; I am still not sure why I did it exactly. Protection, self-preservation, embarrassment? My parents would always tell me that I had to try harder than everyone else just to be seen as a competitor in the United States. I treated everything as a contest; therefore, my identity was rooted in validation from others. I was not always this way. Before I turned six, I lived in perfectly oblivious bliss. Not being conscious of everything around me protected me from the real world. I thought everything was perfect because I was not socially aware of the world around me. I celebrated my Salvadoran culture while eagerly learning about life in the United States. There was no judgment when I expressed myself within both cultures. There is a point in every first- and second-generation child's life when the realization sets in, the divide between self and the United States becomes clear as day. I realized I was different from most of my peers in first grade.

My mother packed lunch for me every single day and her cooking was a godsend in my youthful opinion. One of my favorite things to eat at home was un pan con queso fresco y frijoles (talking about it still makes me hungry). On this particular day, I sat with my predominantly White friend group and began to unpack my lunch. I was so excited to see that my mom had packed my favorite meal—I happily unwrapped it and began to take a bite. Everyone around me stopped talking and I felt their eyes on me. I looked up to find all of them staring with the same expression: disgust. They broke out in seas of "eww" and "gross." If this happened to me now it would obviously not be a big ordeal; I would continue to happily eat my sandwich while they ate their Lunchables. However, as a six-year-old, I could not have been more upset. My friends called my favorite food, and by extension me, disgusting.

After that day, I told my mom to never make my lunch again. I was so angry at her for putting me in that situation. I made all the excuses in the world to protect my blooming American identity, including completely cutting off my own Salvadoran heritage. Everything I did up until recently was to cultivate my newfound identity. I dressed, spoke, and ate in certain ways to make America love me, like I loved her. My idea of the US was not even tangible, it was not real, but for some reason I latched onto it for over 17 years.

Much like Esperanza in *The House on Mango Street,* by Sandra Cisneros, I wanted to fit in with all the "normal kids" at my school. At one point in the story Esperanza mentions that "the special kids, the ones who wear keys around their necks, get to eat at the canteen. The canteen! Even the name sounds important" (43). Much like me, she rejected her mother's home cooking in order to fit in with the kids she wanted to be friends with. I gave up my favorite food for some undercooked pizza and I was perfectly content with it. I wanted to fit in so desperately that I was willing to give up whatever it took in order to achieve that. My food was my culture and my culture was me. Although there was no authoritative figure telling me to stop exploring my native culture, it felt as though I had to assimilate to the American standard. I was restricted in multiple ways from childhood, all to mold me into a perfect American citizen.

Without knowing it, I adopted the qualities of a Nepantlera. According to Anzaldúa, Nepantlera means "boundary-crosser, thresholders who initiate others in rites of passage, activists who, from a listening, receptive, spiritual stance, rise to their own visions and shift into acting them out, haciendo mundo Nuevo" (in Keating 570). The concept of being a navigator between two worlds for my parents inherently makes me a Nepantlera. I am able to figuratively travel through both cultures in order to facilitate my parents' transition to this new country. My parents immigrated to the United States in the 1990s seeking a better life for their future children, as most immigrants do. I am my parents' firstborn, thus I was granted the permanent title of navigator through life. I was immediately forced to learn English when I entered the public school system. It sounded like an amazing opportunity in theory, but I was forced out of my core classes such as math and science to learn a different language. I am still terrible at anything related to STEM; at the time, it seemed like a fair trade-off.

The occupation as a navigator for my parents started as soon as I learned English. At first it was simple tasks like speaking to the cashier at a grocery store, but it quickly turned into me leading them through their daily life in the United States. As a young child, I remember helping my mother through the process of obtaining her permanent residency status. I had no concept of laws, green cards, or even what immigration was. The only thing I could help my parents with was reading the documents and telling them where to sign. It really was not much, but soon enough I was helping them file taxes and apply for government aid programs. I had always thought that every child had gone through the same experiences as I had; when my friends said they had to go help their parents, I imagined them having to go home and make doctors' appointments for their entire families. That was definitely not the case as my peers and I all lived very distinct lives, with polar opposite responsibilities.

Many might think that my parents are bad people for putting me through that, but it was just like doing chores for me. At that point in my life, my identity was formed around servitude and gratitude for my family. I felt as though I had to pay off everything they did for me through my actions. I would give them all I had, and in return I received love and praise. All I ever wanted as a child was to make my parents happy (what child doesn't feel that way?)—although, I still haven't fully recovered from the underlying sense of frustration with my parents for putting me in such difficult situations.

HARDSHIPS OF BEING A NEPANTLERA

As I grew into myself, being a Nepantlera or navigator started to become extremely challenging. In *Borderlands / La Frontera: The New Mestiza*, Anzaldúa expresses that "Much of what the culture condemns focuses on kinship relationships. The welfare of the family, the community, and the tribe is more important than the welfare of the individual" (40). My entire life I have been a giver, it is deeply rooted in me. I gave, and I gave, and I gave. After years of giving, I truly felt like I had nothing else to offer to my family. My identity had been so centered on servitude that I did not really know who I was.

Somewhere on my journey towards self-discovery I concluded that my parents were at the root of all of my frustration. I began to decline the role of navigator; for the first time in my life, I wanted to make decisions for myself. I had spent so much time carefully figuring out my family's path, that I had gone astray from my own. I threw out my core identity of servitude and switched it out for anger. I rejected my parents and everything they stood for; I even went as far as to completely disregard my race and ethnicity. I was not critically thinking about what caused my family dynamic to be this way—what outside forces pushed my family to act in certain ways that made me feel disconnected. Gloria Anzaldúa said, "I remember being caught speaking Spanish at recess—that was good for three licks on the knuckles with a sharp ruler" (Anzaldúa 76). Anzaldúa had to navigate through the same institutions that led to complications within my family. I decided that I would remain in my ignorance and forget about anything that connected me to my past experiences. For the first time, I felt like I had complete control over myself and was not doing anything that I didn't want to.

Soon enough it became extremely hard to communicate with my own parents. During my early teen years, I felt like I was rapidly growing away from them. It seems like an odd concept, but I felt like we were in completely different places. I felt like there was a glass door between my parents and me. They were so close to me and although I could touch them, talk to them, they never seemed to be all there. I distinctly remember trying to tell them about accomplishments or events that were going on in my life, but they would just get frustrated with me and call me a showoff. Or they never understood what my accomplishments were. My parents did not go to school, so every time I brought it up it would be like putting salt on an open wound. I had no one to talk to about anything I did, and they made me feel isolated for years to come.

Being a Nepantlera comes with a massive set of emotional baggage. According to Anzaldúa, "The ambivalence from the clash of voices results in mental and emotional states of perplexity. Internal strife results in insecurity and indecisiveness. The *mestiza's* dual or multiple personality is plagued by psychic restlessness" (100). The navigation weighed heavily on many aspects of my life growing up. In particular, it really shaped the way I formulated relationships with others. I developed this type of 'yes' mentality, in which I was never comfortable with saying 'no' to anyone. Saying yes was ingrained in me from a young age, as I was never allowed to refuse to help my parents. It took me a long time to realize that refusing to do something for somebody else was even an option. Living life with this mentality has been extremely difficult; I manage to overextend myself and get burned out on a regular basis. Things as simple as saying no to a request from a professional or going out with my friends was baffling to me. I believed that saying yes was a way to avoid conflict and keep people in my life. I had always lived in the Borderlands that according to Anzaldúa is "a vague and undetermined place created by the emotional residue of an unnatural boundary where the prohibited, the forbidden and *los atravesados* reside in a place of discomfort as they negotiate between the conflicting forces in such margins" (Aigner-Varoz 49). The Borderlands are a complex space, ever changing. I wanted to feel in control for the first time in my life and one of the few things in my control was my relationship to others. I lived in a constant state of change, but I desperately needed security. In my mind, always saying yes was such a good thing, there was no outwardly obvious negative side effect. I would please everyone around me and in return I would receive that instant gratification, which was more than enough for me at the time.

I have a complicated relationship with the word 'yes' to this day. I value kindness, so I try to say yes as much as possible. However, I also realize that it can rapidly become toxic. It is hard to find the line between being kind and coming off as rude to people. I owe everything to my parents, so who am I to deny them anything? They have given up so much for me, I feel obligated to do the same for them. With my parents, I still am not able to draw a line, and in the end, I am not sure if I will ever be able to refuse them anything.

Since I was a young girl, I have felt a looming sense of guilt resting heavily on my shoulders. I was unable to share my true feelings or experiences with my parents, because my issues were nothing compared to theirs. I discovered recently that it is called *immigrant guilt* (Chick 1). There was an instance in January of 2018 when I really felt the guilt run through me. I was a senior in high school, getting ready to make my final college decision. I had my heart set on Florida State University, and when the results came out, I was not awarded the scholarship I needed in order to attend. I had already planned my entire life around going to that school and in the blink of an eye . . . that opportunity was gone. In desperation, I naturally rushed to my parents and told them that I could not go to my first-choice school and that all my plans were essentially ruined. At this point, I was only seeking understanding—I needed them to realize how deeply the entire situation had affected me. I did not want to hear about how irrational I was being, I wanted them to listen to me for once. I told them the entire story completely in tears, and while I was sitting on the floor, they made the strangest faces at me. I was confused. I expected them to sympathize with me or at least tell me that everything would work out. (That did not happen.)

I am sure that every child of an immigrant has received the "I had to walk 1000 miles to get to school" lecture. They told me that I had the immense privilege of continuing my higher education, something that they could not even dream of. Immediately, I felt guilty. Obviously, I was being too insensitive to them and their unfortunate situations. I felt guilty for even bringing it up; I was so selfish. My mother didn't even get the chance to finish third grade—my problems were minuscule in comparison. "Vos eres tan dramática" she would say over and over again. I sat there on one of the worst days of my life, being lectured over how privileged I was. It was an emotional experience.

I sat quietly, my immigrant guilt sinking deeper and deeper. My problems could never measure up to anything my parents had gone through. Every time I was upset, it would be overshadowed by my parents having to live through the civil war or having to cross the border. My feelings were shot down every single time. I was not allowed to feel anything but gratitude for the life my parents had so graciously provided for me. In the article, "To be the Child of an Immigrant," Kenna Chick discusses the consequences of being the child in an immigrant family. Chick says that "many children of immigrants grow up conscious of the enormous sacrifices that their parents have made and spend the rest of their lives proving to their parents that the suffering was not in vain" (1). My mother did not have paper when she was in school so she would write on banana leaves with her bare fingernails in order to take notes. How am I supposed to compare my issues to that? How can I ever be anything but thankful for the life I lead? Immigrant guilt has just become a permanent part of my identity, as a result of the nature of my relationship with my parents. My issues are so trivial and they have to deal with so much every day. How dare I think my hardships are valid? So, I remain stuck in a place where my parents think I am undeserving of their sympathy.

FINDING MY OWN IDENTITY

My parents had me all figured out. Since I was a little girl my mom would tell me "Angie, cásate con un hombre que tiene pisto." My only career options were to marry rich or be a celebrity. They were obsessed with *Nuestra Belleza*

Latina and we would watch it on Univisión religiously. I remember my mom would dress me up and have me walk on an imaginary catwalk, preparing me for the day that I won la corona for being the prettiest Latina. I went along with their dream; I wasn't sure of any alternatives at the time. I soon realized that I was not tall enough, skinny enough, or conventionally pretty enough to be a model, and I was much too independent to marry rich.

After years of helping my parents and listening to their immigrant narrative, I knew that I wanted to help people. I went straight for the top: I wanted to be the president of the United States. I am still not sure how I jumped from wanting to be crowned the prettiest Latina to becoming the president of the United States. I became completely enamored of politics. I loved the fact that I could apply it to every aspect of my life. The summer before my senior year of high school, I begged my mom to let me go to a local End Family Separation rally. She looked at me funny and said absolutely not—she thought that protesters and activists just wanted to cause radical messes. She did not understand why anyone would be openly against US policy, especially since this country had given them so much opportunity. The United States had given her shelter, food, four healthy children, and a relatively happy life.

I was heading off to college soon and I could completely reinvent myself if I wanted to. I had the chance to be whomever I wanted to be without the judgment of my parents or peers. I was moving one thousand miles away from everything I had ever known. I would have no pressure to do anything anyone else wanted me to do. In my nepantlera journey, I finally realized that "the experience of nepantla 'also involve[s] creating your own meaning or conocimientos'" (Koshy 149). I had associated so much pain with my experience as a navigator that I had tried to reject that role. When I got to college, I did not change into a different person, I simply became who I was always supposed to be.

At first, I worried about my family constantly. I wondered if my siblings had gotten dressed that day or if the bills had been paid. Without realizing it, my family had become one of the biggest components of my identity. When I went off to college, I was left with questions: Who are you really? Who are you, if not a sister or a daughter? I honestly did not think my family could function properly without me there. It made me feel lost, I had been needed for so many years and now I was not. I had spent 18 years making them my priority and now I was not sure how to fill the void.

I decided I would direct my energy to learning of all kinds. I wanted to absorb information from everyone and everything. Within my learning, I discovered my heritage again, I was able to reclaim the fact that I was a Salvadoreña. Since I was away from my family for the majority of the year, I deeply reflected on my life. It was an extreme, out-of-body experience. I was able to comprehend the circumstances that had led my parents to make certain decisions and how those, in turn, had affected my life. There is a great amount of sacrifice that we all had to face, not just me. Yes, I have given a lot to my parents, but what they had given to me was much more meaningful. I had blamed my parents for making my life harder, but in reality, everything they did had led me to this point. I am our future.

WHERE THE NAVIGATION GOT ME

I turn 20 years old soon and the navigation has not yet ended. I am still constantly moving. In the article "New Mestiza, Nepantlera, Beloved Comadre: Remembering Gloria E. Anzaldúa," AnaLouise Keating encapsulates my emotions: I feel like I am still moving "within and among multiple, often conflicting, worlds and [refusing] to align [myself] exclusively with any single individual, group or belief system" (Keating 15). I have learned a lot on my journey and I have so much left to learn. Living in the Borderlands allowed me to learn many lessons that I will carry through life. I have become wiser on my nepantlera journey. The in-between is an uncomfortable and uncertain space to reside, but I have grown used to it now. I thrive in places where there is plenty of pressure and chaos. I have become wiser, more independent, and thoughtful because of my navigation (20). I see myself as an ever-expanding toolbox. I have collected many tools along the way that I can use to help others. My insight can inform my siblings, parents, friends, peers, and professionals.

At this point, since I do not live with my parents, being a nepantlera has taken a new form. It shows itself in my everyday life and it has put me in a place of reflection. I have been able to forgive my parents for any anguish they caused me because I was able to cross consciousness and see where they came from. The longer I reflect on my life, the more learning experiences I spot. Although being a nepantlera is painful and sacrificial, I believe that a lot of good can come out of that space. In *Borderlands / La Frontera,* Anzaldúa says that "in the Borderlands, you are the battleground" (216). My being is a constant battleground, always conflicting and contrasting. My life is different from that of my ancestors, but I am forging a new nepantla culture, a new in-between culture. I am not here or there, I am all of it.

WORKS CITED

Aigner-Varoz, Erika. "Metaphors of a Mestiza Consciousness: Anzaldúa's *Borderlands / La Frontera*." *MELUS*, vol. 25, no. 2, 2000, pp. 47–62.

Anzaldúa, Gloria. *Borderlands / La Frontera: The New Mestiza*. Spinsters / Aunt Lute Books, 1987.

Chick, Kenna. "To Be the Child of an Immigrant." *Mental Health America*, n.d., https://www.mhanational.org/blog/be-child-immigrant.

Cisneros, Sandra. *The House on Mango Street*. Vintage Books, 2009.

Keating, AnaLouise. "New Mestiza, Nepantlera, Beloved Comadre: Remembering Gloria E. Anzaldúa." *Letras Femeninas*, vol. 31, no. 1, 2005, pp. 13–20. *JSTOR*, www.jstor.org/stable/23021509.

Koshy, Kavitha. "Nepantlera-Activism in the Transnational Moment: In Dialogue with Gloria Anzaldúa's Theorizing of Nepantla." *Re-Membering Anzaldua: Human Rights, Borderlands, and the Poetics of Applied Social Theory: Engaging with Gloria Anzaldua in Self and Global Transformations*, special issue of *Human Architecture: Journal of the Sociology of Self-Knowledge*, vol. 4, 2006, 147–162, https://www.okcir.com/product/journal-article-nepantlera-activism-in-the-transnational-moment-in-dialogue-with-gloria-anzalduas-theorizing-of-nepantla-by-kavitha-koshy/?doing_wp_cron=1652125603.2951159477233886718750.

Stoltz Chinchilla, Norma, and Norma Hamilton. "Identity Formation among Central American Americans." Center for the Study of Immigrant Integration, USC Dornsife, Nov. 2013, https://dornsife.usc.edu/csii/identitycentralamericans/.

WHO CAN PUBLISH AUTOHISTORIA-TEORÍA WITH THE ANGER IT DESERVES?

UNCLASSIFIED LLORONAS AND THE ACADEMIC TEXT

SMADAR LAVIE

On October 16, 2009, while teaching at the University of Virginia, Charlottesville's Women's Studies Department, I attended a lecture by Brinda Bose, then an associate professor of English at the Hindu College of Delhi University. The lecture was titled "The Transnational Trials of Taslima Nasrin." Trained as a physician, Nasrin is a Bangladeshi feminist who has written an impressive opus on women's oppression under South Asian Islam. She was forced into exile in Sweden due to multiple *fatwas*[1] calling for her death. Bose delivered her postcolonial lecture in Oxbridge English and a sari. As I listened to Nasrin's globe-trotting, my mind wandered to the logistics of it all. Is Bose a product of India's elite British schools? Who paid for her Oxbridge education? Nasrin and Bose seemed to be on the Global South-to-North traveling star circuit. Who's financing all of this? Even refugees need to pay a hefty fee to be smuggled across borders. Are they middle class? Who can afford to be mobile these days? Yet these kinds of speakers and their topics are in high demand in Northern universities because they speak the language of academe, not the transnational language of Gloria Anzaldúa.

---

1 A Fatwā (Arabic) is a nonbinding legal opinion on a point of Islamic law (sharia) given by a qualified jurist in response to a question posed by a private individual, judge, or government.

THE FACULTY CLUB: NORTH TO SOUTH

Many professors in major universities in the Global South were born into the upper-class, cosmopolitan, national elite. [2] They are either well versed in English or have the funds to translate their scholarship to English—the tyrannical language of academic quotation and promotion. These professors are eager, or perhaps obligated, to apply the United States-United Kingdom (US-UK) formula for academic publication. The formula requires substantiating the anthropological argument's authenticity through the deployment of field snippets. Such snippets emanate from the vagaries of daily life—ethnographic examples, devoid of their organic context—to decorate theories authored in US and European elite universities. As a result, these scholars are perceived by their North American colleagues as the preferred women of color scholars from the Global South. They are the favored alternatives to the in-house American scholars of color. But what about grassroot indigenous or migrant nonacademic, organic *teoría*?

The Global South faculty often conceives of this teoría as an unruly frontier of thought to be tamed or contained in first-tier English journals or university press monographs. Such publications are necessary for their career advancement. Annual international association meetings at five-star hotels present an opportunity to network with editorial board members as well. US-European faculty perceives the Global South faculty as brave interlocutors between the Ivy League and the subalterns of "the field." The Global South faculty (unless they have achieved celebrity status in the North) are often seen as emancipatory "informants" to be theorized by Northern faculty. In turn, these cosmopolitan Southern scholars conceive of nonacademic, grassroot theoreticians as their "informants," and their texts, as data to theorize from. This domino effect of appropriation is laid out in Norma Alarcón's formative 1990 text "The Theoretical Subjects of *This Bridge Called My Back* and Anglo-American Feminism."

Alarcón points at the feminist-of-color theoretical richness underlying the essays, poems, testimonials, and tales in *This Bridge Called My Back* ("Theoretical Subjects"). She writes, "On the [one] hand, Anglo feminist readers of *Bridge* tend to appropriate it, cite it as an instance of difference by subsuming women of color into the unitary category of woman/women" (358). On the other hand, Anglo feminist humanities faculty treated *Bridge* as a mine to theorize from for their merit and promotion publications. They treated feminist theory of color as atavistic repository and ignored its radical, alternative modes of writing up theory as they conjured up the "universal woman," whose class and race were

---

2. These issues stem from discussion of ethnographic authorship in my recent book *Wrapped in the Flag of Israel* (2018).

not as significant as her XX chromosomes. Yet for women of color, *Bridge* was a cornerstone of identification (358–60).

John Gledhill has argued that the US-UK anthropological journal and book formula and its "northern conventions of research, writing, and thinking about the world" has low tolerance for an ethnographer doubling as an indigenous "key informant" who theorizes rather than just tells stories. The anthropologist should not have near-complete overlap between her ethnographic experience and personal and communal biography. Feminist and Cultural Studies scholarship follows and instructs the scholar to avoid victim narratives. The subaltern subject writing the US-UK formula is expected to produce dispassionate scholarship. No wailing, no anger.

Black anthropologist Faye Harrison offers a way out: "The transformed anthropology . . . would recognize that although the profession's institutional centers have been dominated by British, American, and French axes of authority, the intellectual life of the discipline has extended well beyond the North's major metropolitan centers to a variety of sites, typically devalued as peripheral zones of theory around the world" (Harrison 11). Yet her solution does not address the multilayered appropriation operation spelled out by Alarcón. Alarcón's focus is the racial and class hierarchies of US academe. Hers is a made-in-America pyramid whose foundation is the somatic experience of the displaced woman, uprooted from the South and planted in the North to suffer and mimetisize her pain into stories for the Anglo US-UK Women's Studies scholars to theorize. Alarcón conceives of such colored articulations as theory, however. Harrison focuses on decentering anthropology beyond its elite-Ivy-League, US-UK stranglehold, often overlooking the privileged background of Global South faculty such as Brinda Bose. Yet scholars such as Bose, while data-mined for Northern anthropologists, are still the North's client in the patronage system of the academy. Nevertheless, both Northern anthropologists and their Global South constituents, who depend on them for references and tenure letters, created a body of scholarship—one that superimposes itself upon the subaltern woman of the South rather than horizontally dialoguing with her.

In recent years, US-UK anthropology has diversified in forms of theoretical argumentation and in various genres of ethnographic writing. But this diversity, let alone an ethnographer having a near-complete overlap between her ethnographic experience and personal and communal biography, rarely appears in the top tier US-UK journals or scholarly presses. Take for example Ruth Behar. Despite her class privilege, she used herself as a "key informant" through creative writing about disenfranchised Latinas (Behar). She was an anthropologist coming from Princeton and Ann Arbor, so she did not threaten her upper-middle-class colleagues. Even then, her more creative writings rarely appear in top tier anthropology journals. Autoethnographer Zora Neale Hurston never published her story of being an independent scholar living in dire poverty in top journals or academic presses. She died virtually abandoned and destitute at age 69. How ironic and tragic that she only achieved acclaim years after her death for works such as 1937's *Their Eyes Were Watching God*. Anzaldúa died at age 62 from lack of adequate medical care. Her monumental autoethnography, *Borderlands / La Frontera* was published by Aunt Lute Books, a small, underfunded feminist press, because it is believed larger university presses would have deemed it incomprehensible. Overnight, *Borderlands / La Frontera* became an academic and activist bestseller to the dismay of the academic establishment. Mainstream anthropologists opined in 2003 that the book was "an industry" and that Anzaldúa's mestizaje was a "celebration" and "a leisure issue" (Friedman et al. 567).[3] I vividly recall anthropologists offering unsparing critiques of Anzaldúa in various panels at the American Anthropological Association's annual meetings in the early-to-mid-1990s. Perhaps, given the prominence of Anzaldúa's *Borderlands / La Frontera,* these conference presentations were not published as refereed journal articles or book chapters. The quotes from 2003 are the closest example of these critiques I could find in print.

Regrettably, the University of California bestowed upon Anzaldúa a long-deserved PhD—posthumously. In fact, the US-Euro-centered decolonization of anthropology has actually led to further colonization of the discipline as it was mainly unidirectional. Theory continues to be formulated and articulated in US-European metropolitan universities, and the data, now decolonized, continues to come from the Third World or "Third Worlded" Western metropolises (Ribeiro and Escobar).

THE *CONOCIMIENTO* MODEL AND THE STUFF OF LIFE

Gloria Anzaldúa followed the path of Audre Lorde, who, thirty-five years ago, wrote "The Uses of Anger: Women Responding to Racism," where she advocates for the articulation of raw anger in academic texts: "the anger of exclusion, of unquestioned privilege, of racial distortions, of silence, ill use, stereotyping, defensiveness, misnaming, betrayal and cooptation." Lorde argues that anger in academic language should retain emotional power because it is "a liberating and strengthening act of clarification." She discusses the multivocal orchestration of anger as text: "Women of color in America have grown up

3 These quotes are taken from a conversation among three notable European anthropologists, who back in the early 2000s began to explore issues around the ethnography of the right wing. Right wing studies did not become a point of interest in the US academic mainstream until the 2016 election, despite ultranationalism's ever-presence in the Euro-American social fabric.

within a symphony of anger, at being silenced, at being unchosen, at knowing that when we survive, it is in spite of a world that takes for granted our lack of humanness. . . . And I say symphony rather than cacophony because we have had to learn to orchestrate those furies" (Lorde 124–133).

In the early 1980s, Lorde and Anzaldúa continued the groundwork for the post-structuralist analysis of culture from an intersectional-subject position first laid out in 1977 by the Combahee River Collective (Anzaldúa and Moraga; *see* also Moya, 66–99; Alarcón). Shortly thereafter, the US-UK academic world adopted poststructuralism as it continued to trend in France from the previous decade. Yet Lorde and Anzaldúa's contribution to made-in-America deconstructionist theory went, at best, unacknowledged, or ignored altogether. Their theories were dismissed as biographical ruminations, as each wrote from the margins of academia and the mainstream feminist movement of the time.

A key instrument in Anzaldúa's theoretical and methodological toolkit is her use of the word *conocimiento*, or 'knowledge.' *Conocimiento* is not simply 'knowledge,' but rather a model that arranges the innate, underlying, raw emotions from the lived experience of the subaltern, racialized woman. This experience becomes a conscientious, flowing system of insights that derive meanings and modes of being or acting in the world. The model implores the racialized woman to articulate her raw emotion through seven stages: aftershock, the in-between, despair, call for action, putting the pieces together and testing them, rebirth, and spiritual activism (Anzaldúa, "Let Us Shift" 117–159). This model captures the life cycle of subaltern, racialized women and lends itself to contextual cross-cultural comparisons.

Anzaldúa theorizes about the very specific path of the individual woman of color. Her data-set stems from the autohistoria of her own self. She does not, however, follow the self-fashioning formula designated for the construction and deconstruction of the US-UK analytical subject. Rather, her life and words are planted in multiple communities as she contemporaneously crosses borders between and among them all. This is her journey on the conocimiento path.

Written from a marginalized space, Anzaldúa's pathbreaking *autohistoria-teoría* framework was trivialized for years as only testimony. This Anzaldúan framework received only marginal reference in the transnational feminist arenas of scholarship and activism. But, as Anzaldúa writes, we have shifted. *Borderlands / La Frontera* was published by Aunt Lute. *Light in the Dark* was published by Duke University Press, the Ivy League academic publisher.

Conocimiento "requires that you encounter your shadow side and confront what you've programmed yourself (and have been programmed by your cultures) to avoid . . . confront[ing] the traits and habits distorting how you see reality and inhibiting the full use of your facultades" (Anzaldúa, "Let Us Shift" 118).

Anzaldúa's facultades, or agency, cannot be separated from the shadow beast, as the enactment of the shadow beast-facultad involves not only courage but fear. Describing the interplay between the enactment of agency and the very fear of the woman of color from enacting her agency, Anzaldúa writes, "The knowledge that exposes your fears can also remove them. Seeing through these cracks makes you uncomfortable because it reveals aspects of yourself (shadow beasts) [that] you don't want to own" (132).

The rigid US-UK formula standardizes the explication of the stuff of life. But Anzaldúa allows for a range of non-standardized arguments illuminated and interconnected from within, what anthropologist Michael Taussig termed their "epistemic murk" (Taussig 121–135)—the state of being so immersed in violence to the point that it is difficult to identify any particular source for it. The state of constantly journeying into "the heart of darkness" as a subaltern subject, until one experiences both madness and passion. Always moving, yet stuck in the confinement of race, gender, nation, and religion (Lavie, "Staying Put"). Anzaldúa's refusal of Cartesian orderliness is imperative to the decolonization of social theory. The very narration of these intrinsic, disorderly interconnections from within the murk has led to the stymieing of Anzaldúan genres from scholarship. This is not permitted by the gatekeepers, ever dutiful, who oversee the anonymous review process of major US-UK journals and scholarly presses.

Anzaldúa's conocimiento model calls for a reconceptualization of the relationships among communities of subaltern scholarly knowledge. She calls for the replacement of monological and unidirectional anthropology with the multivocal polyphony of autohistoria and autoethnografía, thus paving the way for a more creative and egalitarian environment that is embedded in inchoate communities. Her analytical categories engage the local. For her, the local is not data to be ethnographed by English-language metropolitans, but theory that refuses to adhere to the US-UK pretense of analytical coherence. Anzaldúa refuses to reappropriate informant vignettes as she generalizes her model: "*La mestiza* constantly has to shift out of habitual formations; from convergent thinking, analytical reasoning that tends to use rationality to move toward a single goal (a Western mode), to divergent thinking, characterized by movement away from set patterns and goals and towards a more whole perspective, one that includes rather than excludes" (Anzaldúa, *Borderlands* 79).

LA LLORONA'S TEORÍA TRAVELS TO PALESTINE-ISRAEL

While Lorde's focus is anger, one of Anzaldúa's main figures is *La Llorona*: "a woman who wails, . . . a sight of intersection, connection, and cultural transgression" (Keating xiv). "Betrayed for generations, traumatized by racial denigration and exclusion, we are almost buried by grief's heavy pall. We never forget our wounds. *La Llorona*, our dark mother, with her perpetual, mournful song . . . Our symbol of unresolved grief, an ever-present specter in our psyches . . ." (Anzaldúa, "Let Us Shift" 88). "*La Llorona*'s wailing in the night for her lost children has an echoing note in the wailing or mourning rites performed by women as they bid their sons, brothers, and husbands goodbye. . . . Wailing is . . . [a] Chicana woman's feeble protest when she has no other recourse. These collective wailing rites may have been a sign of resistance in a society which glorified the warrior and war and for whom the women of the conquered tribes were booty" (33). Anzaldúa employs La Llorona, a historical-mythical figure from Latin American folklore,[4] as part of her theoretical and methodological toolkit. La Llorona, the wailing woman, represents the unanswered and unacknowledged cries of pain that she, and other subaltern women of color, endure.

After an impressive genealogy of struggle, North American women faculty of color are finally gaining the ability to express emotions in their academic publications and write in mixed genre—as long as they have tenure.[5] But this feat remains impossible for middle-to-lower class women scholars from the Global South, such as Palestinians with Israeli citizenship and Mizrahim. It is beyond the scope of this essay to address Palestinian feminist scholarship coming from Israel or the non-Western Palestinian diaspora. Nevertheless, stepping into the Anzaldúan tracks, I write here about mi gente.[6]

Mizrahim (Easterners), are Jews from the Arab and Muslim world and margins of the Ottoman Europe and are Israel's demographic majority at 50 percent. Palestinians with Israeli citizenship are about 20 percent of Israel's citizenry. Ashkenazim, Jews originating from Yiddish-speaking countries, are only 30 percent, but control the division of power and privilege in the state. Mizrahi women don't fall under the North American classification of "woman of color." We are expected to use the US-UK formula of dispassionate scholarship

4 La Llorona is a prominent oral legend in Latin America, specifically Mexican folklore. The colonialist lore states that a woman was unloved by her husband, who loved their two sons instead. After catching her husband with another woman, she drowned her sons before drowning herself in a river out of grief and anger. Upon arriving at heaven's gates, she was refused entry until she could find the souls of her two sons. As a result, she cries and wails, taking children and drowning them in that same river. Chicana feminism rescues La Llorona as a hero who drowned her children so that the Spaniards would not enslave them.

5 An excellent, recent example of one such courageous, emotive authorship is Laura Pérez's essay collection, *Eros Ideologies: Writings on Art, Spirituality, and the Decolonial*. Published by Duke University Press, the book challenges the US-UK model of writing culture through a variety of evocative, poetic styles set aside from its academic language.

6 Unfortunately, aside from the Anzaldúan vocabulary, I know no Spanish.

because the underlying assumption is that we are elite—our parents paid for our expensive Ivy League PhDs. My parents drilled me, and I drilled my son to ace his courses, because our only way to receive education abroad (and in English) was by OPM—Other People's Money or performance-based scholarships. No affirmative action for Mizrahim in the United States. No affirmative action for Mizrahim in Israel. Even though we are racialized and minoritized, we are the demographic majority. The State of Israel will never admit to its own intra-Jewish racial formations as it is the designated post-Holocaust Jewish homeland on the lands of British Mandatory Palestine. No rectification. In the Jewish state, all Jews are supposed to be equal, or so Zionist rhetoric would claim.

Zionism is a European ideology of Jewish nationalism whose main goal was to colonize Palestine in order to establish a Jewish state. It can be described as an ethnic by-product of the rise of modernist nationalism in Europe in the mid-nineteenth century. The Jewish state in Palestine was to redeem the persecuted Eastern European Jews through importing European cultural technology to Palestine. Concurrently, it planned to reinforce its conception of European superiority through primitivization of the native Palestinians. Unsubscribing from Zionism is a White, Ashkenazi privilege. It comes with trust funds, inheritances, home ownership, and the ability to pull strings, benefits unavailable to Mizrahim. The best way to silence Mizrahi feminist resistance is through financial deprivation.

Furthermore, Mizrahi feminist author-activists who opt out of Zionism (with or without experiencing the "aftershock" stage in Anzaldúa's model) are not only caught in the US-UK formula. They must fight to carve out a third space between the binarisms available for international public consumption: One is the Jewish state versus its Arab-enemy neighboring states. The other is the Israeli-Palestinian conflict. We are prevented from articulating the in-between, be it W. E. B. Du Bois's 1903 "Between Me and the World" (in *The Souls*) or Chela Sandoval's delineation of the space between Fanon's Black Skin and White Masks in his 1967 autoethnography (Sandoval 83–86). We are not allowed Lorde's anger or Anzaldúa's wailing. Abroad, we are Israeli Jews. In Israel, we are troublemakers—a demographic "in-between" majority, devoid of majoritarian rights, who disturbs the simplistic Palestine-Israel or Arab-Jew binary known to the world. If we sell out, we might fit into the well-funded disciplines of Israeli and Jewish Studies. If not, we still cannot benefit from the welcome boom of critical publications on the Israel-Palestine binary. We are not "Arab Jews" either. That is a historical concept that ceased to exist with the foundation of the Israeli State in 1948, and at any rate, our own communities loathe the term.

We fall into silence when we refuse the containment enforced on our critique of Zionism in the name of Israeli ethnic diversity—diversity that masks itself in the illusion of free speech that lifts once we understand how and how far our criticisms of Zionism are permitted to reach. For us, after the Anzaldúan "aftershock" stage, when we are on the conocimiento tracks and can understand the reality of Israel and the Arab World, Zionism is racism. We fall into silence when we upset the Palestinian national narrative whose secular, academic intelligentsia dialogues with the upper-class post- or anti-Zionist Ashkenazi elites we debunk. Progressive North American feminists of color and Anglo-feminists alike, stuck on the Israel-Palestine binary, label our wailing "polemics" due to our dismantling of the comfortable progressive binarism of the Israel-Palestine narrative. Our grassroot works are omitted from the global circulation of feminists of color texts. What remains for us then? Wailing. So, we wail.

We, Mizrahi feminists, encompass both the shadow beast and la facultad. Mainstream Mizrahi leaders, who align themselves with the Ashkenazi hegemony, and thus deny any intra-Jewish racial conflict, are referred to in Mizrahi-activist slang as "kapos" suffering from "Mizrahi kapo syndrome." Kapos were concentration camp prisoners employed by Nazis as low-level management in exchange for subsistence level privileges. In turn, Ashkenazi mainstream and its Mizrahi kapos judge anyone who speaks out about intra-Jewish race relations as guilty of *le-hitbakhyen*. In Hebrew this means whining and being a crybaby. The term *le-hitbakhyen* is usually deployed by those Ashkenazim who, by default, articulate what they advertise as "the Israeli discourse of pluralist enlightenment." Their pluralism is rooted in meritocracy—equal opportunities based only on the skills, talents, and efforts of individuals devoid of their communal background. To them, entering the academic elite is a result of one working hard, and has nothing to do with money, the color of our skins, or our genders. So when we cannot use the advancement road they delineated for us, they conceive of our failure as personal, not communal. We are simply not enlightened enough to enter the sphere of their US-European renaissance humanism. We are atavistic because we do our best to rescue our traditions they violently attempted to eliminate since they brought us to Palestine as their Jewish blue-collar labor. They are the (post)modernists. We try to rebuild the communities they destroyed, and this makes us backward losers. Therefore, our plights are the wailings of cry-babies who had the bad luck of being born poor in the wrong neighborhoods. This allows them to control the discourse of advocating genuine social justice, as their White privilege permits them to discursively decolonize Zionism. We as the majority, however, must adhere to Zionism—not the discourse but the practice—if we want to make it into their elite time-space. As we enter it, we can enjoy the liberation they envision for us, but only as individuals. Concurrently, our majoritarian communities' adherence to Zionism is the springboard that allows the enlightened Ashkenazim to criticize it while maintaining their privileges harking back to their European colonization of Palestine. And when we wail, they pull out of their sleeve the success of our Mizrahi kapos.

The mindset of the Mizrahi "kapo" is part of the structural-functional Parsonian analytical paradigm (Parsons) so prevalent in universalism vs. particularism's vulgar analysis of Israeli society offered by Shmuel Noah Eisenstadt. From the early 1940s on, Eisenstadt was not only a luminary sociologist at the Hebrew University of Jerusalem, he also designed policies that stripped Mizrahim of their culture, language, and family structure, and oversaw their execution so that Mizrahim degenerated into low-income laborers for the Zionist machine. He and his students remain crucial actors in the revolving door between Israel's academe and regime. To this day, their influence over Israeli social sciences is vigilant, as they continue to edit out scholarship and policy that deviates from this model. Eisenstadt's ideological paradigm impacted Zionist policymakers as they shaped Israel's White-on-White public sphere. Within this sphere, the Ashkenazim are the true, progressive Israelis, and therefore, universalists. Their privilege, transparent. We are left with divisive, primitivist, ethnic particularism. So, we wail.

The most notable examples given for the evocation of *le-hitbakhyen* are the Yemenite Children Affair and the Ringworm Affair. These epitomize the Ashkenazi Zionist's perpetual denial of racially motivated atrocities and trivialization of Mizrahi feminists' legitimate outcries. Those who speak out are deemed as wailing without cause.

The Yemenite Children Affair was the systematic kidnapping of roughly 5,000 light-skinned Mizrahi, Balkan, and Yemeni babies from the 1930s through the 1970s. Health officials alleged that these infants were ill and subsequently died, falsifying documents for their families without providing a body. Ashkenazi Zionist politicians and bureaucrats sold or gave away these children in unconsented adoptions to childless Ashkenazi families in Israel and abroad. While the State of Israel is notorious for its rigorous archival practices, the archives intended to research and educate on this affair remain closed until 2066, with many hospital and court documents having conspicuously disappeared (Madmoni-Gerber). Alternative archives on the affair, established by longtime Mizrahi activists, caught fire during unexplained electrical shortages.

Repeated suggestions by activists to file in the International Court of Justice in The Hague, Netherlands, were refused by the families. Mizrahim paradoxically love the state that continuously tortures them. As a group, they tend to vote for ultranationalist parties (Lavie, *Wrapped*). From the 1880s on, the Zionist socialist parties designed and upheld policies of intra-Jewish apartheid. As Mizrahim became Israel's demographic majority, they refused to endorse the parties that originated their subjugation. Until 1977, the right was the underdog of Israeli politics while Ashkenazi Zionist Socialist parties dominated. Then the system was overturned by the Mizrahi vote. Post-Holocaust, Israeli and diaspora Jews conceive of the Jewish state as the last line of Jewish defense. No dirty laundry revealing otherwise may be washed out at The Hague, before the *goyim* public. Goyim are non-Jews and in colloquial Hebrew, "the enemy."[7]

The Ringworm Children Affair was when roughly 150,000 Mizrahi children were irradiated with high dose x-rays in the 1950s without their parents' consent or knowledge. The monumental documentary film *The Ringworm Children* by David Belhassen and Asher Hemias argues that about 75,000 Mizrahi children were radiated against "ringworm."[8] Current estimates find that this number reflects roughly half of those radiated. In Mizrahi history, this is a key example of the State-sanctioned violence against non-European immigrants. According to Belhassen and Hemias, the experiment was possibly funded by the CIA. These children grew up to develop ailments such as cancer, thyroid problems, and tumors without access to their own medical files from the experiment as they were deemed "classified." They continue to suffer from lifelong disabilities, if not already having succumbed to an early death.

Their ailments, and resulting lack of income or sufficient compensatory funds, made suing the responsible physicians and policy makers impossible. They could not afford to purchase justice in the attorney marketplace and suing a Jewish state for collective crimes against its own people is impossible. The development of these children was documented, well into adulthood, by the Israeli physicians responsible. Their souls rest between the pages of the most prestigious, English-language medical journals. Like the Yemenite Children Affair activism, Ringworm activism was initiated by right-wing Mizrahim. Mizrahim refer to the Ringworm Affair and the Yemenite Children Affair as "our holocaust." I've written elsewhere that in Israel, the "right" is "left" and the "left" is right wing (Lavie, "Staying Put" and *Wrapped*). No dirty laundry washed out in front of the *goyim*. Needless to say that studying this affair from the families' or activists' perspective is taboo in Israeli universities, unless supervised by an Ashkenazi professor patron.

Israel, founded on Mandatory Palestine, conceives of itself as the national home of all world Jewry. Are not all Jews assumed equal in the homeland of

---

7 Due to public pressure, partial segments of state archival documents for the Yemeni Children Affair became available in 2018, but much of the material on these documents has been redacted. The majority of these documents are sealed off indefinitely.

8 For further information about "The Ringworm Affair," please see https://en.wikipedia.org/wiki/Ringworm_affair.

the Jews? But members of Israel's Mizrahi majority find it next to impossible to present any case for racial discrimination in court. Their cases are almost always disarmed and stripped of legitimacy by accusations of *le-hitbakhyen*. Yet, this wailing rarely travels nor transcends the boundaries of the Israeli State where the tyranny of the Hebrew language is one of Zionism's most successful miracles. Author and translation professor at the University of Michigan, Ann Arbor, Anton Shammas is known mainly for his writings in Hebrew and translations of Palestinian literature from Arabic to Hebrew. He told me, "Zionism gave the Jews a territory in the form of language. Hebrew is the only real victory of Zionism. . . . The Hebrew that was resurrected was not the Mizrahi Hebrew. And that was the tragedy" (Shammas in Lavie 1992, 103). Since its establishment in 1948, Israel has had no internationally recognized border. No Oxbridge English in Mizrahi ghetto and barrio schools. No funds for translation, unless provided by the Israeli education ministry that can bear the brunt of the bill. So the Israel-Palestine binary endures. The Mizrahi in-between is not a "legitimate tragedy."

HOW LONG CAN THE REGIME DEPEND ON MIZRAHIS' DOCILE LOYALTY TO THE JEWISH STATE?

Its first blood, a fin de siècle racial wound inflicted by the Ashkenazi Zionist Left. So deep, yet invisible. An apartheid system where everyone knows their place, all entranced by the drumbeat of the miraculous ingathering of the diasporas. Like all Israelis, Mizrahim benefited from the occupation of Palestine. For the Israeli left, protesting the occupation produces international funding for their NGOs. As elites abroad, they enjoy the cosmopolitan lifestyle of the global activist circuits while at home, like all Israelis, they enjoy the constant economic boom the occupation generates for Israel's financial elites. For the Mizrahim, the occupation provides housing solutions in the West Bank settlements—close to Israel's employment sites in its center, yet outside Israel's center's unaffordable real estate bubble.

Creating a third space for Mizrahi lloronas is an ongoing fight for justice. The Israeli regime continues to appropriate Mizrahi identity politics as its veneer of civility to mask from view its racial atrocities. Opting out of Zionism, we remain unclassified. Staying in is tempting. The regime will fund our tours for the North American-European diasporas, performing our songs, poetry, plays, and art as tokens of diversity. The strings attached: not a word on Palestine. Sin frontera. Walls, checkpoints, barbed wire, and minefields. The Israeli Ashkenazi hegemonic center keeps usurping, as its own frontier, the borderzones between European and Arab, Israeli and Palestinian, and Ashkenazi and Mizrahi. Not only is it difficult to distinguish the Israeli nation from its imperialism, but this overlap of nation and empire is imprecise and constantly in flux. Some vestiges of one or the other are always left over. The inner borders where these vestiges meet the larger central area, where nation and empire are fused, might be the only zones remaining for us to create in Hebrew. Because we are unclassified, racialized subjects, our creations rarely travel abroad or get translated to English, the tyrannical language of quotation. There is no "crossover" (*Borderlands / La Frontera* 49). Our wails are in modern Hebrew, a language resurrected by Europeans, that has become our native tongue.

A WAIL

On March 20, 2005, the Mizrahi Democratic Rainbow NGO held a book launch to celebrate Aharon Yitzhaki's book *The Mask: Introduction to Ethnic Strategy in the State of Israel—Comparative Research*. This self-published tome discusses, among other topics, the compliance of Israeli leftist academia with the regime and its apartheid toward Mizrahim. The book refers to Israeli universities' social science and humanities professors as "mercenaries of the pen." Likewise, the book dwells on the docility and lackluster thinking required of Mizrahi intellectuals, male by default, to get a foot in Israeli academe's door. If they are well behaved, they will gain entry. During the discussion, out stood a fierce young Mizrahi feminist. Here is her wail:

> Their racism toward us has gotten so sophisticated in the university. They used to totally shut me up, labeling me as *mitbakhyenet miktzo`it* (one who made wailing about racial issues into an expertise), but I've had it with their kissing ass to the Palestinians, as if our resistance needed a kosher stamp from them (the Palestinians) to be valid. . . . Now they pretend they're listening to our wails. Unlike the Palestinians, we are not a category for teaching about social justice or human rights in the law school curriculum. We belong in their anthropology and folklore departments. As Jews, under the law we have equal rights. But when I insist [that] I am a legal category of racinated discrimination, they just mumble around, so we can move on. I'm the only loudmouth Mizrahi in the classroom, and they're just waiting to see how long it will take me to get worn out and sell out. Enough with this tying everything to the Palestinians! Let them cling to their Ashkenazim, whose racism toward us is now all but undetectable. In my parents' time, it was plain as day. Now we need x-ray vision to see it. That's how we're losing the younger generation. They see racism as just over, because if you see it, it hurts like hell. It's so subtle and so cruel, like cuts in live flesh [where] you can't see the blood.

***

It is my hope that the unclassified, grassroot Anzaldúan scholar from the Global South can shift. That she is no longer given the default elite status. That she is able to publish academically through the conocimiento model of bearing witness to herself and society. This might horizontalize the power dynamics between and among feminists of color in US-European elite academe, feminist faculty in the Global South, and grassroot feminist intellectuals from the Global South. To lend myself to Harrison's vision, we need to listen to, read, and quote feminist theory from ex-centric sites and break away from the anglophone dominance of scholarship. Given that we cannot undo the tyranny of English, now let us shift to translation. Let us shift to the transnational language of Gloria Anzaldúa.

WORKS CITED

Alarcón, Norma. "Chicana Feminism in the Tracks of 'the' Native Woman." *Cultural Studies*, vol. 4, no. 3, 1990, pp. 248–56.

———. "The Theoretical Subjects of *This Bridge Called My Back* and Anglo-American Feminism." *Making Face, Making Soul / Haciendo Caras . . .* , edited by Gloria Anzaldúa. Aunt Look Books, 1990, pp. 356–69.

———. "Anzaldúa's Frontera: Inscribing Gynetics." *Displacement, Diaspora, and Geographies of Identity*, edited by Smadar Lavie and Ted Swedenburg. Duke University Press, 1996, pp. 41–53.

Anzaldúa, Gloria. *Borderlands / La Frontera: The New Mestiza.* Aunt Lute Books, 1987.

———. "Now Let Us Shift . . . Conocimiento . . . Inner Work, Public Acts." Keating, pp. 117–59.

Anzaldúa, Gloria, and Cherríe Moraga, eds. *This Bridge Called My Back: Writings by Radical Women of Color.* London: Persephone Books, 1981.

———. "Combahee River Collective: A Black Feminist Statement." *This Bridge Called My Back: Writings by Radical Women of Color*, edited by Gloria Anzaldúa and Cherríe Moraga. Kitchen Table: Women of Color Press, 1983, pp. 210–18.

Behar, Ruth. *Translated Woman: Crossing the Border with Esperanza's Story.* Beacon Press, 1993.

Belhassen, David, and Asher Hemias, dirs. *The Ringworm Children.* Casque d'Or Films, 2005. Los Angeles Israel Film Festival, 2007. DVD. https://www.youtube.com/watch?v=vMp1tef4lg4.

Bose, Brinda. "words that bleed and fly." Antiserious: Journal of Laughter in Slow Motion, 20 July 2015. https://antiserious.com/words-that-bleed-and-fly-cd5dbc723bbe. Accessed 20 December 2019.

Du Bois, W. E. B. *The Souls of Black Folk.* Penguin, [1903] 1989.

Eisenstadt, Shmuel Noah. *The Transformation of Israeli Society: An Essay in Interpretation.* Weidenfeld & Nicolson and Westview, 1985.

Fanon, Frantz. *Black Skin, White Masks.* Charles Lam Markmann, trans. New York: Grove Press, 1967.

Friedman, Jonathan, Andre Gingrich, Thomas Hylland Eriksen, and Sarah Green. "'Anthropologists are Talking' about the New Right in Europe." *Ethnos*, vol. 68, no. 4, 2003, pp. 554–72, https://lup.lub.lu.se/record/623193.

Gledhill, John. "Beyond Speaking Truth to Power: Anthropological Entanglements with Multicultural and Indigenous Rights Politics." *Manchester Anthropology Working Papers*,

2004, https://johngledhill.files.wordpress.com/2019/10/beyond_speaking_truth_to_power.pdf. Accessed 14 Feb. 2013.

Harrison, Faye. *Outsider Within: Reworking Anthropology in the Global Age.* University of Illinois Press, 2008.

Keating, AnaLouise, ed. *Light in the Dark/Luz en lo Oscuro.* Duke University Press, 2015.

Lavie, Smadar. ""Blow-Ups in the Borderzones: Third World Israeli Authors' Gropings for Home." *New Formations.* 1992, no. 18, pp. 84-106.

———. "Staying Put: Crossing the Israel–Palestine Border with Gloria Anzaldúa." *Anthropology and Humanism Quarterly*, vol. 36, no. 1, 2011, pp. 101–21.

———. *Wrapped in the Flag of Israel: Mizrahi Single Mothers and Bureaucratic Torture.* 2nd ed. University of Nebraska Press, 2018.

Lorde, Audre. *Sister Outsider.* Crossing Press, 1984, pp. 124–33.

Madmoni-Gerber, Shoshana. *Israeli Media and the Framing of Internal Conflict: The Yemenite Babies Affair.* Palgrave Macmillan, 2009.

Moya, Paula M. L. *Learning from Experience: Minority Identities, Multicultural Struggles.* University of California Press, 2002.

Nasreen, Taslima. *No Country for Women.* Vitasta Publishing, 2010.

Parsons, Talcott. *Societies: Evolutionary and Comparative Aspects.* Prentice Hall, 1966.

Ribeiro, Gustavo Lins, and Arturo Escobar, eds. *World Anthropologies: Disciplinary Transformations within Systems of Power.* Berg Publishers, 2006.

Sandoval, Chela. *Methodology of the Oppressed.* University of Minnesota Press, 2000.

Taussig, Michael. *Shamanism, Colonialism, and the Wild Man: A Study in Terror and Healing.* University of Chicago Press, 1986.

Yitzhaki, Aharon. *HaMaseikha: Mavo LaEstrategia HaEtnit Shel HaMishtar BeMedinat Israel The Mask: Introduction to Ethnic Strategy in the State of Israel—Comparative Research.* [In Hebrew]. Kotarot Publishing, 2003

PART III

PHILOSOPHY, THEORY, CULTURE

LA MEXICANA EN LA CHICANA

SOURCES OF ANZALDÚA'S MEXICAN PHILOSOPHY[1]

ALEXANDER V. STEHN AND MARIANA ALESSANDRI

Gloria Anzaldúa once envisioned participating in a plenary panel to be titled "La Mexicana en la Chicana" (Box 122, Folder 11)[2] at the 1991 annual meeting of the National Association of Chicano Studies (NACS), the first to be hosted in Mexico, in Hermosillo, Sonora. The conference theme was Los Dos Méxicos, which resonated with Anzaldúa's dedication of *Borderlands / La Frontera*: "*a todos mexicanos* on both sides of the border" (front matter). Anzaldúa did not end up

1 A different version of this essay was published in the *Inter-American Journal of Philosophy* (Stehn and Alessandri, "La Mexicana"). We are grateful to the journal's editors for granting reprint permission in order to reach a wider audience of Anzaldúa scholars.

2 Handwritten note in the Gloria Evangelina Anzaldúa Papers, Benson Latin American Collection, University of Texas Libraries, the University of Texas at Austin. Copyright © Gloria E. Anzaldúa. Reprinted by permission of The Gloria E. Anzaldúa Trust. All rights reserved. Parenthetical references to box and folder numbers throughout this essay refer to materials available in this archive. A guide to its contents is available on the web at https://legacy.lib.utexas.edu/taro/utlac/00189/lac-00189.html. Parenthetical references to book box numbers refer to the archival location of one of the more than 5,000 books from Anzaldúa's personal library, maintained in the same archive.

participating in this conference, but she attended many other NACCS[3] conferences and was honored with the association's Lifetime Achievement Award in 2005, a year after her death. Unfortunately, Anzaldúa's contributions to philosophy are far less recognized, but this is slowly changing.[4] The fact that Anzaldúa scholars have focused on her relevance for understanding a variety of US-American identities[5]—Chicanx, women of color, queer, etc.—has obscured the fact that Anzaldúa also drew from and contributed to Mexican philosophy, especially *la filosofía de lo mexicano* that flourished in mid-twentieth-century Mexico.[6]

Our essay examines Anzaldúa's critical appropriation of Mexican philosophical sources, especially in the writing of *Borderlands / La Frontera.* We demonstrate how Anzaldúa contributed to Mexican and Chicanx philosophy by developing a transnational philosophy of Mexicanness, effectively participating in what has been recently characterized as the "multi-generational project to pursue philosophy *from* and *about* Mexican circumstances" (Vargas). More specifically, we recover "La Mexicana en la Chicana" by paying careful attention to Anzaldúa's Mexican sources, both those she explicitly cites and those we discovered while conducting archival research using the Gloria Evangelina Anzaldúa Papers in the Benson Latin American Collection at the University of Texas (UT) at Austin. In the three sections that follow, we: 1) pragmatically define the terms *Mexican* and *philosophy* in conversation with Anzaldúa's work, 2) examine the Mexican philosophical sources that Anzaldúa cites in *Borderlands / La Frontera*, and 3) present the other major Mexican philosophical influences on Anzaldúa that we found in the archive. The eight Mexican philosophical sources we discuss here are: José Vasconcelos (1882–1959), Miguel León-Portilla (1926–2019), Juana Armanda Alegría (1938–), Octavio Paz (1914–1998), Samuel Ramos (1897–1959), Rosario Castellanos (1925–1974), Sor Juana Inés de La Cruz (1648–1695), and Jorge Carrión (1913–2005).

---

3 In 1995, the membership of the National Association of Chicano Studies (NACS) voted to recognize the critical contribution and role of Chicanas in the association by renaming themselves the National Association for Chicana and Chicano Studies (NACCS).

4 Examples of recent works that treat Anzaldúa as a philosopher include: Martinez 2014; Pitts 2016; Paccacerqua 2016; Ortega 2016; Newton 2017; Tirres 2019; Pitts et al. 2019; Alessandri 2019; Alessandri 2020; Alessandri and Stehn 2020; Stehn 2020.

5 We use "U.S. American" rather than "American" to refer to people in the United States of America to avoid the narrow provincialism summarized by Edgar Sheffield Brightman: "We [North Americans] arrogate to ourselves the very name of 'American,' which by right belongs to every citizen of North, Central, and South America" (qtd. in Romanell 1952, 5).

6 The best introduction to *la filosofía de lo mexicano* in English is Sánchez and Sanchez Jr. 2017.

DEFINING MEXICAN PHILOSOPHY PRAGMATICALLY

In presenting Anzaldúa as a Mexican philosopher, we face the interrelated problems of defining *Mexican* and defining *philosopher*. The distinctions we make are pragmatic and stipulative rather than metaphysical. In other words, they are calibrated to our present aims of demonstrating Anzaldúa's study of and contributions to the Mexican philosophical tradition. We are not trying to pick out the unchanging essences in the world that are *Mexican* or making transhistorical claims about what counts as *philosophy*. By calling something "Mexican" or "philosophical" we want to draw scholarly attention to unrecognized, understudied, and dismissed features of Anzaldúa's work, while recognizing that Anzaldúa perpetually wrestled with labels for herself and others.

The archival materials associated with the writing of *Borderlands / La Frontera* from 1983–87 fill seven boxes containing 112 folders. In an early draft, Anzaldúa considered dedicating the work to "all Chicanos and Mexicanos on both sides of the border," but also played with the split term "Chicano/ Mexicano" (Box 31, Folder 13). For the final published version she deleted *Chicanos* and code-switched to "*a todos mexicanos* on both sides of the border," which suggests that for her own pragmatic purposes at the time, Anzaldúa was primarily interested in bridging the varieties of Mexican identity. In fact, another draft was "dedicated to all Mejicanos on both sides of the border no matter what they call themselves" (Box 32, Folder 7), which further suggests two things: 1) Anzaldúa recognized that what many people typically conceive as a clear border between Chicano vs. Mexicano or Mexican American vs. Mexican is in fact vague and indeterminate, just as she describes the borderlands that defy the physical boundaries of Mexico and the United States; 2) Anzaldúa recognized that classifying someone as Mexican rather than Chicanx, or Chicanx rather than Mexican American—to take just two examples—risks a certain amount of violence against their self-conception. To avoid contention, the sources of Anzaldúa's philosophy that we identify here as Mexican were all born in Mexico, lived there for most or all of their lives, and practiced philosophy in Spanish or Nahautl—all factors that contribute to why they have not received much scholarly attention in the United States.

It is even more challenging to define and delimit who counts as a philosopher. From Anzaldúa's published works and unpublished notes in the archive, we know that she wanted to be considered a philosopher but felt excluded from what she called the "most closed of male sanctums: philosophy" (Box 234, Folder 14). Anzaldúa reports that she was interested in philosophy beginning in elementary school where she carried around books by Kierkegaard and Nietzsche (Reuman and Anzaldúa 31), and she took several philosophy courses in college and grad school. Long before she died, Anzaldúa imagined her own obituary where she called herself "a great thinker, *philosopher*, writer and humanitarian" (Box 105, Folder 3; italics added), and toward the end of her life she labeled herself a "feministvisionaryspiritualactivistpoet-*philosopher* fiction writer" (*Reader* 3; italics added). In another note, she asked herself "what makes a philosopher?" and answered "scholarly self-study" (Box 102, Folder 5), hearkening back to Socrates and the Ancient Delphic command *gnothi seauton* or "know thyself."[7] In what follows we show how Anzaldúa took up the philosophical project of scholarly self-study by critically appropriating Mexican sources who had been asking "*What does it mean to be Mexican*?" for generations.

EXPLICITLY CITED MEXICAN PHILOSOPHICAL SOURCES IN *BORDERLANDS / LA FRONTERA*

Anzaldúa quotes and footnotes many Mexican sources in *Borderlands / La Frontera* but only two who are clearly philosophers: the historian, anthropologist, and philosopher Miguel León-Portilla (91, 93); and the philosopher and politician José Vasconcelos (99). Of the two, only Vasconcelos is consistently recognized as a Mexican philosopher, but Miguel León-Portilla's groundbreaking dissertation, "La filosofía náhuatl estudiada en sus fuentes" earned him a doctorate from the Facultad de Filosofía y Letras at the Universidad Nacional Autónoma de México (UNAM) in 1956. His previous degree from Loyola University in Los Angeles, California, was an MA in Philosophy earned in 1951 with a thesis on Henri Bergson's *Las dos fuentes de la moral y la religión*.[8]These degrees unequivocally place León-Portilla in the discipline of philosophy—indeed, his work basically established the academic field of Nahuatl or Aztec philosophy—but the fact that he worked almost exclusively on Nahuatl philosophy throughout his career has no doubt led to his being categorized most frequently as a historian or an anthropologist. Reflecting on the Eurocentric disciplinary labels applied to León-Portilla's work suggests that one of the many reasons that Anzaldúa's *Borderlands / La Frontera* is not widely recognized as philosophy may be that it works a great deal with Nahautl symbols and concepts, effectively obscuring the philosophical nature of her project, given the prejudice against the very possibility of indigenous philosophy, or what James Maffie has called "philosophy without Europe" (Maffie 24).

In a similar way, Anzaldúa is most frequently categorized as a Chicana or Mexican American even though she could also very comfortably respond

7 See Alessandri, "Anzaldúa as Philosopher," for a more detailed examination of the archival evidence that Anzaldúa considered herself a philosopher.

8 León-Portilla's prologue to the fiftieth anniversary edition of *La filosofía náhuatl estudiada en sus fuentes* explains that his first transformative encounter with Spanish translations of Nahuatl literature and poetry occurred while finishing his thesis on Bergson's philosophy (9).

to the question "¿Qué eres?" with "soy mexicana" (*Borderlands* 84). The Mexicanness of her philosophical project is also harder for most US American scholars to recognize because they are less likely to know the work of Mexican philosophers like Vasconcelos and León-Portilla. One of Anzaldúa's most important philosophical innovations and contributions to *la filosofía de lo mexicano* was to bridge the histories and philosophies of three different types of Mexicans[9] in order to develop the subtitle of *Borderlands / La Frontera: The New Mestiza*: 1) the indigenous, Nahuatl-speaking Mexicans whose philosophical contributions were recognized by León-Portilla's scholarship, 2) the mestizo, Spanish-speaking Mexicans whose philosophical contributions grew out of the educational system and philosophical milieu established largely by José Vasconcelos, and 3) the Chicana, or those we might call Chicanx Mexicans, who often speak both Spanish and English and whose identities are explored and reimagined throughout Anzaldúa's philosophy.

Chapter by chapter, Anzaldúa weaves together the histories, movements, and identities of Mexicans, Indians, and Americans of many cultures while adding her own mestiza voice to the Philosophy of Mexicanness. The process culminates in what Anzaldúa calls her own "take" on Vasconcelos's idea of *la raza cósmica.* Chapter seven develops *la conciencia de la mestiza,* which in its productive Spanish ambiguity is always both a consciousness and a conscience. Modifying the grammatical gender of the new motto that Vasconcelos devised for UNAM in 1920, Anzaldúa opens the chapter with the words, "*Por la mujer de mi raza hablará el espíritu*" (99). By interpreting the heart of Vasconcelos's vision as one of inclusivity and pivoting toward her own queer identity, the chapter effectively reinterprets the mission of *la raza cósmica* as follows: "We come from all colors, all classes, all races, all time periods. Our role is to link people with each other" (106). It is therefore both ironic and tragic that Anzaldúa's work has not been consistently and emphatically linked with the history of Mexican philosophy.

MEXICAN PHILOSOPHICAL SOURCES NOT CITED IN *BORDERLANDS / LA FRONTERA*

The foregoing sketch should make plausible our reading of Anzaldúa as a Mexican philosopher whose work contributes to *la filosofía de lo mexicano*, but our case is bolstered by archival research. We have examined: 1) many of Anzaldúa's notes and papers from as far back as her undergraduate education, 2) the scholarly sources that she taught, retaught, and tested her students on when she taught courses like "La Mujer Chicana," "The Chicana in America," or

9 It is worth repeating that "different types of Mexicans" operates as a heuristic typology that should not be confused with essentialist claims about Mexican identities.

"Chicanos and Their Culture" while enrolled as a doctoral student at UT Austin in the late 1970s (Sendejo); and 3) the books pertaining to Mexican philosophy that Anzaldúa owned, underlined, highlighted, and wrote marginalia in. The remainder of our paper sketches the archival evidence of the philosophical influence of eight Mexicans on Anzaldúa. The order does not reflect any kind of a ranking but rather our attempt to weave them together in a brief but coherent narrative.

José Vasconcelos (1882–1959)

The Gloria Evangelina Anzaldúa Papers contain five pages of handwritten notes (Box 165, Folder 25) that Anzaldúa took while reading the 1961 edition of José Vasconcelos's *La raza cósmica,* which appears in a footnote in *Borderlands / La Frontera* (119). This means that unlike many other leaders of *el movimiento chicano,* who seem to have merely borrowed phrases from Vasconcelos because they were in the air (Stavans 43), Anzaldúa actually read Vasconcelos's philosophy in order to critically rework it. Anzaldúa also required students in her Summer 1977 course, "Chicanos and their Culture" (Box 229, Folder 1), to read Vasconcelos's "The Race Problem in Latin America." Unlike *La raza cósmica,* it was available in English because Vasconcelos delivered it as a lecture at the University of Chicago in 1926 (*Aspects of Mexican Civilization*). Anzaldúa's bulleted recap of Vasconcelos's work indicates that the mission of *la raza cósmica* is "formar un nuevo tipo humano," the new human type that *Borderlands / La Frontera* would later present transformed as *The New Mestiza.* Anzaldúa's notes also suggest that she was particularly impressed that Vasconcelos "posited that a mixture of races does not create inferiority" and that *mestizaje* evolved much more quickly in Latin America (Box 165, Folder 25).

Miguel León-Portilla (1926–2019)

Anzaldúa's personal library housed in the archive contains more than 5,000 books but none by Vasconcelos. In contrast, it contains eight different books by León-Portilla,[10] at least three of which she almost certainly consulted to write *Borderlands / La Frontera*;[11] it contains two footnotes on page 119 that reference

---

10 Anzaldúa's personal library at the archive technically contains eleven books by León-Portilla, but three are subsequent editions of the same book.

11 From the fact that Anzaldúa inscribed many of her books with the date and place of purchase, we know that she purchased León-Portilla's *Native Mesoamerican Spirituality* on February 22, 1982, and *Aztec Thought and Culture: A Study of the Ancient Nahuatl Mind* on August 15, 1983. We can therefore say with considerable confidence that she read at least three books by León-Portilla before the publication of *Borderlands / La Frontera in 1987.*

Los antiguos mexicanos a través de sus crónicas y cantares (Book Box 27). While not cited in *Borderlands / La Frontera,* Anzaldúa highlighted and wrote marginal notes throughout her copy of *Aztec Thought and Culture: A Study of the Ancient Nahuatl Mind* (Book Box 65) shortly before beginning work on *Borderlands / La Frontera* in 1984. *Aztec Thought and Culture* is a translation of the work that earned León-Portilla his PhD in Philosophy, *La filosofía náhuatl estudiada en sus fuentes.* Unfortunately, the translated English title denies León-Portilla's most fundamental thesis, namely, that there is such a thing as Nahua *philosophy* that can be reconstructed using *Nahuatl* sources.[12] Despite the misleading translation of the title, the heart of León-Portilla's work was not lost on Anzaldúa, who highlighted almost every reference to "philosophy" or "philosopher" in the book. Like León-Portilla, she rejected any unbridgeable divide between poetry and philosophy, highlighting a question and answer from León-Portilla's introduction:

> Had that restlessness of spirit, stemming from a sense of wonder and doubt, manifested itself in the rational inquiry into the nature of things which we call philosophy? . . . The poet is a commentator on life and existence; in his immediate and imaginative way, he is a philosopher. Among the Nahuas, then, as among the Greeks, it was the lyric poets who first became aware of and enunciated the great problems of human existence (*Aztec Thought and Culture* xxi).

Anzaldúa's interest in this quote sheds new light on her comment that *Borderlands / La Frontera* was originally conceived as "a book of poetry, mostly written to Chicanos looking for some symbols of what it meant to be Mexican." Since Anzaldúa felt like the poems would make the most sense if placed into a historical and cultural context she "added the introduction and it kept growing until it became seven chapters, half of the book" (Hernández and Anzaldúa 13). In other words, Anzaldúa's chronological process of writing *Borderlands / La Frontera* as a poet-philosopher proceeded from poetry to philosophy, just like the Aztec *filósofos-poetas* described by León-Portilla. Recovering the influence of León-Portilla on Anzaldúa's writing also helps us understand the way Anzaldúa

12 While most mainstream professional philosophers in the United States would likely consider León-Portilla a historian and/or anthropologist, the fact that he was fundamentally interested in philosophy was obvious to at least one professor of anthropology at Tulane University who reviewed *Los antiguos mexicanos* (the work cited by Anzaldúa in *Borderlands / La Frontera*) for the journal *American Anthropologist* in 1961, two years before the translation *Aztec Thought and Culture* appeared: "The result of this new approach to old material is that [León-Portilla's] style of writing suggests the 20th century philosopher rather than either the historian or anthropologist" (Robertson 1375).

conceived of its pedagogical function, which she further theorized in *Making Face, Making Soul: Haciendo Caras*, whose title references León-Portilla's description of the work of the Nahua sage, *filósofo*, or *tlalmatini* ["one who knows things"] who teaches people "to have and develop in themselves a face" (*Aztec Thought and Culture* 24).[13]

Juana Armanda Alegría (1938–)

Anzaldúa assigned Juana Armanda Alegría's *Psicología de las mexicanas* to her "La Mujer Chicana" class of 1977 (Box 227, Folder 7). There is no copy of the book in the archive, but we speculate that, as in the case of Vasconcelos's *La raza cósmica*, it would have been very difficult for Anzaldúa to purchase in the United States. The use of the book for the course seems to have been Anzaldúa's own innovation because it is not mentioned in the Fall 1976 syllabus or reading list of Inés Hernández Tovar from whom Anzaldúa took the course. For the final exam, Anzaldúa asked questions about all three parts of Alegría's book, although the students who could not read Spanish were questioned on Shulasmith Firestone's *The Dialectic of Sex*. Before Anzaldúa taught the course, it already contained a unit on Chicana psychology that drew upon the work of Chicana feminists like Anna Nieto-Gómez and Martha P. Cotera, so Anzaldúa must have believed that Alegría's book had something important to add.[14] This information supports our thesis about the scholarly imperative to pay more attention to Anzaldúa's Mexican sources, but it also serves as a corrective for standard histories of Mexican philosophy that tend to exclude the work of women by unfairly policing the boundaries of philosophy (del Río). For example, Samuel Ramos's *El perfil del hombre y la cultura en México*, a work in philosophical psychology, is widely considered to be the foundational text that officially launched *la filosofía de lo mexicano* (Schmidt), whereas Alegría's philosophical psychology is typically ignored by philosophers and considered to be *merely* feminism.

What Anzaldúa seems to have found most important in Alegría's *Psicología de las mexicanas* is the way that the three parts of the book address the more general problems of contemporary sexism (Part I) by providing a revisionist feminista history of *la mujer mexicana* (Part II)—going all the way back to the Aztecs and running through various Mexican feminine archetypes including Coatlicue, La Malinche, La Virgen de Guadalupe, Sor Juana, La Llorona, and La Adelita—in order to transform the future (Part III) by rebelling against the

13 Anzaldúa highlighted this phrase in her copy of León-Portilla's *Aztec Thought and Culture* (Book Box 65). On page 13 of the same book, she highlighted a similar passage and wrote "face" in the margin.

14 For more about the history of the "La Mujer Chicana" class at UT Austin, see Sendejo.

"formas estereotipadas de la conducta femenina en nuestro país" to achieve liberation (144). Although *Borderlands / La Frontera* is even more ambitious in historical scope and subject matter, the basic structure resembles Alegría's book with the important exception of the poetry that comprises the second part of *Borderlands / La Frontera*. Indeed, Anzaldúa could have written these words from Alegría's Introduction: "I try to somehow tie everything together from the things that I have experienced myself as a woman and through other women" (Alegría 3; our translation). Both Mexican philosophers also had similar aims: what Alegría terms *concientización*, that is, "becoming conscious of…our circumstances as human beings" (13), Anzaldúa further developed as the philosophical path that leads toward *la conciencia de la mestiza.*

Octavio Paz (1914–1998)

Many of the long block quotes in *Psicología de las mexicanas* establish further organic connections with other important sources of Mexican philosophy that clearly influenced Anzaldúa. For example, Alegría quotes extensively from Octavio Paz's *El laberinto de la soledad*, which Anzaldúa acquired in May 1977 as an English translation (Book Box 3), just as she was finishing teaching "La Mujer Chicana." Anzaldúa heavily underlined Paz's chapter "The Pachuco and Other Extremes." Paz's account of the *pachuco's* "hybrid language and behavior" (*Labyrinth of Solitude* 18) fascinated Anzaldúa, as did Paz's claim that "The pachuco does not want to become a Mexican again; at the same time, he does not want to blend into the life of North America" (14). The year before, in June 1976, Anzaldúa had acquired Paz's *The Other Mexico: Critique of The Pyramid* (Book Box 69), a further development of the lecture he delivered at the University of Texas at Austin in 1969 where he reflected on the student demonstrations and revolutions that were happening throughout the world, including in Mexico and in the United States. Paz's existentialist claim that "The Mexican is not an essence but a history" resonates with Anzaldúa's approach in *Borderlands / La Frontera*, as does his claim that his work on Mexicanness was not "a search for our supposed being" but rather "a vision and, simultaneously, a revision" of what it means to be Mexican (vii). Anzaldúa's archive contains seventeen books by Paz. Although we did not have time to systematically examine all of them, the archival research we present here establishes that there is a substantial organic connection between Paz and Anzaldúa in addition to the literary one so thoughtfully analyzed by Marisa Belausteguigoitia.

Samuel Ramos (1897–1959)

Another work that Alegría quotes frequently is Samuel Ramos's *El perfil del hombre y la cultura en México* (1934), which is widely recognized as a foundational text for *la filosofía de lo mexicano* (Schmidt). Anzaldúa owned the English translation, *Profile of Man and Culture in Mexico*, dating her acquisition "mayo 77, tejas Aztlán." The book was required reading for Anzaldúa's PhD coursework, and when she taught "Chicanos and Their Culture" during Summer 1977, she included exam questions about Ramos's chapter "Psychoanalysis of the Mexican," Paz's "The Sons of La Malinche," and Vasconcelos's "The Race Problem in Latin America," alongside questions on Armando Rendón's *Chicano Manifesto* (Box 228, Folder 7). These juxtapositions in the way that Anzaldúa constructed her course clearly demonstrate that she was thinking about contemporary questions of Chicano/a identity in relation to the longer tradition of *la filosofía de lo mexicano*. Anzaldúa may have also revisited Ramos's book while writing *Borderlands / La Frontera* since a list she wrote in June 1985, titled "Mexican pensadores," names: Antonio Caso, Alfonso Reyes, Samuel Ramos, Octavio Paz, Edmundo O'Gorman, Leopoldo Zea, and José Gaos (Box 32, Folder 10). Below this list, she wrote: "Psychology of the Mexicano / Chicano" and under that: "El Perfil del hombre y la cultura en Mexico 1934 – Samuel Ramos." She also wrote a few bulleted themes, including "fear of inferiority," "self-denigration, self-disparagement," "supposed inferiority of native culture," and "Attitude of a nation which has its origins in a highly developed autochthonous civilization that was later reduced to colonial status. With the Chicano—experienced this twice" (Box 32, Folder 10).

Ramos's basic hypothesis, which Anzaldúa highlighted in her copy of his book, was that "some expressions of Mexican character are ways of compensating for an unconscious sense of inferiority," with the result that "the Mexican undervalues himself, committing in this way an injustice to his person" (9). Like Ramos, Anzaldúa sought to "eliminate the false premises of [Mexicans'] inferiority complex" (Ramos viii). Indeed, the passage where Anzaldúa discusses the inferiority complex of the Chicana reflects the basic structure of Ramos's diagnosis:

> No, it isn't enough that she is female—a second-class member of a conquered people who are taught to believe that they are **inferior** because they have indigenous blood, believe in the supernatural, and speak a deficient language. Now she beats herself over the head for her "inactivity," a stage that is as necessary as breathing. But that means being Mexican. All her life she's been told that Mexicans are lazy. She has had to work twice as hard as others to meet the standards of the dominant culture which have, in part, become her standards (*Borderlands* 70–71; bold added).

According to Ramos, the way beyond the inferiority complex that Anzaldúa represents here is the development of new standards that humanize what the dominant culture has rendered subhuman, and this is just what Anzaldúa does in developing *la conciencia de la mestiza*. By paying more critical attention to the roles of gender, language, sexuality, and spirituality, Anzaldúa's transformation of Ramos's framework makes a critical contribution to Mexican philosophy.

Rosario Castellanos (1925–1974)

The centrality of gender, sexuality, and language in Anzaldúa's work bring us to our examination of Rosario Castellanos and Sor Juana Inés de la Cruz. Anzaldúa most likely considered both poet-philosophers as kindred spirits, but it's unlikely that she would have read Castellanos's MA thesis in Philosophy at the UNAM, "Sobre cultura femenina" (1950), since it was largely unknown even by specialists until it was republished in 2005. Castellanos's thesis directly confronted the trilemma described by Anzaldúa in *Borderlands / La Frontera* that had not changed much since Sor Juana confronted it three centuries before: "For a woman of my culture there used to be only three directions she could turn: to the Church as a nun, to the streets as a prostitute, or to the home as a mother" (*Borderlands* 39). Just as Castellanos's thesis defied the stereotype that women are intellectually inferior, her subsequent work as a poet, literary critic, novelist, neoindigenist, and philosopher confronted the difficult historical fact that the dominant culture has made it almost impossible for women to be both mothers and creative beings.

Although Anzaldúa read at least some of Castellanos's poetry before publishing *Borderlands / La Frontera*,[15] Castellanos's major influence came later. In a work plan titled "Mexican Feminist Theory and Autobiography" that Anzaldúa dated November 9, 1989, she wrote: "Read Rosario Castellanos—novels, theory-criticism, poetry, short stories and critical texts on her work" (Box 91, Folder 6). Anzaldúa had purchased *The Selected Poems of Rosario Castellanos* in January 1989 (Book Box 81), followed by a Spanish collection of her poems in December of 1989 (Book Box 103). At page 208 of this collection, "Poesía no eres tú," we found a bookmark where Anzaldúa had written "Intro to Caras 1st stanza autohistoria 2nd stage self-writing." This note clearly indicates that Anzaldúa was drawn to Castellanos's poetic practices of self-writing and philosophical reflections on self-making, which inspired Anzaldúa's *Making Face, Making Soul / Haciendo Caras*. Anzaldúa also worked on an essay titled "Self-representation and Identity" in 1990 that references Castellanos on page 14 (Box 95, Folder 14). We have not had the opportunity to trace Castellanos's influence more carefully, but Anzaldúa's archive contains twelve books by this author.

---

15 Anzaldúa's handwritten list of readings for ETS 374 La Mujer Chicana included Rosario Castellanos's poem "Silence Concerning an Ancient Stone," which Anzaldúa's notes describe as a "poem about identity, heritage, & creative process—Mexican Poet" (Box 227, Folder 7).

Sor Juana Inés de la Cruz (1648–1695)

Alegría discusses Sor Juana Inés de la Cruz at length in *Psicología de las mexicanas*, as does Paz in *The Labyrinth of Solitude,* which Anzaldúa acquired in 1977 (Book Box 3). In fact, page 111 is dog-eared with "Sor Juana" written on the dog-ear. Anzaldúa highlighted much of Paz's discussion of Sor Juana, and his reference in a footnote to her most famous philosophical letter, "Reply to Sor Filotea" is circled. This passage is underlined: "We can sense the melancholy of a spirit who never succeeded in forgiving herself for her boldness and her condition as a woman" (115). In Anzaldúa's copy of Paz's *One Earth, Four or Five Worlds: Reflections on Contemporary History,* which she acquired in 1987 (Book Box 3), she highlighted Paz's claim that Sor Juana was "not only a great poet but also the intellectual conscience of her society" (139). Anzaldúa's friend and now Anzaldúa scholar Randy Connor gave her a copy of Octavio Paz's book *Sor Juana: Or, the Traps of Faith* in 1988 (Book Box 2). Anzaldúa also acquired Margaret Sayers Peden's *A Woman of Genius: The Intellectual Autobiography of Sor Juana Inés de la Cruz* on October 12, 1988 (Book Box 108). Her copy of *A Sor Juana Anthology* is dated "24 agosto '90 Santa Cruz" (Book Box 65). We did not have the time to examine these books for notes or highlighting, nor could we establish the date of a note card by Anzaldúa that names Sor Juana as a philosopher and her intellectual ancestor, but it reads: "Review: Intellectual Forerunners. What imploded in my consciousness: the fact that this woman (and other lesbian thinkers) are an actuality, that they dared enter the most closet closed [*sic?*] of male sanctums—philosophy. In my own racial background Sor Juana Inez de la Cruz, the first feminist of this hemisphere…" (Box 234, Folder 14).

Jorge Carrión (1913–2005)

Alegría quoted frequently from Jorge Carrión's *Mito y magia del mexicano* (1952), and Anzaldúa owned a photocopy of the book (Box 187, Folder 6). Although this photocopy contains no underlines, Anzaldúa wrote twelve handwritten pages of notes about the book in August 1983 (Box 165, Folder 35), just before she began work on *Borderlands / La Frontera.* These notes add depth to our understanding of the creative process by which Anzaldúa bridged the classic *filosofía de lo mexicano* written by figures like Vasconcelos and Ramos, who, at most, hollowly affirmed the contributions of Mexico's indigenous people in the making of the Mexican, with León-Portilla's scholarly work on Nahuatl philosophy. Published as part of a series called Ensayos sobre el mexicano, Carrión's book opens with reflections on the *choque* between Spanish and Indian that created what Anzaldúa's *Borderlands / La Frontera* later described as "*una nueva raza, el mestizo, el mexicano* (people of mixed Indian and Spanish blood)" (27). Carrión's work brings these two groups of people and cultures closer together by examining the way that Mexicans have relied on a kind of mythical and magical thinking and practice alongside a primitive science in their attempts to interpret and influence reality—all the way from the time of this first *choque* up to the present day *choque* when the souls of Mexicans are colliding with the technical culture of the United States. In Carrión's analysis, Mexicans are thus pinched between the Spanish conquistadors of the past—who imposed their religion, ideas, political orders, and customs—and the North American marauders of the present who impose their science, technologies, and market ideology.

Just as Carrión presented the effects of these *choques* on the Mexican psyche and identity in Mexico, Anzaldúa's work explores their effects on the Mexican psyche and identity in the United States. In fact, Anzaldúa uses the exact same word in Spanish, *choque*, to describe the cultural collision leading towards the creation of *la conciencia de la mestiza*: "*El choque de un alma atrapado entre el mundo de espíritu y el mundo de la técnica a veces la deja entullada.* Cradled in one culture, sandwiched between two cultures, straddling all three cultures and their value systems, la mestiza undergoes a struggle of flesh, a struggle of borders, an inner war" (*Borderlands* 100). While Anzaldúa takes up the Aztec tradition in a very different way from Carrión by engaging in acts of feminist revision, she nevertheless develops something like what Carrión's chapter calls the "Psychological Route of Quetzalcoatl" in her *Borderlands / La Frontera* chapter titled "La Herencia de Coatlicue." This is further developed in her later essay "Let us be the healing of the wound," where she calls it the Coyolxauhqui imperative to heal and achieve integration (*Light in the Dark*).

In sum, Anzaldúa interpolated the philosophical and psychological history of Chicanas into Carrión's philosophical and psychological history of Mexicans. This is clear from the first bullet of Anzaldúa's notes on Carrión's *Mito y magia del mexicano*: "humillada en la carne y la conciencia como mexicano por el español y como chicana por lo blanco, lo gringo" (Box 165, Folder 35). Many scholars have taken up Anzaldúa's call "to recover and reshape my spiritual identity" (*Borderlands* 110) in rebellion against the "white rationality" that wanted her and other people of color "to ignore, forget, kill those fleeting images of the soul's presence and of the spirit's presence" (58), but as far as we know, no one has recognized Carrión as one of Anzaldúa's theoretical sources for this project.

CONCLUSION, LIMITATIONS, AND FURTHER RESEARCH

In Anzaldúa's notes on Carrión, we once again see evidence of her belief that poetry could play a special role in healing the wounds of Mexican people and others: "The poets have a powerful candle for exploring in themselves what is not an impediment but rather a [productive] ambivalence in their magical and logical character. The best works grow out of these antitheses" (Box 165, Folder 125; our translation). Our research has grown out of our conviction that Anzaldúa created many such works—at once magical and logical, philosophical and poetic—and we hope that our essay has succeeded in illuminating them as important contributions that drew substantially upon Mexican sources to further develop *la filosofía de lo mexicano* or the Philosophy of Mexicanness. Anzaldúa's conception of her calling as a poet-philosopher has far more connection and resonance with the long history of Mexican philosophy than scholars have recognized, from the way the Nahua filósofo-poetas are portrayed in León-Portilla's study, to Sor Juana's love of science and poetry, to Vasconcelos's belief that the coming society of *la raza cósmica* should be organized around aesthetic principles.

In a less direct way we also hope to have rendered plausible the claim that Mexican philosophy has a past, present, and future in the United States by demonstrating the continuity between Anzaldúa's philosophical concerns as a Chicana and the philosophical concerns of her eight Mexican philosophical sources. We are certainly not alone in believing that Anzaldúa's work is critical for both Mexican and US-Chicanx philosophy. To borrow language from a book collaboratively authored by thirteen philosophers that makes multiple references to Anzaldúa while exploring the relation between Latin American and Latinx philosophy, we could say that Anzaldúa's work shows how Mexican and Chicanx philosophy "are both related and distinct, and that it is now difficult to draw a non-arbitrary line between them" (R. Sanchez 7).[16]

Setting aside various border disputes, we have attempted to achieve a reasonably comprehensive understanding of the Mexican sources of Anzaldúa's philosophy, but we do know at least two specific ways in which our essay is inadequate and thus calls for further research and commentary. First, Anzaldúa was more heavily influenced by Mexican women writers—typically classified as poets and novelists and feminists rather than as philosophers (del Río)—than we have had time to investigate. For example, the archive contains many hours of audio recordings of Anzaldúa talking to students and faculty about "Contemporary Mexican Women Writers" (Box 155, Folders 32–35; Box 156, Folders 1–9), but we only had time to listen to snippets. There are also far more written materials to examine. Second, although we live and work at Anzaldúa's undergraduate alma mater in the Rio Grande Valley and our understanding of Mexican

16 Anzaldúa's work is discussed in five out of the book's twelve chapters, demonstrating her tremendous importance to both Latin American and Latinx philosophy, as well as the more specific categories of both Mexican and Chicanx philosophy.

philosophy is conversant with much of the excellent scholarship from Mexico, our vantage point is nevertheless from the United States. This not only shapes but also limits what we have been able to see. We hope that others who read this will be able to fill in some of our blind spots and make more connections.

WORKS CITED

Alegría, Juana Armanda. *Psicología de las mexicanas.* Editorial Samo, 1975.

Alessandri, Mariana. "Gloria Anzaldúa as Philosopher: The Early Years (1962–1987)" *Philosophy Compass*, 2020, e12687.

———. "Three Existentialist Readings of Gloria Anzaldúa's *Borderlands / La Frontera*." *Cuadernos de ALDEEU*, vol. 34, 2019, pp. 117–35.

Alessandri, Mariana, and Alexander Stehn. "Gloria Anzaldúa's Mexican Genealogy: From *Pelados* and *Pachucos* to New Mestizas." *Genealogy*, vol. 4, no. 1, 2020.

Anzaldúa, Gloria. *Borderlands / La Frontera: The New Mestiza.* Aunt Lute Books, 2012.

———. *The Gloria Anzaldúa Reader.* Edited by AnaLouise Keating, Duke University Press, 2009.

———. *Light in the Dark / Luz en lo oscuro: Rewriting Identity, Spirituality, Reality*. Edited by AnaLouise Keating, Duke University Press, 2015.

———. *Making Face, Making Soul / Haciendo Caras: Creative and Critical Perspectives by Feminists of Color.* Aunt Lute Foundation Books, 1990.

Belausteguigoitia, Marisa. "Introducción." *Borderlands / La frontera: la nueva mestiza.* Translated by Norma Elia Cantú. Universidad Nacional Autónoma de México, Programa Universitario de Estudios de Género, 2015.

Carrión, Jorge. *Mito y magia del mexicano.* Editorial Nuestro Tiempo, 1952.

Castellanos, Rosario. *Poesía no eres tú: obra poética, 1948–1971.* Fondo de Cultura Económica, 1985.

———. *The Selected Poems of Rosario Castellanos.* Edited by Magda Bogin, Graywolf Press, 1988.

———. *Sobre cultura femenina.* Edited by Gabriela Cano, Fondo de Cultura Económica, 2005.

Cruz, Sor Juana Inés de la. *A Sor Juana Anthology.* Translated by Alan S. Trueblood, Harvard University Press, 1988.

del Río, Fanny. "Notes for an Ethical Critique of the Histories of Philosophy in Mexico: Searching for the Place of Women." *Latin American Feminist Philosophy: Theory Meets Praxis*, special issue of *Essays in Philosophy*, vol. 19, no. 1, 2018, pp. 35–49.

Hernández, Ellie, and Gloria Anzaldúa. "Re-Thinking Margins and Borders: An Interview with Gloria Anzaldúa." *Remapping the Border Subject,* special issue of *Discourse*, vol. 18, no. 1/2, 1995, pp. 7–15.

León-Portilla, Miguel. *Aztec Thought and Culture: A Study of the Ancient Nahuatl Mind.* Translated by Jack Emory Davis, University of Oklahoma Press, 1963.

———. *Los antiguos mexicanos a través de sus crónicas y cantares.* Fondo de Cultura Económica, 1961.

———. *La filosofía náhuatl estudiada en sus fuentes.* Universidad Nacional Autónoma de México, 2017.

Maffie, James. "Philosophy without Europe." *Latin American and Latinx Philosophy: A Collaborative Introduction*, edited by Robert Eli Sanchez, Jr., Routledge, 2019, pp. 13–35.

Martinez, Jacqueline M. "Culture, Communication, and Latina Feminist Philosophy: Toward a Critical Phenomenology of Culture." *Hypatia*, vol. 29, no. 1, 2014, pp. 221–36.

Newton, Margaret. "Philosophical Letter Writing: A Look at Sor Juana Inés de la Cruz's 'Reply' and Gloria Anzaldúa's 'Speaking in Tongues.'" *The Pluralist*, vol. 12, no. 1, 2017, pp. 101–09.

Ortega, Mariana. *In-Between: Latina Feminist Phenomenology, Multiplicity, and the Self.* SUNY Press, 2016.

Paccacerqua, Cynthia M. "Gloria Anzaldúa's Affective Logic of *Volverse Una*." *Hypatia*, vol. 31, no. 2, 2016, pp. 334–51.

Paz, Octavio. *The Labyrinth of Solitude: Life and Thought in Mexico.* Translated by Lysander Kemp, Grove Press, 1961.

———. *The Other Mexico: Critique of the Pyramid.* Translated by Lysander Kemp, Grove Press, 1978.

———. *Sor Juana, or, The Traps of Faith.* Translated by Margaret Sayers Peden. Belknap Press, 1988.

Peden, Margaret Sayers. *A Woman of Genius: The Intellectual Autobiography of Sor Juana Inés De La Cruz.* Lime Rock Press, 1987.

Pitts, Andrea J. "Gloria E. Anzaldúa's *Autohistoria-teoría* as an Epistemology of Self-Knowledge / Ignorance." *Hypatia*, vol. 31, no. 2, 2016, pp. 352–69.

Pitts, Andrea J., Mariana Ortega, and José Medina. *Theories of the Flesh: Latinx and Latin American Feminisms, Transformation, and Resistance.* Oxford University Press, 2019.

Ramos, Samuel. *Profile of Man and Culture in Mexico.* Translated by Peter G. Earle, University of Texas Press, 1972.

Rendón, Armando B. *Chicano Manifesto.* Macmillan, 1971.

Reuman, Ann E., and Gloria Anzaldúa. "Coming into Play: An Interview with Gloria Anzaldúa." *MELUS*, vol. 25, no. 2, 2000, pp. 3–45.

Robertson, Donald. Review of *Los antiguos mexicanos a través de sus crónicas y cantares* by Miguel León-Portilla. *American Anthropologist*, vol. 63, no. 6, 1961, pp. 1375–76.

Romanell, Patrick. *Making of the Mexican Mind: A Study in Recent Mexican Thought.* University of Nebraska Press, 1952.

Sánchez, Carlos Alberto, and Robert Eli Sanchez, Jr., editors. *Mexican Philosophy in the 20th Century: Essential Readings.* Oxford University Press, 2017.

Sanchez, Robert Eli, Jr., editor. *Latin American and Latinx Philosophy: A Collaborative Introduction.* Routledge, 2019.

Schmidt, Henry C. *The Roots of Lo Mexicano: Self and Society in Mexican Thought, 1900–1934.* University of Texas, 1978.

Sendejo, Brenda. "The Space in Between: Exploring the Development of Chicana Feminist Thought in Central Texas." *Chicana Movidas: New Narratives of Activism and Feminism in the Movement Era*, edited by Dionne Espinoza, María Eugenia Cotera, and Maylei Blackwell, 2018.

Stavans, Ilan. *José Vasconcelos: The Prophet of Race.* Rutgers University Press, 2011.

Stehn, Alexander V. "Teaching Gloria Anzaldúa as an American Philosopher." *Teaching Gloria E. Anzaldúa: Pedagogy and Practice for Our Classrooms and Communities*, edited by Margaret Cantú-Sánchez et al., University of Arizona Press, 2020.

Stehn, Alexander V., and Mariana Alessandri. "La Mexicana en la Chicana: The Mexican Sources of Gloria Anzaldúa's Inter-American Philosophy." *Inter-American Journal of Philosophy*, vol. 11, no. 1, 2020, pp. 44–62.

Tirres, Christopher D. "Spiritual Activism and Praxis: Gloria Anzaldúa's Mature Spirituality." *The Pluralist*, vol. 14, no. 1, 2019, pp. 119–40.

Vargas, Manuel. Review of *Mexican Philosophy in the 20th Century: Essential Readings*, edited by Carlos Alberto Sánchez and Robert Eli Sanchez, Jr. *Notre Dame Philosophical Reviews*, 2018.

Vasconcelos, José. *Aspects of Mexican Civilization: Lectures on the Harris Foundation.* University of Chicago Press, 1926.

———. *La raza cósmica: Misión de la raza iberoamericana.* Aguilar S.A. de Ediciones, 1961.

GLORIA ANZALDÚA

INTERSTICIOS ENTRE LAS FRONTERAS DE IBEROAMÉRICA, LA FILOSOFÍA Y LA PAZ

JAVIER ALEJANDRO CAMARGO CASTILLO

> El estirón entre lo que es y lo que debe ser. Creo que al cambiarnos, cambiamos al mundo, que el viaje por el camino de *El Mundo Zurdo* es el camino de un movimiento en dos sentidos —irse al fondo de una misma y extenderse hacia el mundo, una recreación simultánea de una misma y una reconstrucción de la sociedad—. Pero me siento confusa sin saber cómo se logra esto. —*Gloria E. Anzaldúa*

> Coyolxauhqui, it is exactly these times of dislocation/separation that hold the promise of wholeness. We must bear witness to what our bodies remember, what el corazón con razón experiences, and share these with others though we be branded unpatriotic and un-American. These healing narratives serve not just as self-nurturing "therapy," but actually change reality. —*Gloria E. Anzaldúa*

Gloria Anzaldúa es especialmente interesante para el pensamiento iberoamericano, porque justo ella misma, su persona, su cuerpo, su vida y su trabajo de pensamiento rebasan las clasificaciones de país e idioma y muestran cómo en la historia podría caerse en distintas categorías y, sobre todo, se tiene la posibilidad de hacer distintos juegos de identidades como estrategia, que parten del uso de la lengua y no respetan fronteras:

> Nosotros, los Chicanos vivimos a horcajadas en las tierras fronterizas. Por uno de nuestros lados, nos encontramos expuestos constantemente al español de los mexicanos; por otro, escuchamos el vociferar inacabable de los Anglos, así que se nos olvida nuestra lengua. Entre nosotros, no decimos *nosotros los americanos* o *nosotros los españoles* o *nosotros los hispanos*. Decimos *nosotros los mexicanos* (al decir *mexicanos*, no queremos decir ciudadanos de México; no nos referimos a una identidad nacional sino a una identidad racial). Establecemos la distinción entre *mexicanos del otro lado y mexicanos de este lado*. En lo profundo de nuestro corazón, pensamos que ser mexicano no tiene nada que ver con el país en que se vive. Ser mexicano tiene que ver con un estado del alma —no es un estado mental ni una cuestión de nacionalidad—. Ni águila, ni serpiente, sino ambos. Y como el océano, ni el águila ni la serpiente respetan fronteras (Anzaldúa 115).

En este sentido, Anzaldúa permite desbordar los límites lingüísticos, territoriales, nacionales e incluso epistemológicos desde un lugar de enunciación encarnado, que descongela las tradiciones, las desencializa e invita a jugar con ellas para descubrir, *si no escurrimos el bulto,* la importancia de una conciencia mestiza y sus articulaciones políticas, históricas y locales:

> Como cultura, nos llamamos *españoles* cuando nos referimos a nosotros mismos como grupo lingüístico y cuando *escurrimos el bulto*. Es en ese momento cuando nos olvidamos de nuestros genes indígenas predominantes. Somos *indios* en una porción del 70 u 80%. Nos llamamos *Hispanic* o *Spanish-American* o *Latin American* o *Latinos* cuando nos vinculamos con otros pueblos hispanohablantes del hemisferio occidental y cuando *escurrimos el bulto*. Nos denominamos *Mexican-American* para expresar que no somos ni mexicanos ni americanos, que somos más el nombre *American* que el adjetivo *Mexican* (y cuando *escurrimos el bulto*) [...] Cuando no escurrimos el bulto, cuando sabemos que somos más que nada, nos llamamos *mexicanos*, refiriéndonos a la raza y a los antepasados; *mestizos* cuando afirmamos nuestro linaje, tanto español como indio (aunque raramente reconocemos nuestra genealogía negra); *Chicanos* cuando nos referimos, con conciencia política, nacidos o criados en Estados Unidos; *raza* cuando referimos a nuestro ser chicano; *tejanos* cuando se trata de Chicanos de Tejas (Anzaldúa 116).

Gloria Anzaldúa escribe esto en 1987. Más de treinta años después, luego de la globalización y con todas sus consecuencias humanas y, sobre todo, de cara a un escenario en donde la relación de México con Estados Unidos sigue siendo de una desigualdad y sumisión descomunal, tiene gran importancia preguntarnos por nuestro lugar de enunciación y territorialización al pensar, mucho más si este pensar o trabajo con la cultura pretende ser para la paz. La paz no es en abstracto, ni sólo un paraguas comunicativo; tiene que ver con la lucha interna proveniente de nuestro pasado, con nuestra historia, con nuestro territorio y con lo que somos capaces de hacer, empezando por la posibilidad de imaginarnos de una manera rizomáticamente diferente.

Mi primer acercamiento al pensamiento de Gloria Anzaldúa fue a partir de la exploración de las relaciones que podían llegar a tener los estudios de paz y los estudios de género. En ese primer momento me parecía que su figura era muy potente para pensar distintos intersticios que atraviesan las fronteras entre los países, los géneros, las tradiciones académicas y, por ende, la concepción misma que se puede llegar a tener de la filosofía y de la paz. En especial, me parecía pertinente la transformación del lugar para pensar la violencia cultural que plantean algunos autores desde la tradición de los estudios de paz, para pensar ya no sólo en aquellos componentes simbólicos que legitiman la violencia estructural o directa, sino desde los cuerpos y personas cuya cultura los ha traicionado y desafían dichas construcciones culturales.

Anzaldúa fue chicana, de familia obrera, campesina, marxista, y lesbiana. Fue marginada por la academia y tuvo muchas dificultades económicas (Belausteguigoitia 152). Reunió en su vida reiteradas exclusiones, distintas marginaciones, incisivas formas de violencia y, en sus propias palabras, sufrió una traición de su cultura:

> La mujer no se siente segura cuando su propia cultura, y la cultura blanca, la critican, cuando los machos de todas las razas le dan caza.
>
> Enajenada de su cultura madre, sintiéndose "ajena" en la cultura dominante, la mujer de color no se siente segura dentro la vida interior de su ser. Paralizada, no es capaz de reaccionar, su rostro atrapado entre *los intersticios*, los espacios entre los distintos mundos que habita (Anzaldúa 62).

Ahora regreso a estudiar a Anzaldúa desde una perspectiva iberoamericana, a leerla desde un diálogo de contrapunto con los estudios de paz, en particular con la tradición proveniente de la Universidad Jaime I de Castellón. En lo personal, un hito importante dentro de esta escuela es el pensamiento de Irene Comins; en particular, me parece clave su tesis doctoral, presentada en enero de 2003, intitulada "La ética del cuidado como educación para la paz," pues comparte un espacio temporal con algunos de los escritos de Gloria Anzaldúa, así como una pauta de lectura común con relación a la comprensión de la filosofía de la paz.

Brevemente, para esta escuela de la Universidad Jaime I, y leyendo el trabajo doctoral de Comins, habría que resaltar las siguientes cinco características, como punto de partida.

Primero, ven la filosofía con una orientación práctica, como cita Comins refiriendo a su maestro Vicent Martínez Guzmán: "La filosofía ya no se puede hacer desde la vertiente académica en la que repetimos escolásticamente lo que han dicho unos filósofos u otros. Nos urge sacar la filosofía a la calle, al mundo distanciado del reconocimiento de los seres humanos, y confrontarlo con las propuestas de los filósofos" (citado en Comins 13). De ahí que la filosofía de la paz colabora con los estudios de paz que proporcionan la parte empírica para la reflexión filosófica discursiva (Comins 15).

Segundo, conciben "la paz como un proceso y también como empoderamiento, como una recuperación o reconstrucción de nuestras capacidades para la paz" (Comins 16). De modo que la metodología filosófica que plantean tiene que ver con la reconstrucción de posibilidades o competencias humanas para la paz. En el caso de Comins, el cuidado y la preocupación por los otros serían la competencia humana que le interesa recuperar especialmente desde el ámbito de la educación y su vínculo para construir culturas de paz.

Tercero, parten de una perspectiva irenóloga o pazológica, para romper una disonancia cognitiva que busca la paz, pero piensa en la violencia. Más aún, la escuela de la Universidad Jaime I lo hace desde una perspectiva crítica del enfoque planteado por Johan Galtung a partir de lo que señala como dos rectificaciones. La primera crítica es al "esquema antropocéntrico, por estar excesivamente centrado en el ser humano y obviar la naturaleza;" la segunda, proviene de las investigaciones feministas y se refiere al esquema andro-céntrico, lo que hace que el triángulo de la violencia no sólo se deba estudiar a nivel macro, sino a nivel micro (Comins 28-29).

Cuarto, vinculado con lo anterior, el carácter epistemológico de los estudios de paz se aparta del "modelo de ciencia natural como modelo universal y correcto de conocimiento" (Comins 31). Es decir, realizan una revisión crítica del conocimiento, a la par de la crítica de la objetividad que realizan corrientes como las epistemologías feministas y las que pretenden la universalidad de todas las culturas.

Por lo anterior, desde la filosofía de la paz, esta escuela realiza un giro epistemológico que parte de "una noción amplia de epistemología, precisamente como el estudio de las competencias, no sólo como la manera occidental, moderna, blanca y masculina de entender el quehacer científico" (Comins 33). Esta epistemología se compone de cuatro puntos clave:

a) Frente a la objetividad, plantea la intersubjetividad e interpelación mutua.

b) Sustituye la perspectiva del observador distante que adquiere conocimiento por la del participante en procesos de reconstrucción de maneras de vivir en paz.

c) Supera la unilateralización de la razón para hablar de las razones, los sentimientos, las emociones, el cariño y la ternura.

d) Reconstruye, como instrumento de análisis y estudio, la categoría de género (Comins 33-35).

Por último, desde este punto de partida, y por lo que es más frecuentemente conocida esta escuela, está el planteamiento que se desprende del estudio de la violencia cultural respecto a que no existe una cultura de paz, sino culturas para hacer las paces. Ya que, como recupera Comins de Martínez Guzmán, "no existe sólo la cultura; existen las culturas: la pluralidad de maneras en que los seres humanos organizamos nuestras relaciones, con la naturaleza, persona a persona o de manera transpersonal" (citado en Comins 37). A partir de este encuadre, el estudio de Anzaldúa resulta pertinente para establecer un diálogo a partir del lugar de enunciación desde el que escribe, en el que se cruza la epistemología feminista, la indagación cultural del shamanismo y el nahualismo. Sin embargo, su pensamiento también ofrece un contrapunto en donde no sólo se puede enriquecer un repertorio de culturas para hacer las paces, sino también están presentes aportes epistemológicos, nuevas metáforas, lenguajes y prácticas para comprender, y quizás replantear, la filosofía de la paz como una filosofía del mestizaje, en la que una antropología que busca superar la dualidad mente-cuerpo se recompone a partir de una tercera dimensión, la espiritual. En lo que se refiere a las competencias para la paz que es importante recuperar como tarea de una filosofía de la paz, resulta interesante pensar el cuidado desde Anzaldúa en su vínculo con una imaginación encarnada, y la capacidad de sanar las heridas, bajo un imperativo de reintegrar las partes desmembradas, atender las heridas individuales y culturales, en un trabajo continuo, inacabable.

Lo que compartiré a continuación son apenas algunas pisadas de un trabajo en curso, no sólo en el aspecto teórico sino en la invitación latente del trabajo de Anzaldúa para la reescritura de uno mismo, principalmente a partir del primer capítulo de *Light in the Dark: Rewriting Identity, Spirituality, Reality*, publicado póstumamente en 2015, bajo la edición de AnaLouise Keating.

De acuerdo con Marisa Belausteguigoitia, Anzaldúa logra, con una escritura emocional, un dispositivo político pedagógico que combina la narrativa académica con la oralidad, la experiencia, la autobiografía (155). En una época en que las humanidades luchan frente al predominio de la razón tecnológica; las universidades tienen que justificarse en términos ajenos a su lógica y pensarse como empresas y corporaciones; el sentido de la tradición parece colapsar por críticas internas y la impotencia de generar otras instituciones, y hay un vacío, una esterilidad, de imaginación política, Anzaldúa me parece una figura clave para reorientar la búsqueda intelectual, para asumir la perplejidad, para sanar y continuar con una lucha cultural. Para María del Socorro (Coco) Gutiérrez-Magallanes, los escritos de Anzaldúa pueden entenderse como una obra testimonial y autobiográfica con dos dimensiones, "una ética, en el sentido de búsqueda de la verdad y la justicia en relación a la violencia infligida, y otra de carácter estético, vinculada a la creación verbal que narra la historia de un sujeto en el marco de su pertenencia o lucha por transformar a una comunidad y a una na(rra)ción que lo ha discriminado y omitido" (7).

Belausteguigoitia señala, con relación a la obra de Anzaldúa, una particular caracterización del acto de conocer:

> Desde su visión, cada acto de conocimiento significa tender un puente y cruzar, abandonar momentáneamente el territorio que sanciona el significado y transitar al terreno donde sólo es posible y productivo, escuchar observar y transformarse [...] La escritura de Anzaldúa tiene todo que ver con las fronteras, aquellas que cruza, establece y refuerza, pero también las más importantes, aquellas que borra justamente al construir —a partir de su escritura— esos objetos que posibilitan el paso al "otro lado": los puentes (155).

Otro rasgo característico que señala Belausteguigoitia de Anzaldúa consiste en "la necesidad de narrarse a sí misma en la propia construcción del conocimiento" (155). Al respecto, Belausteguigoitia señala lo siguiente:

> Mi interés fundamental es compartir el poder estético, político y pedagógico que tiene su escritura, por el hecho de hablar por sí misma, desde sus experiencias y conocimiento que se asientan muy abajo y se sitúan en múltiples fronteras [...] Respeto mucho los manuales feministas de concientización, los necesitamos; también considero imprescindible la producción teórica sesuda y conceptual, discursiva y deconstructiva; pero también creo en el poder de la escritura desde abajo, con belleza, con cadencia y con ritmo desacompasado por la doble identidad (chicana-mexicana-americana), por la necesidad de decir teóricamente, pero desde el cuerpo (155).

Belausteguigoitia reconoce en Anzaldúa una potencia que no sólo busca explicar el dolor mexicano, sino que "dispara una especie de alzamiento contra el miedo, de la vergüenza que da considerarse menor, una escritura que concentra el dolor y establece una pedagogía para suavizarlo y entenderlo" (155).

De manera provisional, y sólo como una tentativa por acotar el término de filosofía de la paz desde Gloria Anzaldúa, resulta pertinente tener en cuenta las dos siguientes citas. En la primera, aparece una visión de la violencia que recuerda en cierto sentido la pedagogía de la crueldad de Rita Laura Segato, y se plantea la posibilidad de una conciencia que tome en cuenta los sueños, la imaginación y la no separación de las cosas:

> Se supone que no debemos recordar tales hechos sobrenaturales. Se supone que debemos ignorar, olvidar, matar esas imágenes fugaces de la presencia del alma y de la presencia del espíritu. Se nos ha enseñado que el espíritu se halla fuera de nuestro cuerpo o por encima de nuestras cabezas, en algún lugar de lo alto del cielo con Dios. Se supone que debemos olvidar que cada célula de nuestro cuerpo, cada hueso y cada ave y cada gusano contienen el espíritu en sí.
>
> Como muchos indios y mexicanos, yo no consideraba reales mis experiencias psíquicas. Negaba que hubieran tenido lugar y permití que mis sentidos internos se atrofiaran. Permití que la racionalidad blanca me dijera que la existencia del "otro mundo" era pura superstición pagana. Yo aceptaba su realidad, la realidad "oficial" del modo racional y razonador que está conectada a la realidad externa, el mundo superior, y que está considerada la conciencia más desarrollada —la conciencia de la dualidad— [...] Al intentar hacerse "objetiva," la cultura occidental ha convertido en "objetos" a las cosas y las personas al distanciarse de ellas, con lo que ha perdido "contacto" con ellas. En esta dicotomía se halla la raíz de toda violencia (Anzaldúa 83-83).

La segunda cita proviene de una entrevista realizada por Karin Ikas, publicada en la parte final de la tercera edición de *Borderlands*:

> K.I.: ¿Cómo describirías tu propia filosofía?
>
> G.A.: La describiría de la forma en que describo mi espiritualidad, que es el nahualismo, lo que se puede traducir como "chamanismo." Pero el nahual era un cambiante, un chamán que podría cambiar de forma, que podía convertirse en persona o animal. La filosofía que estoy tratando de desentrañar en este momento también se remonta a los tiempos indígenas de México, cuando utilizo términos como *nepantla*, como *conocimiento*, y lo mismo sucede con cosas que proceden de lo indígena, de lo mexicano o lo chicano. Y luego, intento hacer una elaboración filosófica al respecto (284-285).

Para profundizar en las implicaciones que puede tener la lectura de Anzaldúa para una filosofía de la paz considero pertinente la revisión del primer capítulo de *Light in the Dark: Rewriting Identity, Spirituality, Reality:* "Let Us Be the Healing of the Wound. The Coyolxauqui Imperative — La sombra y el sueño," publicado previamente en *One Wound for Another / Una herida por otra: Testimonios de Latin@s in the U.S. through Cyberspace (11 de septiembre de*

2001-11 de marzo de 2002), editado por Claire Joysmith y Clara Lomas. En este trabajo, Anzaldúa nos muestra la preocupación que tiene frente a la violencia de los atentados, cuyas imágenes lastiman el ojo de la mente, hieren a quien las atestigua en su intensa repetición, ocasionan un *shock* y, más aún, provocan una fragmentación, una disociación de sí misma, en la que cada órgano vital de sí se detiene y se produce un estado del cual no se puede liberar, sino que obliga, a ella y a otros tantos más, a estar suspendidos en el limbo, en el espacio intermedio, al que denomina *Nepantla*, a funcionar en piloto automático, desconectada de lo que pasa en su vida misma (9). Gloria Anzaldúa escribe que estaba como *La llorona*, perdida y sola, detenida en el susto, indefensa, cayendo, hundiéndose. No obstante, un punto de quiebre respecto a las opiniones dominantes fue el cuestionamiento del papel que su país había tenido en lo ocurrido y también preguntarse personalmente por la responsabilidad que pudiera tener. Dar cuenta de lo que ocurrió el 11 de septiembre fue difícil, por lo que en ese momento Anzaldúa señala que, al no poder expresar lo profundo de lo que sentía, "se lo tragó." No fue sino hasta meses después que sintió el imperativo de hablar de esa herida abierta y dar cuenta de la sombra colectiva que está en su país, en su nación. De igual modo, recupera la imagen sanadora de la luna, Coyolxauqui, quien también es parte de su herencia cultural, a la que ve como una alternativa para reconectarse con los otros:

> Vulnerable once more, I'm clawed by the talons of grief. I take my sorrow for a walk along the bay near my home in Santa Cruz. With the surf pounding in my ears and the wind's forlorn howl, it feels like even the sea is grieving. I struggle to talk from the wound's gash, make sense of the deaths and destruction, and pull the pieces of my life back together. I yearn to pass on to the next generation the spiritual activism I've inherited from my cultures. If I object to my government's act of war, I cannot remain silent. To do so is to be complicitous. But sadly, we are all accomplices. My job as an artist is to bear witness to what haunts us, to step back and attempt to see the pattern in these events (personal and societal), and how we can repair el daño (the damage) by using the imagination and its vision.

A lo largo de este capítulo, Anzaldúa realiza un repaso de lo que considera una larga sombra cultural que tiene Estados Unidos:

> As I see it, this country's real battle is with its shadow—its racism, propensity for violence, rapacity for consuming, neglect of its responsibility to global communities and the environment, and unjust treatment of dissenters and the disenfranchised, especially people of color. As an artist, I feel compelled to expose this shadow side that the mainstream media and government deny. To understand our complicity and responsibility, we must look at the shadow (10).

En el recuento de esta sombra, critica la retórica del bien contra el mal como si fueran bandos absolutos. Incluso, en un giro y en un llamado a la reflexión, llega a señalar que los actos en respuesta al atentado, que no justifica y denuncia como inaceptable, son también terrorismo, incluso de una mayor escala. Son actos justificados con incongruencias y sin ver que el conflicto está en otra parte y puede ser una oportunidad para sanar heridas, para moverse de un desconocimiento hacia un conocimiento que no duda en llamar *espiritual: spiritual knowledge.*

Si quisiéramos plantearlo en términos de la escuela de paz de la Universidad Jaime I, lo anterior sería congruente con el entendimiento de la paz como un proceso, y habría una pluralidad de culturas de paz. Sólo enfatizaría que cada cultura tiene que revisar su propia sombra, no pensando en que la va a sobreponer completamente, pero sí puede encontrar en ella recursos para luz en la oscuridad (lo que para ellos serían competencias para la paz), a partir de una epistemología encaminada, como se ha dicho antes, a "la conciencia de una nueva mestiza," para la que Anzaldúa proporciona, en cada uno de sus textos, hermosas herramientas.

Los acontecimientos del 11 de septiembre son vistos por Anzaldúa como uno de esos momentos en los que nuestra percepción del mundo se agrieta, en los que la forma en que nos relacionamos con la realidad no puede continuar igual y nos damos cuenta de que la realidad consensuada es una ilusión.

> The world as we know it "ends." We experience a radical shift in perception, *otra* forma de ver. *Este choque* shifts us to nepantla, a psychological, liminal space between the way things had been and an unknown future. Nepantla is the space in-between, the locus and sign of transition. In nepantla we realize that realities clash, authority figures of the various groups demand contradictory commitments, and we and others have failed living up to idealized goals. We're caught in remolinos (vortexes), each with different, often contradictory forms of cognition, perspectives, worldviews, belief systems—all occupying the transitional nepantla space (16-17).

Esta dimensión en la que se requiere entrar para hacernos cargo de nuestra sombra, desmembrarnos como Coyolxauqui, para poder luego desde la herida reconformarnos:

> It is this nuevo mundo, this new order, we need to create with the choices we make, the acts we perform, and the futures we dream. Chaotic disruptions, violence, and death catapult us into the Coyolxauhqui state of dissociation and fragmentation that characterizes our times. Our collective shadow—made up of the destructive aspects, psychic wounds, and splits in our own culture—is aroused, and we are forced to confront it. In trying to make sense of what's happening, some

> of us come into deep awareness (conocimiento) of political and spiritual situations and the unconscious mechanisms that abet hate, intolerance, and discord. I name this searching, inquiring, and healing consciousness "conocimiento" (17-19).

Me atrevo a pensar que Gloria Anzaldúa, desde una lectura de la filosofía de la paz, nos brinda no sólo bellos instrumentales epistemológicos, sino también una profundización, reensamblaje de lo que es un investigador para la paz, en la que se combine no sólo una dimensión reflexiva sobre los estudios de paz, sino una autotransformación, una reescritura de uno mismo, que articule la práctica de la espiritualidad y el activismo político.

> Conocimiento urges us to respond not just with the traditional practice of spirituality (contemplation, meditation, and private rituals) or with the technologies of political activism (protests, demonstrations, and speakouts), but with the amalgam of the two: spiritual activism, which we've also inherited along with la sombra. Conocimiento pushes us into engaging the spirit in confronting our social sickness with new tools and practices whose goal is to effect a shift. *Spirit-in-the-world* becomes conscious, and *we* become conscious of spirit in the world. The healing of our wounds results in transformation, and transformation results in the healing of our wounds (Anzaldúa 19).

"The Coyolxauhqui imperative" sería un nuevo horizonte para pensar y pensarse como investigador para la paz. Si tomamos en consideración los tres elementos que Irene Comins plantea en sus tesis doctoral sobre lo que es un investigador para la paz, desde Gloria Anzaldúa, un investigador para la paz no sólo sería realista, práctico y se consideraría una gente normal y compleja, sino alguien que está dispuesto a transformar la realidad desde la forma en que la comprende y a entrar en el espacio de Nepantla como una forma de epistemología que articula corazón, razón y práctica; no sólo es práctico en cuanto busca ayudar a los necesitados, sino que pretende, a partir de la imaginación y la reescritura cultural –"work that matters"–, encontrar imágenes de pensamiento que les den a los demás acceso a su propio conocimiento; y, por último, en un ligero matiz, consiste en asumir la complejidad humana, aceptar los propios prejuicios, no considerarse ángeles ni héroes, pero sí realizar un trabajo, desvelar un potencial, que no duda en llamar *espiritual.*

> Ultimately, each of us has the potential to change the sentience of the world. In addition to community building, we can transform our world by imagining it differently, dreaming it passionately via all our senses, and willing it into creation. As we think inspiring, positive, life-generating thoughts and embody these thoughts in every act we perform, we can gradually change the mood of our days, the habits of years, and

> the beliefs of a lifetime. Changing the thoughts and ideas (the "stories") we live by and their limiting beliefs (including the national narrative of supreme entitlement) will enable us to extend our hand to others con el corazón con razón en la mano. Individually and collectively we can begin to share strategies on peaceful coexistence y desparramar (spread) conocimientos. Each of us can make a difference. By bringing psychological understanding and using spiritual approaches in political activism we can stop the destruction of our moral, compassionate humanity (20-21).

En trabajos más recientes, de 2018, Irene Comins parece recuperar también esta dimensión espiritual o bien esta experiencia-del-poder-desde-dentro y su papel creativo a partir de la lectura de *El Tao de la liberación. Una ecología de la transformación*, escrito por Mark Hathaway y Leonardo Boff:

> Urge cultivar nuestro poder-de-dentro, ampliar y reforzar nuestra responsividad, nuestra capacidad de responder, de cuidar y de accionar creativamente en el mundo. Urge transitar de una cosmología de la dominación a una cosmología del cuidado y de la responsabilidad universal, potencialmente ganadora de la Tierra y de nosotros con ella. Sabernos capaces de incidir en nuestro entorno, ver los efectos que nuestras acciones de atención y cuidado tienen sobre los demás, sobre la naturaleza y sobre nosotros mismos es la mejor cura para una impotencia interiorizada (Comins 93).

No obstante, Gloria Anzaldúa seguirá siendo un umbral para el estudio de la espiritualidad sin querer regresar, como lo hacen otros al final, a una mera reinterpretación de la tradición cristiana, pues de lo que se trataría precisamente es de lograr un mestizaje espiritual.

REFERENCIAS

Anzaldúa, Gloria. *Borderlands / La Frontera: The New Mestiza.* Capitán Swing, 2016. Impreso.

———. *Light in the Dark / Luz en lo Oscuro: Rewriting Identity, Spirituality, Reality.* Duke University Press, 2015. Impreso.

Belausteguigoitia, Marisa. "Borderlands / La Frontera: el feminismo chicano de Gloria Anzaldúa desde las fronteras geoculturales, disciplinarias y pedagógicas" en *Debate Feminista,* 20 Oct. 2009: 149-169. Impreso.

Comins Mingol, Irene. "La ética del cuidado como educación para la paz". Tesis. Universitat Jaume I, 2003. https://www.tesisenred.net/bitstream/handle/10803/10455/comins.pdf

———. "De la parálisis a la reconexión: por una fenomenología y una creatividad pacifistas" en París Albert, Sonia y Sofía Herrero Rico (eds.), *El quehacer creativo. Un desafío para nuestra cotidianidad.* Dykinson, 2018. Impreso.

Gutiérrez-Magallanes, María del Socorro. "Autobiografía política latinoamericana y autobiografía política chinaca: Discusión teórica, formas de abordaje, deslindes y propuesta de categorías para acercamientos y lecturas," en *La manzana,* 13 de marzo 2016: 6–27. Digital.

GEOGRAPHIES OF TRANSLATION

MAURICIO PATRÓN RIVERA

I would like to share with you the pleasures and challenges I had translating Anzaldúa's "Geographies of Selves," the fourth chapter of her book *Light in the Dark / Luz en lo Oscuro: Rewriting Identity, Spirituality, Reality* from English (and Spanglish, Spanish, Nahuatl) to a Mexican Spanish version that aspires to respect her original polysemic and translinguistic spirit.

My lifeline for this reflection is the research journal I wrote while translating. The impressions I collected there led me to propose to you here the idea of "geographies of translations" as a way to revisit some feminist theories of translation in transcultural contexts. This project started in a literary translation seminar at the University of Houston,[1] which included a translation workshop using the authors of our choice. In this space, we worked together to support and criticize our translations of poems by Natalie Diaz and Safia Elhillo, and essays by Joan Didion and Gloria E. Anzaldúa, among others. Even when this was an individual work, translating Anzaldúa led me to share with others: to read her work and the work of the other poets and essayists as a group, read the translations—all of them from mostly English texts to different variants of

1 Seminar on Literary Translation organized by Professor Mabel Cuesta.

Spanish, comment on each other's works, add a lot of theoretical reading and, finally, come up with a first draft of "Geografías del ser."

In previous years, learning from Anzaldúa connected me with other collaborative experiences. In 2015, I was part of an interdisciplinary critical pedagogy group named MANU(EL)(LA).[2] We were a collective constituted to apply the diversity of decolonial and feminist strategies of the *Cultura Visual y Género* (Visual Culture and Gender) seminar, an interdisciplinary project facilitated by Rían Lozano, Nina Hoechtl, and María del Socorro Gutiérrez Magallanes at the University Museum of Contemporary Art of the National Autonomous University of Mexico. MANU(EL)(LA) functioned as a communicating vessel between the professors and the other students in two semesters titled Traducciones descolonizadoras I y II (Decolonizing Translations I and II):

> Being interested in interdisciplinary knowledges and knowledge productions led us to a liminal (un)teaching and (un)learning space, an interstice, an in-between, a border space where the *bodies in resistance*, those of the participants of the seminar, are a crucial source towards *movidas* [maneuvers] of knowledge and critical knowledge production (Gutiérrez Magallanes, Hoechtl, and Lozano 166).

Gloria E. Anzaldúa's *Borderlands / La Frontera: The New Mestiza* was our guide to ask us about the place of our body, individual and collective, to communicate with otherness and create a map for cultural translations.

In the seminar, the readings, conversations, and artistic practices were focused to realize that reading, writing, and translating, as three key activities of the university, are actions that break through our bodies. With this background, I read *Light in the Dark*'s Chapter 4, "Geographies of Selves," about reimagining the identities, Nepantla, and the new tribalism, allowing me to think of the body as a territory of connection with others. I decided this chapter was my *cenote* to dive into the philosophy of Anzaldúa and to think of the translation of her writing as a practice of being with others. According to Anzaldúa, "If I'm receptive, a new conocimiento/insight will flash up through the cracks of the unconscious, what I call el cenote, la noria interior, a subterranean reservoir of personal and collective knowledge" (*Light* 66).

As follows, I present some reflections on translating Chapter 4 as the first approximation towards a methodology for translating Anzaldúa's writing. The main goal is to set a common ground for an upcoming collective translation of the whole of *Light in the Dark / Luz en lo Oscuro* to Mexican Spanish. The result should be useful for specific reading communities and their located

2 MANU(EL)(LA) was integrated by Axler Yépez Saldaña, Valerie Leibold, Alejandra Gorráez Puga, Amor Teresa Gutiérrez, Toño Hernández, Ariadna Solís, and me.

geographies. It seeks to activate Anzaldúa's Mundo Zurdo among young people—especially gender nonconformists—in Mexico, and it's still in progress. The main hypothesis is that Anzaldúa's work deploys in itself an exercise of reading as translation, and therefore it gives guidelines for its translation to other languages such as mine. To make such an assertion I would like to review the political position of Anzaldúa as a writer beyond the figure of the author; to understand her text as unfolding a territory where the writer, the readers, and the translators meet; and to share three strategies I used in my creative work as a translator.

BEYOND THE FIGURE OF THE AUTHOR

Anzaldúa defined herself as "*esta jotita,* this queer Chicana, this *mexicatejana*" ("Border Arte" 107; original italics) and she writes in that spirit. Her narrative is cross-genre, between academic prose, essay, journal, and poetry. Her stream of consciousness leads her in different directions, putting herself in vulnerable places, delivering concepts, images, and metaphors, sometimes ones within the others. She uses fragmentary writing to depict the thresholds of her theory, as we can read in *Light in the Dark.*

It would not be considered postmodern, but certainly her work is beyond the paradigm of modernity. Following Chela Sandoval's *Methodology of the Oppressed* in her critique of Frederic Jameson's *Postmodernism, or, the Cultural Logic of Late Capitalism,* in the epistemic fight between modernity and postmodernity there was no space for "an anticolonial, mestiza, US feminist of color, queer, and differential conceptualization of the subject" (Sandoval 33–34).

Sandoval states that:

> Indeed, the fragmentation or split subjectivity of subjection is the very condition against which a modernist, well-placed citizen-subject could coalesce its own sense of wholeness. Such wholeness of being became the modernist "solid identity" that now has the opportunity to move toward a "critically distant" relation to the dominant. . . . Indeed, the condition recently claimed as the "postmodern splitting of the subject" is one of the conditions that conquered and colonized Westerners were invited to survive under modernist and previous eras, if survival were a choice (33).

Doubtless, Anzaldúa is one heiress of the survivors referred to by Sandoval, and her work is a constant effort to acknowledge this condition. She writes using "the survival skills and decolonizing oppositional practices that were developed in response to such fragmentation under previous cultural eras" (Sandoval 33), which necessarily implies the fragmentation of the modern author.

It is what Anzaldúa calls *the wound,* "First you must recognize and acknowledge la herida. . . . Rupture and psychic fragmentation lead to dialogue with the wound" (*Light* 89). She locates herself in the wound as a place from which the text flows, as a place of recognition of the wounds of others, too. But what happens to readers when we confront a wounded text? I read in her texts, and so many others by outsider writers, a broken language. Her imperfect use in standardized terms of the imperial languages becomes a locus of enunciation, of turning the tongues. She writes and rewrites, circling that wound, braiding a connection with our own broken readings.

In *The Death of the Author*, Roland Barthes talks about the end of the traditional form of reading. In the opening, Barthes questions the figure of the Author but also the monolithic concept of the text as closed and finished, and therefore the idea of the reader as a unidirectional consumer. He says:

> Nevertheless, the feeling about this phenomenon has been variable; in primitive societies [*sic*], narrative is never undertaken by a person, but by a mediator, shaman or speaker, whose "performance" may be admired (that is, his [*sic*] mastery of the narrative code), but not his [*sic*] "genius." The author is a modern figure, produced no doubt by our society insofar as, at the end of the middle ages, with English empiricism, French rationalism and the personal faith of the Reformation, it discovered the prestige of the individual, or, to put it more nobly, of the "human person" (142–143).

Anzaldúa, following Barthes, is more of a mediator or a shaman than an author. When writing, she creates spaces to encounter with others, like the Greek *agora* or, as I prefer to depict it, a public park. Therefore, her texts are more a *plaza pública* than a private room of her own.

I am writing this as I remember Anzaldúa—in "Speaking in Tongues: A Letter to 3rd World Women Writers"—compelling us to "Write in the kitchen, lock yourself up in the bathroom. Write on the bus or the welfare line, on the job or during meals, between sleeping or waking. I write while sitting on the john" (170). In reading these much-read and much-quoted lines, I find myself with her and her community. Her texts were not only written without a private room, but without the pretension of her being the owner of those words. As mediator, she makes a "performance" and is recognized by her readers (us) for her "mastery of the narrative code" (Barthes 142–143). For her, writing (and publishing) is to be with others:

> The danger in writing is not fusing our personal experience and world view with the social reality we live in, with our inner life, our history, our economics, and our vision. What validates us as human beings validates us as writers. What matters to us is the relationships that are important to us whether with our self or others. We must use what is important to us to get to the writing. *No topic is too trivial* ("Speaking in Tongues" 170).

In Anzaldúa's words, she was a Nepantlera, an in-betweener; and that interstice hosts the creation of a non-identitarian practice. Her writing is a liminal space between the writer and the readers, the mediator. She uses textuality to turn the tongue and create places for an "oppositional consciousness" (Sandoval 54–55); this conception contrasts with the modern figure of the author, which at times appears ubiquitous but bodiless. Anzaldúa's writing is devoted to the creation of a territory, and not to the affirmation of herself as an author. She offers "Geographies of Selves" where the identities of *author* and *reader* open their limits. In this territory, as we'll see, reading is a form of translating.

READING AS TRANSLATING: "GEOGRAPHIES OF SELVES" AS A TERRITORY OF CROSSING

An open text like *Light in the Dark* transforms the traditional contract between the writer and the reader. It demands the active work of the reader to relocate the meaning of the book in their own terms. Published in 2015, thanks to the editing and work in the archive by AnaLouise Keating, *Light in the Dark / Luz en lo Oscuro* is the latest and posthumous book by Anzaldúa, where she reunited what could have been her PhD thesis. It's a text full of experimentation, rewriting (as we can tell by reading the extensive notes and appendices), of deep reflections on the self and the community, and of struggling with the university as a place full of contradictions, especially for outsider corporalities.

In the whole book, but in particular in Chapter 4, there is a constant use of translation at the core of its creation. Following the scheme of translation made by Susan Bassnet from Roman Jacobson's article "On Linguistic Aspects of Translation," (both Jacobson's article and Bassnet's book are considered milestones in translation studies), there are three types of translations: the interlingual translation or translation proper; the intersemiotic translation or transmutation; and the intralingual translation, or rewording (Bassnet 23).

In "Geographies of Selves" these three kinds of translations are present:

> The interlingual (or regular translation) when she uses words from Spanish, Spanglish or Nahuatl and explains its meaning: "El árbol de la vida (the tree of life)" (*Light* 67).
>
> The intersemiotic use of language and images. She includes drawing as a parallel thought system (*Light* 70, 72, 78, 80).
>
> And the intralingual translation when she selects key words and develops them to her own extended meaning.

Anzaldúa's writing uses these types of translations to create what she calls *conocimiento*. Let me unfold the idea of her intralingual translation, to state how she closes the gap between reading and translating. The intralingual translation, or rewording, refers to the expansion of the meaning within the same language, like in a synonyms dictionary, or for that matter, any dictionary. In fact, an intralingual translation is what readers do when understanding a text. In Anzaldúa's creative writing, the intralingual translation becomes a language game, her equivalence creation—or translation within the text—is a central part of both her literary style and epistemology.

In "Geographies of Selves" she tells us different personal stories. I selected two of them to show how she translates them from the anecdote to the theory: her relationship with the "árbol de la Guadalupe," and a moment in her life in New York City. After she recalls the memory of her Guadalupe tree, she deepens the *new tribalism* concept:

> Today I walk to the ocean, to my favorite tree, what I call la Virgen's tree. . . With my back against its trunk, I meditate, allowing it to absorb my body into its being; my arms become its branches, my hair its leaves, its sap the blood that flows in my veins. . . . El árbol de la vida (the tree of life) symbolizes my 'story' of the new tribalism (*Light* 67).

Later she links her experience living in New York with the *geographies of selves* concept: "As a queer Chicana living in New York City in a Puerto Rican neighborhood, surrounded by Russians, Jews, and other 'racially' different peoples, I bore my 'differentness' and negotiated my identity. . . Our bodies are geographies of selves made up of diverse, bordering, and overlapping 'countries" (*Light* 68–69).

Anzaldúa makes sure to let us know that her theory comes from specific episodes of her life and closes the gap between them: "Struggling with a "story" (a concept or theory), embracing personal and social identity, is a bodily activity" (*Light* 66). In other words, she translates episodes of her life into opportunities to create *conocimiento*. As AnaLouise Keating summarizes, *conocimiento* is:

> A Spanish word for "knowledge" or "consciousness," Anzaldúa uses this term to represent a key component of her post-*Borderlands* onto-epistemology. With conocimiento, she elaborates on the potentially transformative elements of her earlier theories of mestiza consciousness and la facultad. Like mestiza consciousness, conocimiento represents a nonbinary, connectionist mode of thinking; like la facultad, conocimiento often unfolds within oppressive contexts and entails a deepening of perception. With conocimiento, Anzaldúa underscores and develops the imaginal, spiritual-activist, and radically inclusionary possibilities implicit in these earlier theories. (243).

With conocimiento as a "connectionist mode of thinking" and "deepening of perception," Anzaldúa is doing a nonbinary "Intralingual translation" (Bassnett 23); rewording between her stories and concepts to create a way of reading in translation.

I feel that after reading her, I need to do my own rewording or translation, to generate a friction between my reading and my life to grasp the text and knit my own conocimiento. In this way Anzaldúa asks for active readers, ready to translate her words with their own interconnected Cenotes: "To be in conocimiento with another person or group is to share knowledge, pool resources, meet each other, compare liberation struggles and social movements' histories, share how we confront institutional power, and process and heal wounds" (*Light* 91). That's why I wanted to understand the process of translating Anzaldúa through the "reading as translation" idea, because she writes looking for a constant relocation of her readers. That opens the idea of translation as a system involving the readers, the writer, but also the borderlands between them: interlinguistic translation, publishing, distribution, reading communities, etc.

TRANSLATING "GEOGRAPHIES OF SELVES": THREE STRATEGIES AS A TRANSLATOR

It was just after reading *Light in the Dark*, translating it to my own voice, that I was able to start thinking about the interlingual translation into Mexican Spanish. "Translation is the most intimate act of reading," explains Spivak in *The Politics of Translation.* "Unless the translator has earned the right to become the intimate reader, she cannot surrender to the text, cannot respond to the special call of the text" (400). I started from framing some questions regarding the challenge of translating "Geographies of Selves": What happens with the grammatical gender and its political sense in the moment of the translation? How can we translate a book from English, with a lot of Spanish, with a mix of both, and vocabulary from Nahuatl, to one dialect of Spanish, the Mexican? Why is it a matter of ethics to acknowledge the reading communities at the moment of translating? How can translation strategies expand the borderlands, and lead the readers to inhabit a Nepantla state in different languages?

> Tanto en México como en los EE.UU., se legitima por medio de políticas lo que se debe de hablar, cómo se debe de hablar, dónde se debe de hablar, pero también 'en qué idioma' se debe de hablar para ser parte de la cultura dominante. El español en México y el inglés en los EE.UU. se promueven como medios legítimos y superiores de comunicación (Invasorix 162).

The official state languages, like English and Spanish, says Invasorix, are a source of colonization, they create the line of belonging or ostracism, of normalization or violence (te chingas o te jodes, they say in Mexico), and as part of that model of globalization the translation has been an instrument to enforce and legitimate those languages over others. That's why translation is a critical space for the connection of social movements and the search for justice.

Standing from the critical perspective of the translation studies, I tried to answer these questions by creating a methodology that implies that translation is a creative work that departs from another creative work by trying to apply the translator's experience as a reader. Therefore, if the idea of fidelity exists in a translation—a fidelity to the readers and to the writer as a mediator of her culture, not to the writer as author—it is also a fidelity to the certainty of the untranslatable; translating is a political action that aims to bridge the "us" with the "others," it is to dwell in the hyphen in *nos-otras*.

While the dialogue with other translations and translators is helpful and necessary, I support the idea that a methodology of translation should be built from the act of reading. In *Gender in Translation*, Sherry Simon quotes this statement by Lise Gauvin: "My translation practice is a political activity aimed at making language speak for women. So my signature on a translation means that this translation has used every translation strategy to make the feminine visible in language" (Simon 15). That statement challenges any idea of neutrality in a translation; it stands for the visibility of the translators and our responsibility in the work we do, both the decisions and the mistakes. From this approach, the moment of translating is as creative as the moment of writing or the moment of reading. And even more, it is not a solitary task. Translating with Gloria Anzaldúa is to follow her writing prompts, or what I call a theory of feminist and Chicana translation inside the text itself.

The following are three of the various strategies I am using to translate Anzaldúa's work. I am not pretending to provide a manual, but on the contrary, to share my thoughts with her readers after my own reading of "Geographies of Selves."

1. Translate with Others / Do It With Others (DIWO)

For my translation, I looked into other translations of Anzaldúa's works. Not only to figure out the semantics but also to acknowledge the politics of translation. Sherry Simon says: "The feminist translator affirms her role as an active participant in the creation of meaning. In theoretical texts, in prefaces, in footnotes, she affirms the provisionality of meaning, drawing attention to the process of her own work" (29). Therefore, I consulted the translations of *Borderlands / La Frontera: The New Mestiza* to Italian by Paola Zaccaria; to Spanish in the Mexican translation by Norma Elia Cantú; and the Castilian translation by Carmen Valle. All of them are books with introductions, forewords, footnotes, and other paratexts to situate the new creations. While translating I felt accompanied by them.

In her introduction to the Mexican edition, Norma Elia Cantú remembers: "Recuerdo con gran claridad que al terminar de leer *Borderlands* sentí que me habían dado permiso para escribir. Nunca había leído un texto que, como chicana, me inquietara y a la vez afirmara mi vida de tal manera" (49). In the metaproduction surrounding other translations it is possible to find useful strategies to do your own and dig into your understanding of the text. It's a way of learning from others with a similar reading experience to yours. Maybe it is because of that willingness to be translatable, that Anzaldúa's work permits you to write, like Cantú says. She is giving her approximation to *Borderlands* from an affective point of view and acknowledging her position between the readers and the text. Cantú delivers its translation only after a profound personal transformation, clarifying the idea of the translation as a creative and political task.

The work of the translator is also informed by other theoretical and literary publications. In the use of "every translation strategy," as Gauvin says (Simon 15), we are accepting translation as an interpretative act, and therefore as a limited and partial view reinforced by researching the theory of translation, the context of the book like other Chicana and Latinx texts, and again the critical apparatus of Anzaldúa and her translators. It's a moment when I expand my reading beyond the chapter I wanted to translate. To *Do It With Others* means to be open to being affected by the experiences of the otherness, from the "nos" to the "otras," to work with other translators, writers, and readers, to exchange comments and critiques on the drafts, to be ready to improve your word selections, and to go deeper into the meaning of a line.

2. The Grammatical and the Metaphoric Gender

In translating from English to Spanish there is a dissonance between genders in a grammatical sense. In Spanish we use grammatical gender, meaning that words have their own gender that could be feminine, masculine, or neutral. "This form determines the way the word will behave grammatically as regards the agreement of adjectives, articles and pronouns. Grammatical gender is a formal property and has nothing to do with meaning," explains Sherry Simon (17).

In the English language there isn't grammatical gender, "it is attributed not by form but by meaning" (Simon 17). This phenomenon is called "metaphorical gender" and shows that the gender structures in language go beyond its morphology, "It shows that gender is relational, and is in fact an extension of the binary, oppositional structure that pervades all our thinking" (Simon 18). These differences are important to acknowledge at the moment of translating any text, especially from a perspective of feminist translation, but when we are translating a text about feminism and decoloniality, the gender roles became fundamental.

In *Light in the Dark / Luz en lo Oscuro*, and in particular in "Geographies of Selves," there are neutral pronouns that I am translating to the feminine in

Spanish and others in the masculine, following the possibilities of the text. For example, in the section "*Shadow aspects emerge in conflict,*" Anzaldúa writes:

> We may feel threatened by those who possess a different viewpoint or different kinds of knowledge/conocimiento. Fear and ignorance (desconocimientos) of the other—those who come from a different race or class; have a different skin color or gender; dress, speak, or are "abled" differently—may be the source of our problems. Fear and ignorance produce conflict (77).

I translated it using the first person plural, marked by *we* in the feminine at the beginning, and then the third person plural, marked by *those* in the masculine, like this:

> Podemos sentirnos amenazadas por aquellos que poseen otros puntos de vista u otros tipos de *conocimiento.* El miedo y el *desconocimiento* de los otros—aquellos que vienen de una clase o raza diferente; tienen un color de piel o género distinto; tienen capacidades diferentes, hablan o se visten distinto—podrían ser el origen de nuestros problemas. El miedo y la ignorancia generan conflicto.

I decided to go with the feminine first person plural (we/nosotras) when the text is developing a thought that vindicates ideas referring to the formation of identities; or in other words, for the moments when she is giving clues on how to create a *new tribalism* (84). I chose the masculine first person plural (nosotros) when she is writing about fixed identities that are getting the benefits (or privilege) from the state of being (4).

Anzaldúa gives cues about the metaphorical use of gender constantly, and sometimes chooses to change to Spanish to make the grammatical gender present in the text. Under the section "In the cracks between the worlds; dwelling in liminalities," she uses *Mestiza* in the feminine:

> Negotiating with borders results in mestizaje, the new hybrid, the new mestiza, a new category of identity. Mestizas live in between different worlds, in nepantla. We are forced (or choose) to live in categories that defy binaries of gender, race, class, and sexuality. Living in intersections, in cusps, we must constantly operate on a negotiation mode (71).

And I just follow her cue to respect her decision:

> El resultado de negociar con las fronteras es el mestizaje, una nueva hibridación. La nueva mestiza, una nueva categoría identitaria. Las mestizas viven entre diferentes mundos, en nepantla. Nos vemos forzadas a (o elegimos) vivir en categorías que desafían los binarismos de género, raza, clase y sexualidad. Viviendo en las intersecciones, en los vértices, debemos negociar constantemente.

From the close reading, I chose some general rules for all the translations. In these two cases, the decision was to follow with the same grammatical gender when she makes it explicit, like in *Mestiza*, and to translate to feminine the collective voice of the *we*.

3. Contra-Translation

Probably one of the more prolific discussions around translating Anzaldúa's work is the one related to the multilingual aspect of her work. She uses a diversity of languages and its possible combinations as an explicit intention to talk with *la raza*, her people in the borderlands. In Valle's introduction to *Borderlands*, the translator says she uses a technique she calls "contra-traducción" (31) that consists of leaving in English some concepts with the same evocative force that they have in Spanish and are easy to deduce. For example, keeping the double word in Spanish and English when it helps to clarify the contrast of cultures. In *Borderlands* she translates: "Las fronteras están diseñadas para definir los lugares que son seguros y los que no lo son, para distinguir el *us* (nosotros) del *them* (ellos)" (42).

This strategy generates an exchange of political and cultural weight between two colonial languages and at the same time acknowledges the border as a place of the bilingual colonial wound. In her translation to French, Paola Bacchetta decides:

> One of the first steps we took was to respect Anzaldúa's refusal to suppress linguistic hybridity. Her refusal is evident performatively in *Borderlands/La Frontera*, with its several languages and logistic codes. . . . To respect Anzaldúa's linguistic multiplicity, her multi-vocality, but also her priorizations and her linguistic affective relationalities and intimacies, we decided to translate only the English(es) in the plural into French(es) in the plural and to leave, as Anzaldúa herself did, all other languages intact, untranslated, as they are" (178).

Here she decides to give account of the impossibility of the total or perfect translation, but offers a compensation in opening footnotes every time she considers it necessary. Bacchetta strategically points towards the silences or dark places, accepting that some meanings will remain enclosed between the Spanish speakers, others between the Latinx, the Chicanx, and even just with mexitejanas.

These translators, Bacchetta, Valle, Cantú, and Zaccaria, are excellent guides to enter into the Nepantla state of translation. Departing from their reflections I decided to give a it try, translating the English (most of the text) into Spanish, but also leaving in the original all the other diversity of languages. Here is a fragment of "Geographies of Selves":

> *Estamos peliados*
>
> While speaking at various universities, I've witnessed gente in professional disciplines a grito herido (with loud cries) badmouth each other. Palabras picantes like jabañer nasal spray sting the air and, like the slash of whips, scar the skin. Jíjole. For people of color and other outsiders, the academy is a wounding field. Our cuerpos are riddled with emotional scars. Heridas fragment and disrupt the self, disturb who and what we are (*Light* 76).

And here is my translation:

> *Estamos peliados*
>
> Luego de hablar en varias universidades, he visto *gente* en disciplinas profesionales insultándose *a grito herido. Las palabras pican* en el aire como un espray nasal de habanero y como latigazos, abren la piel. *Jíjole.* Para la gente de color y otras marginadas, la academia es un campo hiriente. Nuestros *cuerpos* están plagados de cicatrices emocionales. Las *heridas* fragmentan e interrumpen el ser, interrumpen lo que somos y lo que hacemos.

I keep the original Spanish words signaling them in italics, respecting also the ones that reflect the oral expression and cultural value of its context. For example, *peliado,* instead of following the canon (the Royal Academy of the Spanish Language) with *peleado.* I eliminate the clarifications made by Anzaldúa in parenthesis—"(with loud cries)"—and try to eliminate also the duplicity of meaning, for example with "palabras picantes" and "sting in the air," I choose to transform the adjective *picante* into a verb, *pican,* so that I could keep the original selection of Spanish, "*Las palabras pican* en el aire" that preserves the word game made by the use of *sting* instead of *hot.* With these strategies, among a multiplicity of other line-by-line decisions, I'm trying to transmit to the readers in Mexican Spanish the importance that Anzaldúa gives to the use of multilinguistic writing; but I'm also trying to do it in the simplest possible way.

Being completely in Mexican Spanish, my translation certainly misses the strong contrast between languages, which in the original version represents the epistemic violence in the border lived by the migrants and fronterizos with an open wound at the edge of the empire. Nevertheless, I think that the reproduction of that structure in a different context, for example among young outsider Mexicans, couldn't have the same effect. I imagine the ideal reader of this translation as a young queer student who exists in a transnational context but doesn't have the privilege to read in English.

I chose to bring these three of many translation strategies to share an approach of walking through Anzaldúa's geography. In *Translations as Trans-*

humance, Mireille Gansel—translated by Ros Schwartz—says that translation is just provisional and momentary, and she compares it to the work of the shepherds: "transhumance: the long, slow movement of the flocks to distant places, in search of the greenest pastures, the low plains in winter and the high valleys in summer. . . . So it is with the transhumance routes of translation, the slow and patient crossing of countries, all borders eradicated, the movement of huge flocks of words through all the vernaculars of the umbrella language of poetry" (75).

CONCLUSIONS

I have reviewed some of Gloria Anzaldúa's fundamental concepts, framing text as geography. As a shepherd, she takes care of the words in the flock, and as shepherds too, we read them, taking them with us to new geographies. This movement from writer to reader and then to translation is fluid in Anzaldúan territory because she writes to be translated. I believe this happens for two reasons. First, Anzaldúa as a writer, but also as a philosopher, mexitejana, spiritual activist, lesbian, and overall as a new mestiza, makes the physical and intellectual work of creating an oppositional consciousness. This conocimiento situates her outside the (modern and postmodern) figure of the author. Second, as a Nepantlera, Anzaldúa exercises a self-intralingual translation, embroidering embodied memories with the elaboration of her concepts to theorize. Reading her we can learn from her creative process. Dwelling in her territory, I can say that translation is an act of bridging, is to inhabit the hyphen in Nos-otras, exchanging it for the diagonal (/) transitorily. Translating is a moment when we can be the other. After translation, you go with your version and I with mine until next time. The words maybe are animals, just like us, tearing the grass of the landscape, and letting it grow again in different geographies of selves.

WORKS CITED

Anzaldúa, Gloria. "Border Arte: Nepantla, El Lugar de la Frontera." *La Frontera / The Border: Art About the México/United States Border Experience*, catalogue for the exhibition. Centro Cultural de la Raza and Museum of Contemporary Art, San Diego, 1993.

———. *Borderlands / La Frontera: The New Mestiza.* Aunt Lute Books, 2012.

———. *Light in the Dark / Luz en lo Oscuro: Rewriting Identity, Spirituality, Reality.* Edited by AnaLouise Keating, Duke University Press, 2015.

———. "Speaking in Tongues: A Letter to 3rd World Women Writers." *This Bridge Called My Back: Writings by Radical Women of Color*, edited by Gloria Anzaldúa and Cherríe Moraga. Kitchen Table: Women of Color Press, 1983.

———. *Terre di confine = La frontera.* Italian translation by Paola Zaccaria, Palomar, 2006.

Bacchetta, Paola. "Wild Tongues / Transnational Crossings: Reflections on Translating Anzaldúa into French." *El Mundo Zurdo 7*, edited by Sara A. Ramírez, Larissa M. Mercado-López, and Sonia Saldívar-Hull, Aunt Lute Books, 2019, pp.173–85.

Barthes, Roland. "The Death of the Author." *Image, Music, Text.* Fontana Press, 1977.

Cantú, Norma Elia, trans. *Borderlands / La frontera: La nueva mestiza* (Mexican Spanish), by Gloria Anzaldúa. PUEG-UNAM, 2015.

Gansel, Mireille. *Translations as Transhumance.* Translated from French by Ros Schwartz, Feminist Press, 2017.

Invasorix. "Me duele la cara de ser tan güerx." *Transborder Matters: Circulaciones literarias, transformaciones culturales mexicanas y chicanas. iMex Revista,* México Interdisciplinario / Interdisciplinary Mexico, year 9, No. 17, 2020/1, doi:10.23692/iMex.17.10.

Keating, AnaLouise. Appendix 1: Glossary. In Anzuldúa, *Light in the Dark / Luz en lo Oscuro.*

María del Socorro (Coco) Gutiérrez Magallanes, Nina Hoechtl, and Rían Lozano. "Decolonizing the public university. A collaborative and decolonizing approach towards (un)teaching and (un)learning." *Tijdschrift voor Genderstudies*, vol. 21, no. 2, Amsterdam University Press, 2018.

Sandoval, Chela. *Methodology of the Oppressed.* University of Minnesota Press, 2000.

Simon, Sherry. *Gender in Translation: Cultural Identity and the Politics of Transmission.* Routledge, 1996.

Spivak, Gayatri Chakravorty. "The Politics of Translation." *The Translation Studies Reader.* Routledge, 2000.

Valle, Carmen, trans. *Borderlands / La frontera: La nueva mestiza* (Spanish for Spain), by Gloria Anzaldúa. Capitán Swing Libros, 2016.

Zaccaria, Paola, trans. *Terre di confine = La frontera* (Italian), by Gloria Anzaldúa. Palomar, 2006.

ARTICULATING METHODOLOGIES FOR A DISSERTATION PROJECT

EMBODIED EXPERIENCE TO TELL A STORY OF (COLONIAL & FORCED) MIGRATION

BERNARDITA M. YUNIS VARAS

> *Our bodies are geographies of selves made up of diverse, bordering, and overlapping "countries." . . . Like a map with colored web lines of rivers, highways, lakes, towns, and other landscape features en donde pasan y cruzan las cosas, we are "marked." . . . As our bodies interact with internal and external, real and virtual, past and present environments, people, and objects around us, we weave (tejemos), and are woven into our identities.*
>
> *- Gloria Anzaldúa, "Geographies of Selves"*

As Gloria Anzaldúa writes in her posthumously published work *Light in the Dark / Luz en lo Oscuro: Rewriting Identity, Spirituality, Reality*, our identities are developed of crisscrossing histories and realities, past and present tejidos of our experiences and relationships. In preparing to embark on my dissertation project,[1] engaging with feminist and women-of-color methodologies like Anzaldúa's work is not only an obvious choice, but becomes necessary as I attempt to tell this complex, interlocking history. This essay develops methodol-

1 Since May 3rd, 2022, I am now a Ph.D. candidate at the University of Colorado, Boulder, receiving a doctorate in Communication Studies.

ogies for writing a recovery project in an effort to tell the (his)stories of (colonial and forced) migration of a family from Latin America (Chile) to the United States, and previously from Palestine to South America. I claim that narrating this journey through performative writing, autoarcheologies, oral histories, and other forms of embodied retellings grounded in Anzaldúan and women-of-color feminist thought is vital for developing a narrative that is true and begins to do justice to the journeys embarked on by my diasporic Palestinian Chilean family and me.

By laying the groundwork with feminist, Indigenous, women-of-color methodologies like Gloria Anzaldúa's, these methods directly and indirectly challenge White-supremacist, patriarchal, colonial research methods that limit my own experiences. Taking on this narrative recovery project demonstrates how colonial (his)stories reshape family narratives of diaspora through—often violent—erasure of histories and lived experiences. I attempt to do the work that Anzaldúa describes as writing to survive: "I write to record what others erase when I speak, to rewrite the stories others have miswritten about me, about you" (*Borderlands* 169). Grounding my work in these methodologies allows me to articulate how these Indigenous feminist texts that center Indigenous histories and women-of-color theories facilitate a recovery project where I can research and express the narratives of diaspora and migration that led to my ancestors' migration from Palestine to Chile, and then my own migration to the United States.

FEMINIST AND INDIGENOUS METHODOLOGIES

Feminist and Indigenous methodologies have provided me the language and new understanding of how to challenge White-supremacist and colonial research methods. As Linda Tuhiwai Smith writes in *Decolonizing Methodologies*, the "context in which research problems are conceptualized and designed, and . . . the implications of research for its participants and their communities" are the starting point of what needs to be challenged as White, colonial methods (ix). Through this project, I articulate how these Indigenous feminist methodologies facilitate the recovery project I undertake in my dissertation. As feminist, women-of-color writers articulate, by grounding my work in these methodologies, I access the language and tools that allow my existence to exist, to be written, and valid. Because if work by authors like Anzaldúa, Smith, Chela Sandoval, Katherine McKittrick, Elizabeth A. Povinelli, and Jasbir K. Puar is created in the borderlands of crisscrossing lands and lived experiences can narrate the stories of their existence, survival, and resistance, then so can mine. Feminist methodologies establish that stories of migration cannot be examined without considering how Indigeneity and displacement by colonial, imperial, and White-supremacist structures have shaped each journey. Therefore, these new theoretical understandings provide the why and how these methodologies are vital for sharing these stories.

My family's journeys have been or have become political. My grandfather's displacement from Palestine to Chile, as retold by my father, is a deeply political journey of escaping to survive and build a different, flourishing life in a new land. While the extent of this story as I have known it is limited, my earlier exposure to Middle East politics in college courses has taught me that it is deeply complicated and nuanced. In my dissertation project, while searching and retelling the (his)stories of these journeys, I contextualize and understand how my grandfather and his family's story fit in the historical and political contexts of the time. Grounding my own family's history in the Middle East and in global histories creates a space for understanding the complexities of the political story and the impacts that these broader sociopolitical events have on day-to-day experiences of individuals caught in the crosshairs. While I did not experience the journey, I have carried with me the story of migration and persecution of Palestinians from the Ottoman Empire through World War II and the creation of the state of Israel (Bowler; Dawn). The impacts of events from over a century ago live on today in the lives of displaced and diasporic Palestinians like myself and my family.

Because of the political and hegemonic powers that forced the migration of these populations throughout the world, I engage these feminist methodologies to situate and understand the stories of diaspora and Indigeneity interplaying, creating, and cocreating, challenging and restructuring each one. As part of a Palestinian diaspora and as a Chilena expatriate, my own movements through the world in search of stories, information, artifacts, and experiences for my "research" (to use the traditional, White academic term) are vital as embodied experiences in my process. To that end, the following are some of the methodological practices I utilize:

- In July 2019, I embarked on a journey to Palestine, a place I had visited only in my dreams. During the "Know Thy Heritage" leadership program trip to Palestine, for the first time I experienced and explored the homeland of my Palestinian people. While I never thought I would visit this place, as a Palestina Chilena, I have known that it is my land of origin. Chile has the biggest population of diasporic Palestinians in the world ("Los palestinos"). And our heritage is vibrant, alive, and constantly present. My hope is to visit Palestine during subsequent summers.

- I also plan to travel back to Chile to visit my Palestinian and Chilean families and record oral histories, view and collect artifacts, which will become part of the research and autoarcheological historical tales that complement the hegemonic historical and political retellings of these journeys.

- Broadly, moving to Denver, Colorado for this doctoral program is also a part of a journey back home. The Rocky Mountains are a reminder of the mountain range of the Andes where I was born, in Viña del Mar, Chile. The fortuitousness of being in this program, located in this geographic region is a compromise between my immigrant journeys. While I cannot go home to Chile to partake in this research in a communication studies program, I can experience similar home landscapes in the Colorado mountains. Being an immigrant for over twenty-three years in the United States, this is the first time I have moved West enough to enjoy natural and environmental sightings familiar to me, which bring me closer to my original home and birthplace. Therefore, this location is far too alive in my body for it to be accidental and I must consider it part of my research methodologies of embodied experiences. As a constant, embodied reminder of the view from my childhood home I have a hand-poked tattoo of the mountains. These choices—deliberate or accidental—all bring me to my present work and these feminist methodologies bind them together as purposeful and significant.

In this work, I invoke the "differential consciousness" that Chela Sandoval defines in *Methodology of the Oppressed* as the "mode of social movement" that provides a space for "whatever is not expressible through words" and is "accessed through poetic modes of expressions: gestures, music, images, sounds, words that plummet" (138–39). Through the use of non-Western methodologies delineated in Smith's, Sandoval's, and Anzaldúa's works, among others, I articulate and develop a methodology that allows me to theorize how personal trauma and experiences can ground my work, be productive for telling these stories, naming these struggles, and creating space for these repressed, erased lineages and histories to be reclaimed.

My family's and my historical migration experiences as well as my own methodological choices entangle our stories in a deeply colonial history that necessitates a questioning and challenging of racist and oppressive practices. Colonialism is ever-present in my own history in critical ways. It begins with the Ottoman Empire and the displacement of Palestinians abroad through the creation of the State of Israel. It continues in my birth and life in Chile and the United States, both countries that were colonized by European imperial powers. It continues today with the settler colonialism present in Palestine through Israeli colonial forces. All these histories demand that decolonial and Indigenous methodologies be part of my process if I am to recover the true stories that created my family's journey. I must, therefore, delineate the concepts of decoloniality and Indigeneity that will guide my research processes.

DECOLONIALITY

As Anzaldúa writes, "My body is raced; I can't escape that reality, can't control how other people perceive me, can't de-race, e-race my body, or the reality of its raced-ness "Geographies" 65). Decolonial methodologies provide my narrative a grounding I have been seeking as an individual. I am part of the "US society [that] is gendered and racialized," and as Anzaldúa tells us, "If you're a person of color, those expectations take on more pronounced nuances due to the traumas of racism and colonization" ("Geographies" 65). Smith writes, "There are numerous oral stories which tell of what it means, what it feels like, to be present while your history is erased before your eyes, dismissed as irrelevant, ignored or rendered as the lunatic ravings of drunken old people" (30–31). I see myself and my own story, as a product and a generation born out of this erasure. Through this project, I intend to reach and reclaim the histories and lineages that colonialism and imperialism attempted to take away—and arguably succeeded in taking—from diasporic peoples like my family. Smith explains that "for most of the past 500 years the indigenous peoples' project has had one major priority: *survival*" (111, original emphasis). For my family's history, and to further elaborate on stories of the Palestinian diaspora, my project exists in reformulations of the Indigenous peoples' project as part of the recovery element that moves beyond and outside of Western research approaches, which I consider living remnants of colonial forces (121-22). These considerations are critical for understanding how the stories I plan to write are enveloped in colonial histories and yet, will attempt to challenge these forces.

Because part of my research project involves the actual movement of my body and my person through new and old spaces, this project comes alive as a "recovery of meaning through movement" as Sandoval defines in *Methodology of the Oppressed.* This process then becomes embodied in me as, through my writing and my research, I am acting and "bursting" the self into a "re-formation" and "conversion" (130). The process of this research project will become the "threshold" through which I will attempt to recover meanings and transfigure the histories that created my story and my family's, and I will not be able to help being changed by it—as I have already started to be (131). This "place of crossing, of transition and metamorphosis" for me is my research, my doctoral program in Boulder, Colorado in the Rocky Mountains, my dissertation project, my travels through Palestine and Chile to recover, transition, metamorphize, and then disperse the histories, knowledges, and stories I am gaining (131).

Through these embodied practices, traveling, and movements, I will recover and record my/our histories. Thus, the writing, stories, retellings, and reinterpretations I collect—in oral histories, autoarcheologies, autoethnographies, testimonios, and more—will be the new interpretations of how colonial histories have erased us. Feminist methodologies then offer the power to reclaim and rewrite the history of my family, and the minimized version of Chilean Palestinian history. *The Chile Reader*, a 640-page tome that covers Chile's 500-year history, includes only one footnote about its Palestinian diaspora—the largest in all the world as noted above (*Chile Reader*; "Los palestinos").

It is in the telling and retelling of this story—one that literally exists on the margins of history, as an afterthought, and the inconvenient details that pierce the master narratives the White men in power want to tell—with this project, that I can participate in a resistance of the White-supremacist, colonial ideals that force my people and other immigrants in the United States and South America into shadow places and invisible statuses. Looking at this project through the lens of decoloniality—removing colonial impacts and arriving at the Indigenous truths of these various physical and colonial histories of my family's journey—provides me with insights for framing my dissertation as an important decolonial project, lifting the veil of whitewashed histories.

Aside from utilizing a decolonial lens, what Sandoval labels a "radical mestizaje" (169) is also critical for my project. She states, "Like the 'mestiza consciousness' described under US thirdworld feminism, which, as Anzaldúa explains, arises 'on borders and in margins' where feminists of color keep 'intact shifting and multiple identities' with 'integrity' and 'love,'" so must my work exist in these borderlands (168). While Anzaldúa writes of the mestizaje lives in the borderlands of the United States and Mexico, I find myself in her and in Sandoval's work because my own "raced" body is birthed of borderlands (Anzaldúa, "Geographies" 65). Not only am I a daughter of the Palestinian diaspora, but I am also part of the White and Mestizo groups of Chileans.[2] In remembering colonial histories, it is critical to acknowledge that Chile is not just a country of Latin American success. It is a place where brownness and Indigeneity are erased, often violently.

INDIGENEITY

My move to write as a decolonial practice does not remove my responsibility to Indigenous folks, but rather highlights it. As a diasporic individual living on

2 The vast majority of the Chilean population is White and Mestizo, a mix of White (European) and Amerindian ancestry. The latter is a term that refers to the Indigenous (native) people of North and South America. The main Chilean racial type was produced by a mixture of Spanish ancestry, principally Andalusians and Basques, and the indigenous Mapuche. There have been, however, immigrants to Chile from England, Germany, Switzerland, Italy, France, and Eastern Europe. Chileans with European ancestry are those who are usually part of the political elite, run important financial sectors, or important manufacturing operations.

the stolen land of the Indigenous Mapuche, Aymara, and Quechua whose lands were taken and pillaged, and whose people were raped and murdered, I must write these stories and these truths of Indigenous folks in my various homes ("Chile").[3] Anzaldúa's posthumously published work reminds us that, "'El árbol de la vida' (the tree of life) symbolizes my 'story' of the new tribalism. Roots represent ancestral/racial origins and biological attributes; branches and leaves represent the characteristics, communities, and cultures that surround us, that we've adopted, and that we're in intimate conversation with" ("Geographies" 67). My histories are tied to, interlaced with, connected to, shaped by, and reformed through their relationship to the Indigenous communities of the lands I have lived in. To begin to do justice to these violent histories that live in my body and those of my ancestors, I must acknowledge these conflicting realities of diaspora and Indigeneity and begin to account for how I will encounter these in my broader project. Through my dissertation, I want to explore and write of how my own raced, diasporic body attempts to participate and reclaim, honor and recover, while also doing violence to Indigenous life by my very existence in lands that are not mine to claim.

Because of these identities as a diasporic Palestinian and Chilean immigrant in the United States, I exist in a constant state of displacement where my own positionality is at fault and at risk. We are a displaced people, living on lands made available through the displacement of others—whether it is the Mapuche and others in Chile, or the various Indigenous tribes of the United States. This narrative of displacement and recovery must bring to light the painful perpetual and circular violence for multiple peoples by colonialism, a system that produces a continuous reliving and perpetuation of violence. Through this specific project, I attempt to define a methodology that draws on personal experiences and uses them as a launching pad for conversations that extend far beyond the Yunis Varas family tree.

As Guillermo Gómez-Peña writes in *The New World Border*, we discover that "here/there, the Indigenous and the immigrant share the same space but are foreigners to each other. We have all been uprooted to different degrees, and for different reasons, but not everyone is aware of it. Here/there, homelessness, border culture, and deterritorialization are the dominant experience, not just fancy academic theories" (6). Indeed, it is critical through this project of recovery that Indigenous lands and histories not be ignored and for me to acknowledge that I come from a place (Chile) where at the time of colonial take-over, the

3 Chilean Ethnic groups, according to CIA's World Factbook: White and non-Indigenous 88.9%, Mapuche 9.1%, Aymara 0.7%, other Indigenous groups 1% (includes Rapa Nui, Likan Antai, Quechua, Colla, Diaguita, Kawesqar, Yagan or Yamana), unspecified 0.3% (2012 est.).

enslavement of Indigenous folks "was an everyday practice" ("To Sell" 98). In *The Chile Reader: History, Culture, Politics,* Elicura Chihuailaf Nahuelpán, a Mapuche Chilean poet and author, writes in the essay titled "The Mapuche Nation and the Chilean Nation":

> One student asked me, "But why do you insist so much on talking of Chileans and Mapuches? Are you not Chilean? Do you not feel Chilean?" I told him, "I was born and raised in a Mapuche community where we see the everyday and spiritual worlds in our own way. We view the world through Mapudungun and in the later imposed Spanish, in our brownness, and in the memory of the arrival of the Chilean state that 'gave us' our nationality. It was 'also' certainly the arrival of large landholdings from which we were excluded" (Chihuailaf 569).

This conflict in identity and of existing with this violent history in our bodies, is not only my own, but the history of every Chilean. Therefore, this acknowledgment must exist in my project if it is to truly take on the practice of recovery and liberation of both my history and migration trajectory and that of the lands that my family has called home.

Similarly, when exploring the journeys that the Yunis Varas relatives have taken throughout the United States, I cannot ignore that Miami, Florida, exists on land stolen from the Seminole tribe. The land of Washington, DC, which I called home for many years, is land stolen from the Pamunkey tribe. The land from which I write today in Denver, Colorado, belonged to the Arapaho, Cheyenne, Ute, and Sioux tribes. Beginning with my birth in Viña del Mar, Chile, in 1985, I have since traversed native lands of nearly a dozen tribes who were violently removed so White colonizers could live and flourish from the benefits of these Indigenous lands. If my journey in this project is to recover histories and homelands taken from me/us by imperialism, colonialism, and capitalism that forced our migrations one way or another, I must honor and recognize the rights of native folks to be named as the rightful indígenas of the lands I have called home.

As Chihuailaf claims, "One of the most important tasks that we have taken on has dealt with making our rights as a community respected. We have worked on recovering these rights" (571). If I want to do the same with my story, "to record what others erase" and take back the stories that have been "miswritten" about us, as Anzaldúa urges us, I must not do so by taking advantage of my native brothers and sisters ("Speaking in Tongues" 169). For the Mapuche, as Chihuailaf writes, "land is the most important thing for us" (Chihuailaf 571). If I do this work, with women-of-color, feminist methodologies as my foundation, then I cannot continue to inflict violence on Indigenous folks by ignoring their true histories and erasing their stories. If my story is to be honored, I must also honor Indigenous folks' fight for their communities. My effort to recover my family's story must be bound to the fight for Indigenous people's rights because, while complicated by my participation in violence against them as part of the immigrants that continue the colonizers' missions, I am also fighting for my own freedom from colonization. While "[n]o one is immune to the virus of internalized colonialism," I know this fight must be fought with them (Gómez-Peña 7).

I consider my identity as a diasporic Palestinian Chilean immigrant in the United States as one that creates space for an alliance. As Gómez-Peña states, I too "oppose the old colonial dichotomy of First World/Third World with the more pertinent notion of the Fourth World—a conceptual place where the Indigenous peoples meet with the diasporic communities" (7). In this Fourth World, Gómez-Peña tells us, we "live between and across various cultures, communities, and countries. And our identities are constantly being reshaped by this kaleidoscopic experience" (7). Thus, I take seriously his call that we must "elaborate the new set of myths, metaphors, and symbols that will locate us within all of these fluctuating cartographies" (7). I see myself and this project as that of a child of the Fourth World, birthed of migrations and diasporas and displacement; my own truths and identities are kaleidoscopic experiences. Therefore, I must take an approach that challenges the "existing cartographic rules [that] unjustly organize human hierarchies *in place* and reify uneven geographies in familiar, seemingly natural ways" (McKittrick x, original emphasis). My story, which traverses different geographic journeys, exists in a new terrain that reshapes colonial landscapes.

MY DIASPORIC STORY WEAVES RECOVERY

Honoring the history of Indigenous lands connects me further to the violence inflicted on the Palestinian people in the Middle East. While McKittrick grounds me on the land in the Western Hemisphere where I have lived and where I am writing, thinking about land and boundaries connects me and this work further to the Palestinian struggle. This project is my own fight and "desire for mobility," as Jasbir K. Puar writes in *The Right to Maim* (161). The desire for my migratory, diasporic story to be told, to be acknowledged, is a fight for it to be viewed as a valid Palestinian narrative, an immigrant story. As diasporic immigrants, I/we exist in a constant state of displacement. While I have not lived in or been removed from our land in Palestine, the ancestral fight for land exists in my body and it remembers. Having been in Palestine one summer, seeing, witnessing, and experiencing the occupation, displacement, and efforts to erase my people, I understand and feel its secuelas in my body and life.

With this project, I see how my own story is an inheritance of the settler, colonial occupation that displaced my people. As an immigrant in the United States, I have felt I have no home. I have no claim to my ancestral lands because I do not know the land of my ancestors. Yet when I crossed into Palestine on that hot July day in 2019, my body recognized this new place as its home, its birthplace. I am a product of the displacement imposed on my people by settler colonialism in the Middle East and in South America. inded me of how important it is to acknowledge that what is going on in Palestine cannot be separated from Indigenous histories across the Americas because that very effort is part of a "project of elimination" that Puar writes about where Indigenous peoples are erased through genocide, assimilation, and other methods of ethnic cleansing (144). So instead of further participating in what Puar calls the "framing of settler colonialism," I choose to unmask it, to name it (144). I connect with the stories of Indigenous folks because I am Indigenous to Palestine, and because, as Gómez-Peña tells us, "everything is interconnected, all destructive and divisive forces have the same source" (15). My recovery project is bound up to an Indigenous people's project for survival and resistance. As a White-passing Latina and Palestina, it is both my privilege and my responsibility to name the oppressions of Indigenous folks in the United States and Latin America and link them with the Palestinian struggle for freedom from the Israeli settler colonial state. These stories are both unique and birthed from the same powers of colonialism that attempt to diminish, destroy, and disappear entire cultures and peoples.

CONCLUSION

My name is Bernardita Maria Yunis Varas. My name carries histories. My Spanish first and middle names honor my mother and my Chilena identity. My last names carry the histories of colonialism and Palestinian displacement. In the telling of my story and my family's diasporic, immigrant history, I reclaim my Palestinian ancestry and the legacy of Latin America to which my name alludes. As Anzaldúa teaches us, our identities are crisscrossing borderlands, colorful tejidos that narrate painful and beautiful histories. The tapestry of my family history is vibrant and yet obscure for me as a second-generation Chilena and immigrant in the United States. Recovering our stories, connecting to my ancestors, and discovering what I do not yet know, motivates my life. Anzaldúan thought and Indigenous and women-of-color feminisms provide the tools for doing this work of recovery, discovery, reclamation in just, nonviolent, life-giving ways. My methodologies must acknowledge and connect with other fights for survival and resistance. My work must be grounded in women-of-color, Indigenous, feminist methodologies in order to reclaim and expose the stories of my peoples as Palestinian and Latinx communities whose lives have been displaced and erased. Therefore, as Anzaldúa reminds us, "I write to record what others erase when I speak, to rewrite the stories others have miswritten about me, about you" ("Speaking in Tongues" 169). I write to state and honor the names of those removed, destroyed, replaced, and erased.

WORKS CITED

Anzaldúa, Gloria. *Borderlands / La Frontera*, 3rd edition. Aunt Lute, Books 1987.

———. "Geographies of Selves—Reimagining Identity: Nos / Otras (Us / Other), las Nepantleras, and the New Tribalism." *Light in the Dark / Luz en lo Oscuro: Rewriting Identity, Spirituality, Reality.* Duke University Press, 2015, pp. 65–94.

———. *Making Face, Making Soul / Haciendo Caras: Creative and Critical Perspectives by Women of Color*. Aunt Lute Books, 1990.

———. "Speaking in Tongues: A Letter to Third World Women Writers." *This Bridge Called My Back: Writings of Radical Women of Color*. Edited by Cherríe Moraga and Gloria Anzaldúa. Kitchen Table: Women of Color Press, 1983, pp. 165–74.

Bowler, Hannah. "Giving Away Other People's Land: The Making of the Balfour Declaration." *Journal of Palestinian Refugee Studies*, 2016. Gale in Context: Global Issues, http://bit.ly/2A6X8e9. Accessed 23 May 2022.

Chihuailaf Nahuelpán, Elicura, translated by Ryan Judge. "The Mapuche Nation and the Chilean Nation." See Hutchison, et al. *The Chile Reader*, pp. 568–74.

"Chile." *The World Factbook*. Central Intelligence Agency, https://www.cia.gov/library/publications/the-world-factbook/geos/ci.html. Accessed 20 Mar. 2019.

Dawn, C. Earnest, *From Ottomanism to Arabism: Essays on the Origins of Arab Nationalism*. University of Illinois Press, 1973.

Gómez-Peña, Guillermo. *The New World Border.* City Lights Books, 1996.

Hutchison, Elizabeth Quay, Thomas Miller Klubock, Nara B. Milanich, and Peter Winn, editors. *The Chile Reader: History, Culture, Politics.* Duke University Press, 2014.

"Los palestinos miran con esperanza su futuro en Chile sin olvidar Gaza e Irak." *El Economista (EFE),* 2 Feb. 2009. https://ecodiario.eleconomista.es/sociedad/noticias/1028142/02/09/Los-palestinos-miran-con-esperanza-su-futuro-en-Chile-sin-olvidar-Gaza-e-Irak.html. Accessed 19 Mar. 2019.

McKittrick, Katherine. *Demonic Grounds: Black Women and the Cartographies of Struggle*. Minneapolis: University of Minnesota Press, 2006.

Povinelli, Elizabeth A. *Geontologies: A Requiem to Late Liberalism*. Duke University Press, 2016.

Puar, Jasbir K. *The Right to Maim: Debility, Capacity, Disability*. Duke University Press, 2017.

"Revolution in the Factory: Interviews with Workers at the Yarur Cotton Mill." See Hutchison, et al. *The Chile Reader*, pp. 393–99.

Sandoval, Chela. *Methodology of the Oppressed.* Minneapolis: University of Minnesota Press, 2000.

Smith, Linda Tuhiwai. *Decolonizing Methodologies: Research and Indigenous Peoples*. Second Edition. New York: Zed Books, 2012.

"To Sell, Give, Donate, Trade, or Exchange": Certification of Indian Enslavement." *The Chile Reader: History, Culture, Politics*. See Hutchison, et al. *The Chile Reader*, pp. 98–108.

LAS INVISIBLES

THE WOMEN OF THE TEJANO MUSIC INDUSTRY

GLORIA VÁSQUEZ GONZÁLES

We arrived at the ballroom for that night's performance. I got off the bus and went to find the promoter. He came out of his office, and I introduced myself. We made small talk, such as finally putting a face to a voice since we had been talking on the phone for a couple of years. I told him I was there to collect the deposit for that evening's performance. He started telling me that he did not understand why the boss was treating him that way because they had been working together for years and shared other complaints. He failed to mention that he had not paid the band for their previous performance. I told him my instructions were to collect the cash deposit before the band would unload and set up. If he did not have the money we were to keep traveling home. He was very surprised by that and told me "But we have already sold a lot of presale tickets for tonight." Again, I told him "Those are my instructions." We went into his makeshift office, we sat at a long folding table, and he placed a briefcase on it. He opened the briefcase and told me "See I have it." In the briefcase were bundles of cash and what seemed like a huge gun. I was scared and puzzled because I did not know what he was going to do. I did not think that this situation called for a gun. He never offered to give me the money and he kept stalling which scared me even more because I did not know what he was waiting for. We were there for about twenty minutes, but it seemed like hours. He continued to complain about my boss' stance because of their long personal and working relationship; the bus driver walked into the office. I was so relieved! The promoter seemed surprised to see the bus driver, but I was very thankful to see him. The driver saw the opened briefcase with the money and the gun. He placed his briefcase on the table, opened it, and to my surprise he also had a gun in his briefcase. I was totally freaked out. The promoter proceeded to recount to the driver the same grievance he had previously shared with me, and the driver told him:

> My instructions are to get back on the bus and keep driving to Texas if she does not get the deposit. The band members are all on the bus waiting, the equipment rig is behind the bus and the roadies are waiting to unload or keep traveling. They are all waiting for the signal from her. The boss and the agent are waiting at the airport for her to let them know if they should book a flight here or to Austin.

The promoter said "No, no, I was telling her that I have the cash." He took the gun from the briefcase and pushed the briefcase toward us. The driver and I counted the money, and I gave him a receipt for the cash. I transferred the money to my briefcase, the driver and I left for the bus. When I got on the bus and told the band they were staying they started clapping. They were aware of the situation. I called the agent to inform them that I had the deposit.

I know that the promoter was trying to intimidate me by having the gun in his briefcase. I do not know what his plan was had the driver not shown up with another gun. Perhaps because I was a woman, he was just going to show me the money and try to get out of handing it over to me. As soon as the driver walked in and opened the briefcase with his gun, the situation changed completely. The bus driver told him the exact same thing I did, but my statement was not taken as seriously.

I use this scenario as an example of some of the challenges I encountered in my eighteen plus years in the Tejano music industry. The women I interviewed for this article encountered similar scenarios as they navigated careers in this male-dominated industry. For the most part, women and their labor were deemed menial. My insider experience provided me with a unique insight to the industry and the ability to gauge the depths of women's participation in the creation, production, and distribution of *Tejano* music. Once I decided that my experience in the *Tejano* music industry in the mid-1970s through the mid-1990s qualified as academic research for a dissertation, I set out to find a means to explain how women, including myself, have navigated through this patriarchal industry. After being introduced to Gloria Anzaldúa's *Borderlands / La Frontera: The New Mestiza*, I realized I had undergone the various processes of her conocimientos (stages of awareness) to navigate my own achievement in the industry. I became convinced that other women who worked in this industry also unknowingly went through this progression, so I set out to substantiate my perceptions.

Toward that objective, I completed four oral histories with the following women: Christie is the current business manager of her family's music-based company and the proprietor's daughter; Irene handled publicity for a *Tejano* group cofounded by her brother; Mickey is a conjunto performer, musician, and producer; Nelda is operations manager at a *Tejano* radio station. Their oral histories resulted in my dissertation, "*Las Invisibles*: The Women of the *Tejano* Music Industry." In this essay, I use excerpts from that dissertation. My intent is to give a brief overview of the ways in which the participants spoke about their experiences as women in an historically male-dominated industry. I seek to illustrate the ways in which these women negotiated their presence and intervention in the *Tejano* music industry to successfully fill various roles.

FROM BORDERLAND ATRAVEZADA TO MESTIZA CONSCIOUSNESS

I incorporated Anzaldúa's *culture of tyranny*, *borderlands*, *nepantla*, *Coatlicue*, *Coyolxauhqui*, *la facultad*, and *mestiza consciousness* as concepts that articulate an understanding of the ways in which *Tejanas* experience the *Tejano* music industry. I began with the culture of tyranny to describe the ways in which values, beliefs, and behaviors are employed to reproduce power and retain what was construed as legitimate authority in the industry. The women entered the industry through relationships and internal connections. They were often assigned traditional clerical tasks, whereby the labor of men was perceived as more valuable than the work of women, even when the female employees were professionally prepared and had amassed abundant experience in their positions.

Through her concept of a culture of tyranny, Anzaldúa examined Chicana/o culture. According to her, our cultures formed our beliefs as we were socialized "to perceive the version of reality that it communicates" (16). Thus, cultural paradigms, as created by men who exercise cultural power and are the architects of society, become transmitted and reinforced by women. As women, we learned and internalized notions that a good woman was subservient to her man. Moreover, women were socialized to emulate that which privileged society in the image of males who had the power and control. In Chicano culture, these norms were reproduced by women to sustain the culture and power of the patriarchy. While women in the *Tejano* music industry resided as borderland persons who navigated between two worlds, the state of nepantla served as a place where change and growth were tangible options. The borderlands for these women entailed living inside painful experiences, whereby one's sense of self had been broken, forcing those who lived between two worlds to navigate spaces that were painful, uneasy, and harmful, amid a state of invisibility and transition. The nepantla state served as an intermediate space whereby one would experience multiplicities of realities simultaneously, and it was this experience that opened the possibilities for change and growth.

According to Anzaldúa, being in the Coatlicue state was to be on the verge of experiencing a life-altering event. This event was the premise for the self-change these women would experience. Those in the borderlands, whose culture was not the dominant one, often experienced an identity crisis between the various cultures of their lives, and it was an empowering term for describing their internal conflict. This was the place from which they gained options to remain in the state of confusion or to pursue the transformation that awaited them and begin a state of nepantla. Thus, it was here that they accessed the ability to recognize the fragmentation for which the Coyolxauhqui imperative could facilitate rebuilding—after having gone through a process of conocimiento and having gained la facultad to see the world in a different way. It was here that their awareness emerged, and they set out to put the pieces together again and to continue working on becoming whole.

Anzaldúa defined la facultad as the ability to capture the depth of the soul, the self, which broke the habitual modes of seeing reality and the patterns of consciousness, which resided not in reason but in the body. Having reclaimed the self and its mind-body-spirit, mestiza consciousness was a "shift out of habitual formations … toward a more whole perspective, one that includes rather than excludes" (79). Framed within Anzaldúa's theorization, this article was guided by a discussion on the culture of tyranny, nepantla, Coatlicue, Coyolxauhqui, la facultad, and mestiza consciousness in the context of the shared narratives provided by the participants.

CULTURE OF TYRANNY IN THE BORDERLANDS: BOYS WILL BE BOYS AND THEY KNOW BEST

Mickey's homesickness resulted in her taking a leap of faith and forming her own *conjunto* group. Mickey moved to Puerto Rico to accompany her husband to his native home. There, she gave up her cultural expressions, particularly *Tejano* music, which was a felt absence in her life. She elaborated, "Even though I loved salsa and merengue y todo eso, I really missed my culture." It took a divorce and her return to Texas to reclaim the beloved music of her life; she was saddened by a displacement that had kept her away from a cultural expression that she loved. Mickey was inspired to explore the feasibility of creating her own group—a conjunto in which she would be the lead singer. She saw this venture as a part-time hobby, rather than deciding to pursue conjunto music as a full-time job. However, because she was one of the few women who played the accordion, unexpected attention and quick success came to the group, creating a dilemma for her and the members, and this led to their eventual breakup. She elaborated: "When I first got in, it was just going to be a hobby, just for enjoyment—*lloraba tanto mi música,* my culture's music that I just wanted to . . . it was just for fun. I didn't think that we were going to take off so fast."

When Mickey set out to form a group for which she would be the lead singer and perform the music she had longed for in Puerto Rico, she quickly discovered the difficulty of finding an accordion player who would commit to only being a member of her group. They all wanted to head up their own group and to be the lead vocalist. It is important to note that in *Tejano conjunto* the accordion player is usually the lead vocalist and generally the band leader. It was her mother who planted the idea that Mickey should learn to play the accordion. She elaborated, "I couldn't find an accordion player. Y mi 'amá me dijo, 'oye, pero ¿pa' qué andas batallando?' Mami tenía un acordeón viejo, 'Ahi 'tá el acordeón.' If you want respect as an artist, the accordion 'ahi 'tá el instrumento y hazlo tú.' I was like pos sí ¿verdad?"

Mickey took accordion lessons and restructured her life to enable her to start up her own *conjunto.* The lessons only lasted a year, "porque yo estaba apurada, I wanted to just have my band already. I wanted to perform." The group she gathered enjoyed local success, performing on most weekends in the local conjunto venues. The group's performance at the Guadalupe Cultural Arts Center Tejano Conjunto Festival in San Antonio put them in the state and national spotlight. The Tejano Conjunto Festival is the oldest and longest-running festival of its kind in the nation. In her estimation, this new spotlight was one of the factors that led to the group's demise.

Surprisingly, Mickey was unaware of the politics of gender in the industry. For example, she had not thought about the ways in which bands and their roles are organized. None of the members of her group, including her, were willing to give up their financial security to pursue the promise of fame. Mickey found herself missing family experiences that may have seemed routine in daily life but are absent to persons who dedicate themselves to a full-time career in touring on the *Tejano* music circuit. She explains, "That's the part where I say I did not expect. . . it wasn't what I imagined it was going to be. It was pulling me away from my family, my nieces, and nephews. I don't have children, pero, my nieces and nephews—I missed out on a lot with my family." As a performer, Mickey would learn that women did not have it as easy as men. Anzaldúa stated that "the culture expects women to show greater acceptance of, and commitment to the value system than men." This cultural practice referred to as marianismo prescribes "dependence, subordination, responsibility for domestic chores and selfless devotion to family" (Espinoza 319) and the women in the *Tejano* music industry were not exempt from these expectations. The men had someone who took care of everything when they went on tour. Nonetheless, Mickey made the decision to step out of her comfort zone.

NEPANTLERAS IN THE MAKING: ENTRE-MEDIO OR MUSICIAN BUT ONLY WITH AN INSTRUMENT

Like Mickey, Nelda Saenz lacked experience in the *Tejano* music industry. In the family as well as at work, Nelda found herself in the in-between space of daily life and performance. In her job, she was no longer satisfied. With a dream of playing music on the radio, Nelda set out to explore her options: "I was in the medical field before. And I had a very good job. I worked with an endocrinologist; I was his assistant. And it was very good pay. But I couldn't take the responsibility anymore. I wanted music. That's what I wanted to do." Her love of music, perseverance, and willingness to take risks enabled her to search out her dream. She recalled, "One of the station owners just happened to answer the phone when I called one day, and I said, "What do I have to do to become a deejay?" He said, "Well, what are you doing tomorrow?" I said, "Nothing." To her surprise, he asked her to come to the station. "Why don't you come in, we'll train you, we'll see how serious you are, and we'll go from there."

Mickey and Nelda threw caution to the wind and entered the music business without a clue as to what it would take to become successful. For Nelda, soon after starting her new job, she learned that being a radio disc jockey entailed much more than just spinning records. Her on-the-job training taught her all the duties that came with her deejay role.

On the other hand, Irene Lichtenberger and Christie Cruz, who had familial ties to the industry, had a different type of experience. They had to navigate perceptions of those inside and outside the music business—whether real or imagined—who assumed that their positions within their respective companies were based on privilege rather than on their qualifications. Both felt a need to prove themselves as capable of excelling in their respective positions within their families' businesses. Christie's goal was to be acknowledged as a worthy professional, rather than because, "she's the daughter, let's do it. You want to know it's getting done because it's a good idea, it's a good project, or it's the best or the most efficient way, and it's not just because of who you are related to."

As per her own role in the business, Irene did not want her peers to think that her success was solely based on her family connection or her appearance. Calling for respect, she explained, "It's hard. I'm not trying to be vain or anything . . . [As] an attractive female in the industry, it was either I'm sleeping with someone in the band, or the opportunity was given to me." Clearly, she was adamant about things not having been easily or readily handed to her. "Nothing was given to me even though my brother was in the band. I had to work for everything, I worked hard for it all." As she recalled, "It was very challenging, getting respect and showing that I am for real." The need for respect and to be taken seriously in the music industry emerged as significant obstacles in both Irene's and Christie's quest for success. In Irene's case, once she became a publicist, her most persistent challenge became the need to be taken seriously. Irene spoke about a strategy whereby business relationships are needed to get things done. She emphasized:

> It's first building that relationship, getting that door open. I would never take "No" for an answer. I kept active in the local scene, by attending networking events, communicating with the right people, and staying in touch with everybody I met. I just collected business cards, built my own portfolio of contacts, and just kept on it.

She went on to build a portfolio that served her very well and enabled her to become very effective in her position. Irene built working relationships with experts in the *Tejano* music industry. She overcame conflicts and challenges and became accepted as an equal by her peers.

Conflicts and challenges would also surface inside the culture of the family. For example, Christie spoke about a confrontation with her father. She had tried to warn him that the manager at the time was not handling the business in the most efficient way. She recounted, "We went through a hard time with one of our business managers." Even so, she recognized that "it was business, and, at the same time, [Dad] was going down the wrong road." In her view, her father "was trusting in the wrong person." Her warning was not heeded because she was deemed unqualified to speak on the subject. Her persistence on the manager issue led to her being fired by her father. Her knowledge was not deemed valuable and considered irrelevant although her observation was well informed and based on her formal business education. "Tú no sirves pa' nada – you're good for nothing. Eres pura vieja," (Anzaldúa 83) alluded to Christie's situation. Her place was not to inform but to be silent and let the men handle the business decisions. In time, her father did acknowledge the accurateness of her observation and asked her to return to help him fix the problem.

Each of the women risked their reputation. They challenged how others perceived them as women, as newcomers to the industry, as relatives—sister or daughter of musicians—and as inexperienced workers, compared to their peers. The women's risk-taking illustrated the process of nepantla. Recognizing that they were between two worlds, the women realized change and growth. Nelda and Mickey were novices, Irene and Christie were both in spaces of family and business. Their challenge to the status quo could easily have knocked them out of the industry. Opting for change, they negotiated the culture of masculinity and its devaluation of women. These experiences allowed them to expand their awareness of self and raised their mestiza consciousness in the context of their everyday experiences as workers and women in the *Tejano* music industry.

THE BEGINNING AND THE END: ENTERING THE SERPENT OR CREATING AN ALTERNATIVE PERSPECTIVE

To participate in the music business, the women had to relearn to see themselves and their value as individuals in the context of a patriarchal environment that misperceived them as commodities for profit or sexual gratification. To examine the ways in which the participants dealt with these travails, I rely on Anzaldúa's theory of the Coatlicue state to assess the ways in which they decided whether to continue their chosen path in the *Tejano* music industry or remain in their comfort zones. As they reflected on their experiences, the women spoke about acquiring knowledge that advanced their understanding of the industry. They recognized that not accepting the mistreatment of women in the music industry as culturally designed left room for regret. The decision to leave would mean they had to recognize it as a sign of failure, that they had been unable to survive in the industry. The women interviewed acknowledged that they did not *pay to play* and decided to stay. The expression "pay to play" refers to enduring everything from sexual comments to the sexual harassment of women. The consensus was that it "came with the territory" and "was no big deal." Not accepting that consensus meant an uphill struggle for women in the *Tejano* music industry and some chose to not challenge the status quo. These women chose otherwise. They persevered and set out to learn and became experts in their respective fields.

It was in the Coatlicue state that Nelda came to the realization that being a deejay entailed so much more than she knew or expected—power relations were implicated in the duties she would discharge. She recalled, "I didn't know that coming into radio there was more to it. I just thought I was going to go in there and play music. That was it." She recounted:

> One day I was deejaying, and one of the sales guys came in and said, 'You need to do this commercial.' I said, 'I need to do what? I'm not here to do that. I'm just here to play music.' They go, 'Oh, no, this is included in your job title.' I was like, 'Oh my God, what am I going to do from here?' It was all new to me. Then it was just another script, and another script, and by the time I knew it, I was doing production.

She went on to master all the duties entailed in becoming a deejay. Her determination to succeed and her ability to challenge male expectations enabled her to conquer her fears in the Coatlicue state.

Not only did these women contend with the conflict and difficulties of work culture, but they also assessed the balance of work and family. Christie was jolted to the realization that her role placed a heavy burden on her personal life in and out of the business. She explained:

> I deal with every aspect of my parents' life, including the company—it's very mingled together. It also extends to my father's brothers and sisters. If they need anything, they always come to me first or if they go to dad he will say, 'I have to ask her. Let me ask Christie if it's possible.' When I took this position, I took the position of caring for everyone, even aunts and uncles. I stepped into a role that was bigger than me. I thought it was going to be 'I'll just do my job and go home.' Because it's family, I take it home. It's a twenty-four/seven job.

Without realizing it, she had lived inside a job training environment since she was young, albeit carrying a traditional female role—taking care of everyone. She expressed her insight:

> I'm like a mother figure to them. Even though my other brother is older, they always come to me with work problems, personal problems. They say someone in the family is chosen. I was the second child. . . I was chosen to run every aspect of my parents' life—their medicine and bills, company, and personal—[things] the boys would have never even wanted to deal with.

Even though Christie reproduced gender as a structure of inequality, she accepted the responsibility as it pertained to employment and her role as the only female child in the family, thus reproducing expectations found in the culture of tyranny. *Tejano* culture marked her path when she decided to marry. She married a musician. "It's like, that's all I ever knew, people being gone. My father being gone and now my husband being gone—it's all-encompassing." As the only daughter, Christie saw her role in the family inside the dynamics of a traditional female family member, and as one who embraced those responsibilities. In her job, she was also a caretaker, problem solver, and confidant to her brothers and the extended family. Expectations for her were different from those for her brothers, based on gender roles:

> It was easy for my brothers. Since they were babies, and my dad being gone so much, my mother was always like, "You have to take care of your brothers." I babysat and if they had problems at school I would go talk to the teachers, I talked to the principal. My older brother, he was always on the road with my father.

Christie found herself as the surrogate parent, not only for her siblings but also for the extended family. Those expectations remanded her to the domestic space of the home. She explained: "That left me at home taking care of everything at a young age. And, when I took over the company, we all gelled because they already knew what to do. They knew if they had problems to ask me." This traditional role served her well, when running the family business. Even though she was the head of the company, she remained intensely loyal to her brothers and made sure not to minimize their roles within the company. She emphasized her brothers' importance within the company and in the family structure, almost as if to provide a place for them to belong, while minimizing her own value.

The conflicts experienced by each of these women in the *Tejano* industry demonstrated the ways in which each woman dealt as they engaged in the Coatlicue state. Conflict emerged in the context of personal tension and within the structural inequalities they discharged, given the responsibilities they have taken on in the industry or their family business. Mickey reasoned that treating all members as equals would result in a deep investment to the group and all would strive for it to succeed. She recalled, "Porque yo me metí en la mente de que if I paid the musicians evenly, then they would be satisfied; they would feel important and I would keep them happy." Even though she owned the band, she paid herself the same as the other musicians, "I didn't pay myself more because I was the owner of the band. Whatever I put into the band; I saw it as this is for my benefit." In her view, her group was like a family: "That's the way I wanted it to be, for us to be a family, a group. Pero once the promoters started pushing more toward Mickey, it became a problem. I lost my band and I lost everything." Her intention was to be an equal with her group members. However, Mickey lamented, "It did not develop as I had planned."

Las mujeres de la música Tejana marked the Coatlicue state as the ability to negotiate difference, to cross over from one world into another. Thus, understanding the different terrains, including the local and national spotlights, was a benefit for Mickey to grasp the reality of her investment, yet the group's unexpected success became the end for them as a group. The collapse of the group was a disappointment from which she would not quickly recover. There were also several other factors that presented obstacles for Mickey.

In the recollection of her efforts, Mickey realized that being the leader of a musical group where all members, except for her, were males was challenging. She focused on the interactions the various male members had in the band, particularly their toxic masculinity. She recalled:

> I would not deal with a machista person. Yo personalmente, I like dealing with people that are open-minded and easygoing, porque así soy yo. I don't have boundaries, and I don't like people that have boundaries; . . . a machista, I wouldn't deal with him. If you're not open-minded; you're limited, you're handicapping yourself. Así pensaba yo entonces. Whenever I would run into a machista, I would try to work with them

> for a little bit then I [would] move on. . . A lot of the men that I worked with were very, very, very respectful, and open-minded men.

Men were in positions of power and they dominated the music industry. As such and under a patriarchal system, they modeled the disinclination of men to acknowledge a woman's authority. Coatlicue presented Mickey with some unexpected, rather hard realizations. In contrast, Irene saw the reality of her situation and proceeded to create a strategy to navigate through the challenge she faced. Irene had to take matters into her own hands, because of the lack of people in the industry ready and willing to help her. She described her strategy:

> I made it a point, everywhere that we went, I would find the radio stations, find the local newspapers, magazines, whatever was there in the market we were hitting, and I would send all the press materials to them. I would coordinate all these things on my own, like radio stations. I would do photo shoots on my own. . . I would just reach out on my own and I didn't rely on anybody else to do it for me.

Following that strategy enabled Irene to become a very effective publicist, as well as a resource for others in the field. When word got out about her decision to step away, Irene was highly sought after by others in the industry. However, she was ready to move in another direction.

COYOLXAUHQUI, AND LA FACULTAD—UNVEILING A MESTIZA CONSCIOUSNESS

In the Coyolxauhqui stage, however, those who experienced the fragmentation of self had the option to put the pieces together again. As such, the process was one of reconciliation with the self—a point of self-acceptance and self-appreciation. It was the process of putting the self together, not only at the individual level, but also in relationship to the social, political, economic, and emotional context in which one lives. Thus, it was imperative to recognize the multiple influences one has been exposed to and recognize multiplicity as part and parcel of one's own identity.

As the women went about learning their respective fields, they also knew that they had to navigate those fields by encountering and engaging with their male peers. Very quickly they learned the importance of having the respect of their male peers, but only as it was given to them, as it was encumbered within the reciprocity of mutuality—what was good for one, was good for the other. All the women agreed that to be able to perform their jobs in their area of the *Tejano* music industry—respect was essential. Without respect, the women would have been unable to give their all to the enterprise. It was concluded that respect in the industry must be earned because it was not automatically given to women. It was also not as easily achieved by women as it was by their male counterparts.

It was achieved by showing their peers that they were serious about their jobs. If at any time their counterparts suspected that they were not serious, women lost very important negotiating leverage. It was also earned by being a quick learner and showing their peers that they were knowledgeable about what they wanted to accomplish, whether it be a performance booking or commercial advertisement sales.

Mickey also concluded that a woman was not taken seriously or considered a legitimate musician if she were merely a singer. It was only when one played an instrument that they were considered a true musician. She explained:

> I ran into difficulties with my back. I have a back injury. Y me tumbó madre, I can't even pull the accordion now. And I thought about going and getting back into it nomas as a singer like I started off, pero I hesitate por que hay una falta de respeto when you're just a singer. Porque no las respetan igual, you know if you pick up an instrument, entonces you are part of the band, pero if you're just a singer, como que, you're just a singer. I don't know why it's like that but that's how I see it.

With this perspective about the music industry, Mickey circumvented any possibility of a comeback. In addition, health issues with her back would not allow her to play the accordion for any extended period. This was compounded by the realization that being the leader of a male musical group brought personnel issues with which she did not want to contend. This insight led her to decide that if she ever put another group together, the personnel management duties would be delegated to a male member of the group. She understands that personnel management conflicts did not always have to be hostile; sometimes they just took the form of one person carrying an unequal share of the duties in the workplace.

Nelda was promoted to operations manager of her radio station. This was something that she proudly touted, proclaiming "I am the owner's right hand—not the right-hand man—but the right-hand woman." Her duties were all encompassing: "I'm overseeing the whole radio station. I do everything. I do a bit of sales, the programming; I do the commercials. I do pretty much everything." When referred to as a one-person radio station, she quickly placed the credit elsewhere, stating: "Well, no, we do have a secretary. We have our disc jockeys, and of course, the owner's there." Still, she recognized the ways in which her work intersects with other personnel at the station. Her multitasking skills allowed her to perform these additional duties. All this effort also earned her the respect of male peers. They acknowledged her work: "They know that Nelda does everything. Nelda fixes everything. Everything, Nelda, Nelda. I'm like, 'Oh, come on, guys.' They say, 'I don't know how you do this. You have so much on your plate.' I don't know how I do it, either, but I'm able to deal with it." As she talked about her responsibilities, I noted that she performed the tasks of two to three people. She acknowledged my observation. "That is true, but you know what? You do it so much that you don't even think about it at times." She articulated that women should be able to handle multiple tasks, whereas that was not the expectation for men. However, she did not challenge that expectation. This philosophy enabled her to succeed in her dream job, but it also locked her into meeting stereotyped behaviors that reflect a strong, motherly, caregiving employee who tended to family and workers as her own children, privileging men over women. It was in this way that she colluded with the gendered practices that encumbered her with much responsibility, rather than delegating some to male employees who could carry out these duties.

To piece herself together as the point person for the business, the Coyolxauhqui imperative came to Christie when her father blessed her with the leadership baton, and she became not only the financial head of the family business but also the financial caretaker of the immediate family, as well as the extended family. In her hands laid the approval or disapproval of all business and family decisions. Those decisions are respected by the people she deals with, whether family or business associates.

Irene earned the respect of her peers, which signaled her arrival at the Coyolxauhqui stage, as she began taking on the assignment of putting a performance together from beginning to end. She proudly reminisced:

> I was given one challenge, they said "Irene, this is what we want you to do, we want you to call around on dates, you know when the band tours they book something in between from one city to the next so that the band can keep working." They said, "we're going to do this show, we want you to buy the ads, do all the publicity for it, market it, get the tickets printed, work the door, buy the radio ads, do everything." And that's what I did.

Her understanding of the processes entailed in carrying out all those responsibilities gave her the confidence to do the work. Irene's first successful event demonstrated to the group leaders that trusting her was the right decision. She showed herself to be an asset to the company and became an integral part of the *Tejano* music industry.

In the Coyolxauhqui stage, the women learned to navigate challenges presented to them. By demonstrating that they were professionals in their respective areas, the women used their insight and awareness, thus showing entry into la conciencia de la mestiza. To arrive at this juncture, these women demonstrated la facultad to engage as critical thinkers who understood the value of their work and their relationships and position within their enterprise. Nelda's positive attitude was an asset to her. Mickey's tenacity allowed her to form her conjunto group and enabled her to enjoy quick, unexpected success. Christie and Irene stepped up to accept the opportunities presented to them. In turn, they successfully confronted the challenges. The mestiza consciousness became part of their new identities and they all enacted it and performed it daily. They redefined their positions, not only in their own eyes, but also in the eyes of society.

LESSONS LEARNED: COMING TO SELF AS CREATORS AND REPRODUCERS OF TEJANO MUSIC

Each of the women risked her reputation. They challenged how others perceived them as women, as newcomers to the industry, as relatives—sister or daughter of *Tejano* artists—and as inexperienced workers, compared to their peers. They succeeded in negotiating through a culture of masculinity and devaluation of women, which enabled each one to grow both personally and professionally. These experiences allowed them to expand their awareness of self, raising their mestiza consciousness in the context of their everyday experiences as workers and women in the *Tejano* music industry.

All in all, these women were not meek. They were not tamed women who were uncomfortable challenging others. From their experiences, we learn that one must defend the right to find out who one is and who one wants to be without having others telling them the roles they should play. To participate in the music business, the women had to relearn, to see themselves and their value as individuals in the context of a patriarchal environment. By gaining their self-confidence and realizing their actual self-worth, the women rose to the top of their respective fields. Through their terca rationale, they chose the music industry as the site for personal change. They altered their lives and paved the way for future generations of women interested in entering the various areas of the *Tejano* music industry. Their influences still reverberate in the *Tejano* music industry and culture.

Las mujeres de la música Tejana experienced a journey that was unique to each one of them. Their personal stories illustrate their navigation through the *Tejano* music industry. They shared the ways in which negotiation through a sexist culture that maintains power over this cultural expression allowed them to excel. All the women achieved recognition in the *Tejano* music industry as women who are professionals and experts.

WORKS CITED

Anzaldúa, Gloria E. *Borderlands / La Frontera: The New Mestiza*. Aunt Lute, 1987.

Cruz, Criselda Z. Interview. Conducted in Temple, Texas by Gloria V. Gonzáles, 28 Sept. 2012.

Espinoza, Roberta. "The Good Daughter Dilemma: Latinas Managing Family and School Demands." *Journal of Hispanic Higher Education,* vol. 9, no. 4, pp. 317–330. *Sage Journals,* doi:10.1177/1538192710380919.

Gonzáles, Gloria V. Las Invisibles: *The Women of the* Tejano *Music Industry*. Dissertation. University of Texas, San Antonio, 2019.

———. Personal journal. 27 Feb. 2013.

Lichtenberger, Irene. Phone interview. Conducted by Gloria V. Gonzáles, 08 Feb. 2018.

Mendoza, Mickey. Phone interview. Conducted by Gloria V. Gonzáles, 14 June 2018.

Saenz, Nelda. Phone interview. Conducted by Gloria V. Gonzáles, 15 June 2018.

NEPANTLERA OF BLACKOUT POETRY

A CONVERSATION ON ART AS HEALING

SAMANTHA CEBALLOS

The world demands a lot from us. Every day, there is something new to worry about, blocking us from reaching inner peace, leaving a mark on us. It feels as though we are taking permanent residence in Nepantla instead of moving in and out of this state. I fear turning on the television and watching the atrocities happening in my backyard. I fear picking up a newspaper or reading an online article because I risk falling into a state of panic or depression. I have learned to stay off news sites while at work or I risk coloring my day with emotions I may not be able to control. This is a reality a lot of us live in, whether we realize it or not. Gloria Anzaldúa describes Nepantla as, "places of constant tension, where the missing or absent pieces can be summoned back, where transformation and healing may be possible, where wholeness is just out of reach but seems attainable" (*Light* 2). The world thrives off tension that then flows into us.

Actively trying to become whole and heal is an act of rebellion and survival. How do we navigate through this state as people traumatized by events from the past and events in the present? Marian MacCurdy states that trauma does not always mean mental instability; trauma is also bodily harm or moments of witnessing (161). Trauma causes tension within and around us. We may discover that we are not whole beings, meaning that we, as individual people, have experienced trauma that has caused great harm to us physically, spiritually, or mentally—that has disturbed us. We try to repair ourselves when we realize we are shattered in one form or another.

Through creating art, we are healing and becoming whole. The tension that causes trauma on our psyche and on our bodies shows that we are "vulnerable to spiritual anxiety and isolation, suspended on the bridge between rewind and fast-forward, swinging between elation and despair, anger and forgiveness, you think, feel, and react in extremes" (*Light* 127). In Nepantla, we pull into ourselves. The remolino we enter knocks us into realities that we do not know how to navigate. The emotions we feel, the confusion, the uncertainty, are all valid. We all have the right to heal and we all have our own ways of healing.

Through art, people express themselves without having to verbally explain the meaning behind their artwork. Some people feel comfortable in the space allotted through the arts and thus feel relieved when creating. This relief aids in the healing of trauma. As a writer, I feel as though I am in limbo trying to figure out what I need mentally, spiritually, and so forth. Where does this trauma come from? How do I take this trauma I have deep inside and transform it into something new, something beautiful, something creative? Entering the site of transformation, I become a Nepantlera. I navigate this traumatic space in numerous ways. My default way of healing has always been through writing. As a poet, I give shape to my hurt and use my words to piece myself back together. The process of recuperation takes time and many cycles through the stages of conocimiento. Anzaldúa is correct, Nepantla is the stage in which we spend most of our time. Poetry allows me a space to heal. Blackout Poetry has given me another avenue of peace and healing through the creation of art and literature.

Through Blackout Poetry, I have found a way to kick-start my writing, create a work of art, and most importantly, a way to heal the wounds I accrue daily. I am a Nepantlera of Blackout Poetry working to heal myself. In the process, I put myself back together, like Coyolxauhqui so that I may continue working to change the world by changing myself.

WHAT IS BLACKOUT POETRY?

One writer describes Blackout Poetry as the following: "the poet takes a found document, traditionally a print newspaper, and crosses out a majority of the existing text, leaving visible only the words that comprise his or her poem; thereby revealing an entirely new work of literature birthed from an existing one" (Miller par. 2). Blackout Poetry became popular after

Austin Kleon, a writer, posted his newspaper masterpieces online. However, Blackout Poetry is not a new concept. There exists a long history of blacking out words in documents out of boredom, out of privacy, out of secrecy. Poets shape a poem from words, groups of words, or stitched words to create a new piece of art-literature. Blackout Poetry breaks away from traditional ideas of poetry by discovering what the poet is capable of creating with an already present form.

Blackout Poetry has a 250-year-old history, according to Austin Kleon. Before Kleon, there was Tom Phillips, who took pages from books and painted them. Phillips created a lifelong project titled *The Heart of the Humument*. Phillips first published this in 1973, and he continues to revise and transform his work. He got his idea from William Burroughs's method of cutting up writing and piecing it together (Kleon). Burroughs got the idea from an artist friend, Brion Gysin. About thirty years before Gysin, a writer named Tristan Tzara would pull words from a hat and perform them as poetry. Caleb Whittcford, sometime in the 1760s, would read the newspaper columns straight across instead of up and down. He eventually created puns and stories with these readings (Kleon). There are countless other examples of repurposing and remixing literature throughout history that still need to be found and documented. From the musician Stravinsky to the FBI, people have always found ways to take documents and make them new. The main concept Kleon discusses revolves around the idea that we must "steal like artists." He points out that nothing is wholly original. A good artist acknowledges this idea. Kleon states, "Imitation is not flattery. Transformation is flattery." Transformation is healing.

Psychologist Sophia Richman writes, "through the symbolic or direct expression of the trauma experience, the survivor can bring some order into emotional chaos. Creative self-expression provides an opportunity to mourn, to find meaning, and to regain some sense of continuity and connection" (13). It is through the taming of chaos that we are better able to analyze our trauma. We give ourselves permission to let the trauma manifest in a creative form. The chaos written in the newspaper becomes an arrangement of thoughts, feelings, ideas that we are better able to explore through. The poetry on the page acts as a launching point to a greater realization or a greater peace. Creating is a way to step out from inside ourselves. Anzaldúa's words ring with truth: "Writing is a gesture of the body, a gesture of creativity, a working from the inside out" (*Light* 5). Estamos sacando lo de adentro en un jale, and that jale is helping us produce a piece of art that lives in Nepantla.

HOW DO WE ENACT NEPANTLA THROUGH BLACKOUT POETRY?

Blacking out harmful words, words of hate, words of discomfort causes us to stop floating in Nepantla and pushes us into a new state. Blackout Poetry is itself Nepantla. A Blackout Poem made from newspaper is the product of an in-between state, a state that lands between the logic of the article and the emotions being revealed. This amazing creation combines two worlds into one, and readers witness the heart, the hurt, and the transformation within the art. Through Blackout Poetry, we are not stealing like artists, we are healing like artists. We are transforming a document and transforming ourselves.

Anzaldúa wrote, "my job as an artist is to bear witness to what haunts us, to step back and attempt to see the pattern in these events (personal and societal) and how we can repair el daño (the damage) by using the imagination and its visions" ("Let us" 304). Similar to Anzaldúa, I, too, believe art is transformational and medicinal. I enact the medicinal and transformational healing of Blackout Poetry in an attempt to ground myself and navigate through trauma. Many personal accounts tell about the power of writing and the power of art. Writing is art and vice versa. Blackout Poetry shows the power of words that are elevated by an image or a blacked-out page.

Writing is a cathartic act. We cleanse ourselves as our eyes travel around the page looking for those words that speak to us, the words that cause an emotional reaction, good or bad. As the mind wonders, the emotions hidden in the subconscious bubble to the surface and become conscious thought. Cathartic writing helps mend the soul. Writing with the idea of healing in mind opens the possibilities of reaching into the dark place deep inside and sticking the mess onto paper. The article "Cathartic Poetry: Healing Through Narrative" describes the process of cathartic poetry as a means to help people with chronic pain express their pain in a new way: "The poem and the person endeavor to make sense of the chaotic thinking, restoring a feeling of balance and of wholeness in oneself through words" (Hovey et al.). Blackout Poetry aims to achieve similar goals. We as media consumers are bombarded with negative stories of people being detained and held in inhuman conditions. People are being targeted for being different. Forests are burning, and the lungs of the earth are dwindling. Some people become desensitized to the sight of human suffering, but those who are aware of their situations and circumstances are more vulnerable to falling into Nepantla. These individuals have la facultad, or "the capacity to see in surface phenomenon the meaning of deeper realities, to see the deeper structure below the surface" (Anzaldúa, *Borderlands* 60).

Through this process of poetic healing we are learning things about ourselves. We are in the act of re-membering ourselves while re-membering

Coyolxauhqui. The shattered pieces are being put back together in the form of art and words. We are moving through Nepantla, while creating a piece that will forever represent the in-between of our creativity. Shaun McNiff points out that "the adult has fallen from the imaginal grace. Image dialogues are threatening because they are not part of our habitual mode of conversation. . . The ideas in our minds block the expression of new images" (107). We are not able to re-member Coyolxauhqui if we are not able to move past the blockage within. The act of coloring a page relaxes us. Think of the simpler times when coloring brought joy. The scratching of colors on paper, there begins transformation. The page becomes a new piece of art. We have expressed ourselves through images, now let us remix an article to create something new.

"Cathartic Poetry" offers this thought, "this transporting process moves our internal thoughts onto the written page, creating a space for our inner thoughts to be in the world in a tangible way," which is seen in Blackout Poetry (Hovey et al.). As we continue to live through difficult times, the act of finding the words to heal helps us pull out our internal chaos/anger/disappointment from within and place the narrative in a space where we can rewrite and heal. I am often reminded of the following passage in *Borderlands*: "Because writing invokes images from my unconscious, and because some of the images are residues of trauma which I then have to reconstruct, I sometimes get sick when I do write. . . But, in reconstructing the traumas behind the images, I make 'sense' of them, and once they have 'meaning' they are changed, transformed. It is then that writing heals me." (92). As a writer, I reflect and process the horrors going on around me while healing myself into a better mental state.

We are the shamans to our own healing and Blackout Poetry allows us that opportunity: We as artists must enter a shamanistic state remembering that, "shaman-like nepantla moves from rational to visionary states, from logistics to poetics, from focused to unfocused perception, from inner world to outer" (Anzaldúa, *Light* 108). We as Blackout poets are moving from a logical state presented in the newspaper story into the poetics of the finished product. Put in a different perspective, we are talking through words and visuals. McNiff describes the process of communicating through visuals as a "free-association technique of early psychoanalysis, which enabled 'unconscious' expressions to circumvent the 'conscious' mind. Freud described the artist as 'leaving' reality to become immersed in creative fantasy, whereas we see the artist as a person who moves among different realities and psychic states" (106). Reading this, I think of what it means to be a Nepantlera. I navigate this space so that I may be able to move on to a new stage of conocimiento.

We as Nepantleras/os can use poetry to help others heal. In true Anzaldúan fashion, "we must use creativity to jolt us into awareness of our spiritual and political problems and other major global tragedies so we can repair el daño" ("Let us" 312). This is why, I think, newspapers are used for this form of poetry. Though I have used regular book pages before, newspapers become obsolete after a new tragic story takes its place, but the damage of the news stories remains on and within us. Transformation takes over and creates a new piece of literature that lives on from the words of tragedy.

We become the spiritual activists fighting to change the policies and voice our stories through art. We navigate the space as scholars, writers, activists, and heal our traumas through the act of creating art. Blackout Poetry bridges image and poetry. As a poet, you are reconstructing your trauma and recontextualizing the words on the page. Blackout Poetry is a launching point into healing. What you produce can lead you to writing more on the topic at hand, or it can take you to another topic hidden in your unconscious mind. Either way, this is the beginning of a never-ending cycle of healing that we must go through as artists.

BLACKOUT POETRY EXAMPLE

I created the following Blackout poem using a snippet from "Asylum Policies Wearing Down Many at Border," written by Jose A. Del Real, Caitlin Dickerson, and Miriam Jordan. The article appeared in print in *The New York Times* published on Sunday, February 17, 2019.

Criminal

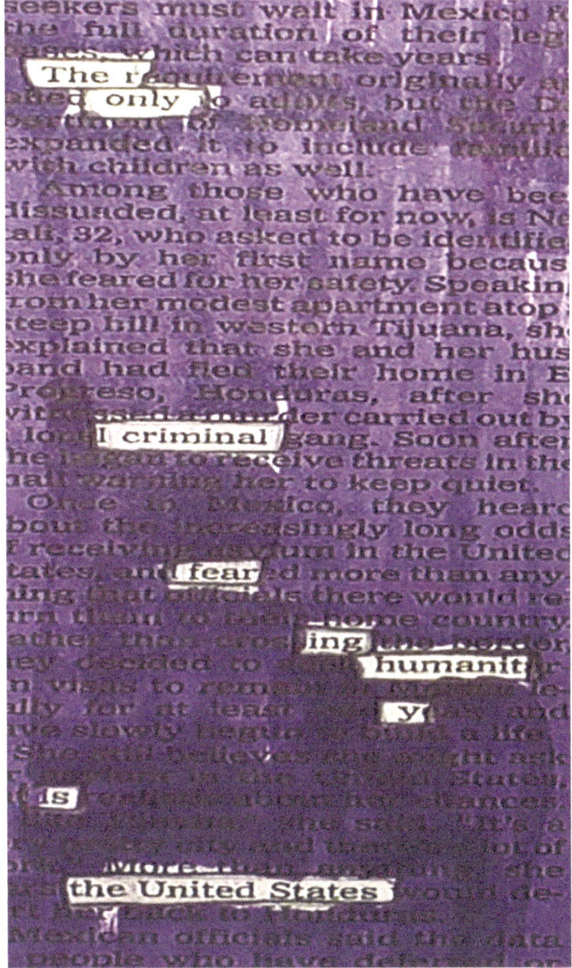

Figure 1: Samantha Ceballos, "Criminal," April 10, 2019. Blackout poem, marker on newsprint

The only criminal
fearing humanity

is the United States.

WORKS CITED

Anzaldúa, Gloria. *Borderlands / La Frontera: The New Mestiza*, 4th ed. Aunt Lute, 2012.

———. "Let Us Be the Healing of the Wound: The Coyolxauhqui Imperative—La Sombra y El Sueño." *The Gloria Anzaldúa Reader*, edited by AnaLouise Keating, 2009, pp. 303–17.

———. *Light in the Dark / Luz en lo Oscuro: Rewriting Identity, Spirituality, Reality.* Edited by AnaLouise Keating, Duke University Press, 2015.

Ceballos, Samantha. "Criminal" (blackout poem). 10 Apr. 2019.

Del Real, Jose A., Caitlin Dickerson, and Miriam Jordan. "Asylum Policies Wearing Down Many at Border." *The New York Times*, 17 Feb. 2019, p. A1.

Hovey, Richard Bruce, Valerie Curro Khayat, and Eugene Feig. "Cathartic Poetry: Healing Through Narrative." *The Permanente Journal*, vol 22, 2018, doi:10.7812/TPP/17-196.

Kleon, Austin. "Steal Like an Artist: Austin Kleon at TEDxKC." *Youtube*, uploaded by TED, 12 Apr. 2012, www.youtube.com/watch?v=oww7oB9rjgw.

MacCurdy, Marian M. "From Trauma to Writing: A Theoretical Model for Practical Use." *Writing and Healing: Towards an Informed Practice (Refiguring English Studies).* Edited by Charles M. Anderson and Marian M. MacCurdy, The Council of Teachers of English, 2000, pp. 158–200.

McNiff, Shaun. "Talking with Images." *Art as Medicine: Creating Therapy of the Imagination*, Shambhala, 1992, pp. 105–08.

Miller, E Ce."What Is Blackout Poetry? These Fascinating Poems Are Created From Existing Art." *Bustle*, 28 Aug. 2017, www.bustle.com/p/what-is-blackout-poetry-these-fascinating-poems-are-created-from-existing-art-78781. Accessed 29 Oct. 2019.

Phillips, Tom. "A Humument." *Tom Phillips*, www.tomphillips.co.uk/humument. Accessed 30 Oct 2019.

Richman, Sophia. "Out of Darkness." *Mended by the Muse: Creative Transformations of Trauma*, Routledge, 2014, pp. 10–29.

PART IV

HEALING, POETRY, AND ART

ERIKA GARZA-JOHNSON

POET'S STATEMENT

My connection to Anzaldúa comes from my home in deep South Texas. I was raised in Elsa, Texas, not far from Hargill. I became a real poet when I read *Borderlands* for the first time. I attended Gloria's funeral in 2004 and she inspires me every day to be a poet and an educator.

A bruja, a healer, an academic, someone who lives and breathes her words.

Who goes to the source . . .

She is my guardian angel. My muse. And I hate muses.

Unless it is Her.

Shade

She threw shade with every namaste.
"Namaste bitches," she uttered after yoga class.
"What a bunch of shit, I'm making an ass of myself."
She would leave, smoke a cigarette.
Curse the soccer moms and their perfect lives.

She failed at the current trends of spirituality.
She was condescending, lonely, a hateful,
hate-filled witch.
No spells, no sacred shells,
no indigenous prayers or chants,
no songs and danzas passed down by ancestors.
She bought sage once, it made her cough,
smelled like armpits.
The crystals got lost in her office,
in all her mess of papers and bad poems.
She had bought oils for relaxation and they made her eyes burn.
She tried to have a moon circle but one woman got sick.
Said she had absorbed the bad energies
of others who claimed they had been cleansed.

Her tarot pack was missing cards.
The nine of swords, the three of cups, gone.

Yemaya made her house flood.
Oshun made her infertile.

Her spirit was a mess,
an overflow of uselessness of pop culture references.
Misogynist rap songs were earworms.

Her spirit an ashtray of cigarette butts, crushed beer cans,
red bologna casing ribbons, reminders of failed attempts at veganism,

healthy living.
Her lotus blossom withered.

Bitterly she meditated and maldiciones were a mantra.
Fuck the world. Fuck this place. Fuck my life.
A mala mujer with unbalanced chakras.

In vain she tried to garden.
She had a black thumb.
Lattice fences were plagued with choking weeds
and suffocating vines.
No morning glories, no wisteria.
Her only gift was killing succulents.

She visited graveyards
Cleaned the tombstones of historic healers and poetic prophets.
Gloria Anzaldúa wanted nothing to do with her.
She found snakeskins on her grave that made her afraid of returning.
Don Pedrito Jaramillo visited her in a dream telling her to stay away.

Some nights she would sit alone under
a waxing gibbous moon with hope in her soul.
With this wish to start again.
However, she had ostracized herself.
It was too late for magic, for peace,
for a coven,
for a mystic existence,
for healing.

These Walls

So many walls to climb
The walls are your own DNA.
The wall is "Don't cry boy, be a man."
Wall is "You are an hocicona. Shut up, angry bruja."
The wall is "Don't be a puta."
The wall is "You are fea because you are brown."
Always looking on the other side of the wall to see your own beauty.
The wall is "Don't speak Spanish."
The wall is "We don't talk about our history. Some things are best forgotten."
The wall is "You are so gorda. Why do you eat so much?"
The wall is "You don't eat enough. Don't be vegan. You'll be malnourished."
Wall is "Don't act so tough. No one will marry you."
Wall is "When are you getting married? When are you having another kid?"
Wall is "You forgot where you came from."
Wall is "Te crees muy muy."
Walls in your hometown.
Wall is "Why did you marry a white man?"
Wall is you are "Still here but so far away."
Wall is you want to leave this place. However, you cannot.
A pipe dream to go somewhere with no walls.
Wall is "You are an outcast in Gringolandia. You bring down the property value."
Wall is "You are too educated. You lost your street cred."

Wall in your own heart always building a ladder to see your old self.

Wall, your four walls in your office, as you learn how to educate others to break down walls.
Wall, always walls to climb, you must exist to reclaim your voice, be heard, be outspoken, resist.

You were a stranger to walls, brought up in a neighborhood with no fences. But all these walls break you down. You want to break down. You find solace in the moon, the sky, the palmas, the urracas, the church of nature, you pray to the wind, worship the rain, and the walls won't be ignored, but will come down.

You are a wall. Strong, protective, vines like words, wisdom, song, holding in the ideas and thoughts of your own, a fortress for your folklore.

To keep out intruders meant to shatter your dreams.

The walls of your home to be a place for so many more artists, poets, philosophers, teachers, brujx, activists, curanderx, revolutionaries, to flourish.

I will use my walls to protect anyone who needs shelter.

Coatlicue Status

She was yelling at the flowers to help them grow, again.
Trying to paint rainbows in sheer darkness.
Humming "You Are My Sunshine" to her void.
Sang lullabies to the sunrise
when she would put her fears to bed and face the day.
On her mirror, post-it affirmations.

"You'll get through it."
"Just be happy."

But she was starving.
She was sick of eating, too.

She thought if she fed every stray,
helped everyone who had no smile,
told stories to the dying,
she would be sated.

The aloe vera was thriving.
The bougainvillea blossoms, burning fuchsia.

Today she would heal the burns
she gave herself
when she hated her own reflection.

MARÍA L. M. GARCÍA

POET'S STATEMENT

Community Art-iculation

As a recent member of the community—El Río Grande Valley, El Valle, El RGV, the 956—I am finally home. Before reading Gloria Anzaldúa, I had limited language to describe my otherness. I had no language to describe the feeling of not belonging. I had ideas but no theory. Since reading Gloria Anzaldúa's *Borderlands / La Frontera: The New Mestiza* in 2014 and again in summer of 2019, while working with young mothers and the LGBTQIA+ community workshop, Queering Cuentos (sponsored by an Aunt Lute grant from the Alice Kleberg ReynoldsFoundation [AKR]), I am changed and my world expanded. This new conciencia—awareness of states of being, historical grounding, inner work and outer acts—is the work I needed to read to become familiar with my unknowings, to acknowledge my facultad (60): that intuition that comes to women as a result of traumas, but is repressed through the practice of oppressive systems, such as patriarchal patterns of silencing women, the cultural tyranny of women transmitting rules made by men (38). The ultimate challenge for me now is a new conocimiento of self that facilitates spiritual change through activism in community. What to do? The only option is to make visible in the community at large, in all places, but especially cultural spaces, the idea that through art, people change, and when people change, life changes, and when life changes, history is made. Like Gloria said, "*No hay más que cambiar.*"

My challenge since my arrival to the RGV in 2017 has been to seek and immerse myself in the arts. I hesitate to describe myself as an artist, a poet. If others refer to me as one, I feel uncomfortable. It's still foreign to me. Why? Because the arts were essentially out of reach for me as an activity for learning and intellectual growth. As an immigrant child of seven years and growing up in the United States, everything was new terrain—language, customs, people, food, clothing, traditions—and had to be learned more like symbols than real things. The emphasis was on learning English and doing well in school. An appreciation and immersion in the arts was a distant ideal for my parents and family. This focus on academic education, at that time, did not include art—the study of music, dancing, painting, creative writing, acting, drawing—until I could experience it as an elective in middle school and high school in Los Angeles. As life evolved, interest and attention was placed on improving my own economic standing. The idea that art exists and is a way of sharing our lives in a beautiful, colorful, lyrical way became even more distant. Eventually, I realized patterns have to be broken before the idea of art makes its way through the eyes, the ears, the nose, the mouth, the hands—anything broken feels like shards of glass or shrapnel. And it hurts to touch broken pieces.

The real world, then, has us holding a broken glass nopal with sharp crystal thorns; and that's where art lives, in manos espinadas. Working as a K–12 teacher in rural communities for fifteen years made me keenly aware of the lack of art in schools. But, it's not so evident. And it's not so distant. Maybe because it feels unnecessary within the structures of power. Maybe because of the belief that art belongs in a museum or a gallery and it's only for certain people. But, it is easily accessible if we want it to be. The perception of artistic expression is changing and maybe it has even localized itself on the human body through the extensive use of social media and memes. What evidence of the practices of art have I witnessed in the RGV? Who is creating art? Where is art hiding? Where is art making itself known? Art is everywhere waiting for eyes to see it, ears to hear it, nose to smell it, mouth to taste it, hands to make it. Every person carries art in their body. Few seem to know art manifests itself in our everyday lives. I didn't know that growing up. I know it now. I have attended and participated in poetry readings, marches, and protests. I have met many artists through workshops and pláticas, book launches, classes, and book festivals. As I have leaned toward retirement and caring for my aging mother, I have also made time to immerse myself in literary interests that seemed out of reach while growing up and working.

A question I now pose to the Mundo Zurdo community concerns the function of living in the herida abierta between borders of identity and countries: Is it a womb where the thoughts of all that gather there gestate and give birth to new creations, of ways in and ways out, of bridges, of that liminal space called Nepantla? The opportunities to participate in bringing Gloria Anzalduúa's *Borderlands* prose work and poetry to high school students and the LGBTQIA+ RGV community during that summer has inspired me to continue this work through the opening of a cultural space dedicated to youth artistic development. It was encouraging to hear comments of support during the El Mundo Zurdo conference and the mantra of "doing work that matters." Face the fears. "*The possibilities are numerous once we decide to act and not react.*" (*Borderlands* 101)

WORK CITED

Anzaldúa, Gloria. *Borderlands / La Frontera: The New Mestiza*. 4th Ed., Aunt Lute, 2012.

About the Medio (Found Poetry in the Borderlands)

Atravesada
Never comfortable
Mi México, es el otro México de aquí
Because homeland means (in)security
ICE, maga—instead of Valle de Magia

The herida, open to new blood
Has a new name—*Nepantla*
Ahora te entiendo
Todo está en el medio
En el ambiente caliente
De cara pura
El nuevo México de aquí

My new language is mixed
I don't code switch
Join me, listen to the similarities
Say my name, say my name
María José 1521
La nueva raza se forma y crece

1848 some feet were rooted, some left
Either way
We stayed.
The medio of the river whispers
The names of many dead
As they cross from there to here
And here to there

Those *movimientos*
De cultura y rebeldía
Son la resistencia:
Brujería, jotería,

Intersticios, ejercicios
Lloronas y Chingonas
Machos, Mojados y Secos

In ten years time, in 1531
The mujer was virginized
Guadalupe substituted Coatlalopeuh
Or Coatlicue, She with dominion over serpents
The Raza of today has three misunderstood mothers—
Malinche, Llorona, and Guadalupe

Así que usa tu *facultad*
Use your "sensing,"
Perception, feeling, awareness
Mediated by the pictures in your head
Learn your unknowing ways
Look in the mirror until
You see your Self

The espinas, the rajas
The fear, the shame
The addictions—feed them to the snakes
When the snakes appear
Or let them all take you to the depths of darkness
Of life and death, of beauty and horror
But don't stay there

Retorna

Del *susto*, del *embrujamiento*
A la *travesía,* y cruza territorios nuevos,
una y otra vez
Ese es *el quehacer*
¡Hazlo Ya!
No hay más que cambiar.

En el Medio

—After Gloria Anzaldúa's poem
"To Live in the Borderlands
Means You"

En el Medio
To live in the Río Grande Valley means you
Live in the know, but don't know
What you have lost
You are no longer Hispana, Latina, or
Chicana
You don't claim India
Mucho menos Negra
Quieres descender de Españoles
Te mezclas con bolillos, pan francés, y potato bread
Reniegas de ser Mestiza o Mulata
You don't know where you come from
You don't know where to go
In the Borderlands you live
with the colas largas, twisted tales of
La Malinche and La Llorona
at the crack of your door
Hungry ghosts with clanging chains
Put them there just for you—
Your father and your mother
Their fathers and their mothers
Feeding you *men*-tiras
Stealing your song, teaching you
to hush, to bury you, your spirit

En la Frontera no hay ley
Puro espacio cruzado
Pintado de dolor verde
Aire contaminado con liquified natural gas
Tierra violada como mujer callada
Con tubos y tubos de sangre negra
envenenando su agua

En la Frontera el cuchillo se esconde
En bolsillos de trajes con corbata
The shootings always on the other side
The kidnappings, the panty trees, the worn out shoes in the monte
Leave uneven snake trails only trained eyes can follow
and no sage can clean
Too much too much too much for our ears?

Living in the Frontera means
You do, make do and re-do
You mix and match to renew what is trapped
Between the Río and the Checkpoint
In the Miles, the Milpas, the colonias of
Hidalgo, Cameron, Willacy and Star Counties
Tacoviche, pupusas, arepas, empanadas, pastelitos
Wok-A-Mole, Bar-Ba-Coa, Sandwichón,
Mostachón, hamburguesa con frijoles y jamón
Our fusion, our comfort
Cuando vives en la frontera
Te buscas en el espejo y no te ves
El chupacabras te desangra
El payaso te pinta
Te quieres conocer pero no te ves
If you want to survive the Borderlands
Amasa conocimiento, usa tus facultades
Atraviésate ¡Vive sin Fronteras!

SOPH/SPENCER MARGULIES

WHO AM I?: UNDERSTANDING MY BORDERLANDS USING POETIC INQUIRY

De dónde eres (2017)

Where are you from?
This question may seem a quick answer for some but for me it causes a full range of emotions.
How do I respond? Do I state the place my family and I have lived for six years now?
Or do I state all the countries that I have lived in throughout my life?
But Who Am I?
Pues no sé, y describing myself is like trying to build a puzzle of a thousand pieces.
It is hard. It is confusing. But all in all, it is mostly frustrating.

In society's eyes, I am seen as a White American female.

In my dad's eyes, I am seen as a Hispanic American female.

In the eyes of all the surveys I have ever taken, I am seen as a Hispanic White female.

But back to "Where are you from?"

The answer is, I do not know.

The answer is, I am still trying to figure that out.

But what I do know is that

I am the daughter of a diplomat who has had the privilege of living around the world my whole life.

I was born in Asunción, Paraguay, and since then I have lived in Mauritius (which is an

island off the coast of Madagascar), Perú, Honduras, y la República Dominicana.

What I do know is that

I know that in society's eyes, I am a White American female.

I am seen as such because of my light skin.

I am seen as such because of my appearance.

I am seen as such because of the way I speak English.

I know my privilege and I know where I am marginalized.

Although I am light skinned and am regarded as White, I am Hispanic.

It is an identity that I own, what makes me, me.

Not that it has been easy being me.

Whenever I tell people that I am Hispanic

They gasp. They gawk. They grin.

And they say "Yeah right."

But what do they know?

They do not know that I was born in a Hispanic country.

I am proud of being Hispanic.

Or am I?

I am afraid of speaking out and correcting people when they categorize me as a "White American."

It is an unconscious decision.

Until I think back to my first memories in an institution.

This was during kindergarten in Lima, Perú.

There I was considered "Gringa" or "American."

And I played along.
Not that being "American" put me in the dominant group.
I was not considered the "norm" abroad.
My "Americanness" and being "Hispanic" always classified me as part of the subordinate group.
In the United States, things were not any easier.
Sure, I was considered "White" but I was not "American" enough.
My experiences made me different.
A never-ending cycle of not being part of a category.
So, I stopped correcting others and I pause when trying to answer the question
"Where are you from?"
Why?
Porque I am still trying to answer the question
"Who Am I?"

Belonging (2018)

Abrí la puerta de tu oficina
My inside screamed
No sabía cómo decirte de qué encontré entre ese poema que escribe para la clase.
Estoy más confundida de quién soy
Ayúdame pues
Please
I feel torn between two identities dos vidas
two lives dos experiencias
two histories dos personas
No se qué hacer
Como qué
hago yo en este cuerpo que no amo y del que el mundo no se da cuenta
Trato de hablar con otros en español pero me miran como si fuera loca
I try English instead
They laugh
No puedo ganar en este juego
Y pues aquí me siento
Con mi sándwich en mano
Solita
Solito
Alone

Complicado (2019)

My body is complicated
My blood churns with the memories of those before me
Pictures capturing moments long forgotten
I am the flesh of a line of bodies that led me to exist
I wish I could meet them all
Hablar con todos
I own que soy Paraguaya
I own que soy Estadounidense
Soy los dos in one body
Soy ella
Soy él
Soy los dos
Pero ninguno
Sin fronteras
Sin crossroads
I define them as they come
It is how I introduce myself
Latinx/e
Pero eso no ayuda porque
Me parezco White
I cannot hide that
I have privileges that come with that
Advantages of being able to code switch
Surprising everyone when I do so
Pero quiero usar mi posición para ser una voz en este terreno político
No sé si me van a escuchar
Pero vale la pena

JOSÉ DAVID "PEPE" GARCÍA GILLING

POET'S STATEMENT

In 1948, John Huston directed the film *The Treasure of the Sierra Madre*, which recovered more than the $3 million spent on production and has rave reviews from sites like Metacritic and Rotten Tomatoes. In the Western-thriller, Mexican actor Alfonso Bedoya plays the role of Gold Hat and Hollywood legend Humphrey Bogart plays Fred C. Dobbs. The tagline on the Internet Movie Database reads:

> *"Two Americans searching for work in Mexico convince an old prospector to help them mine for gold in the Sierra Madre Mountains."*

At some point, Bogart's character encounters Gold Hat, the leader of a local bandit gang in the area, disguised as "mountain police." In their initial confrontation, Fred Dobbs asks Gold Hat to show his badge to prove that they are in fact the federales. Gold Hat responds:

"We Don't Need No Stinkin' Badges!" Remake

EXT. SIERRA MADRE – DAY
Passport? We ain't got no passport.
We don't need no passports
I don't have to show you any stinking passports
Gold Hat doesn't say *passport.*
Gold Hat says *badges.*
Maybe Alfonso Bedoya took the role
Because of the screens America stole
It wasn't only Bogart searching for
Gold in the Sierra Madre
American producers hunted
Treasure in *Mexican*
Gold(en Age) sierras

EXT. BORDER RANCH – DAY
Camera shot of an
Immigrant shot for trespassing into
A White man's lot.
So what does
Hollywood want us to see?
I guess Brown is also chroma key.
Question: This land of the free,
How does it show Mexicans on screen?
Answer: Does it?

INT. OFFICE – EVENING
To properly wash your film
Do your laundry in White
For Zapata, make the skin light
Marlon Brando seems right
Get Natalie Wood to say *buenas noches*
In West side stories, love wins
For the role of Anglo Zorro

Get Anthony Hopkins
Supply Pacino with a machine gun
Violent Latinos are always fun
Or so says the NRA.
Cause who's to say
Latinas are more than just a maid?
Lupe Ontiveros played over a hundred of 'em
Don't worry, she got paid.
H'bout that gangbanger, Hector?
What movie was he in?
Oh, yeah. That's right.
It was Noel Gugliemi in all of them.

INT. STUDIO – NIGHT
Two men sit behind a table. Our hero, Salma, walks in.
"Hi, my name is Salma."
"Hi, *Selma*, what part are you auditioning for?"
"Naturally for
the maid
the hot Latina
the prostitute
the spit-fire lady
the immigrant mother."
"The role is yours."
"Hi, my name is Gael."
"Hi, *Gale*, what part are you auditioning for?"
"Naturally for
the gangbanger
the gardener
the fieldworker
the immigrant
the drug lord
the lazy Mexican."
"The role is yours."

The casting director whispers to the producer:
"When Mexico sends its people, they're not sending their best."
Yeah . . . Cuarón, Iñárritu and Del Toro
Are losers
Cause they don't
Make films of
Violent bandits grabbing
Hypersexualized mamacitas
by the pussy.

EXT. SOME PLACE ON THE BORDER – DAWN
All we got is
Burning Brown-made celluloid
Sparked with spit-fire
Chingona dialogue of
Fuck your Gold and palms
My heroes reduced to
Comic-relief ant men
Fire ant men
Get your extreme close up
of scene 3A, take two
many times
we'll cross the border
of the frame
so track your shot
and zoom in on my badge:

Acción. ACCIÓN. ¡ACCIÓN!

CHRISTEN SPERRY GARCÍA

POET'S STATEMENT

Nepantleando as Art Practice

My practice as an artist/writer/educator centers on nepantla. Working at an Hispanic-Serving Institution (HSI) on the South Texas border wherein the work of Gloria Anzaldúa is not broadly taught, my art practice and pedagogy is driven by the work of Gloria Anzaldúa. Nepantla + Spanish gerund (ando) = nepantleando. Shifting from ideology to action, nepantleando joins art making and teaching with fragmented experiences of living in between worlds, a space that Anzaldúa describes as ambiguous, tense, and contradictory. From a Chicana artist's perspective, nepantleando focuses on emotional, geographical, spiritual, and metaphorical borderlands spaces, and challenges nepantla through art practice. Nepantleando engages Anzaldúa and Keating's feminist conception of a Chicana border artist, and explores existing in-between worlds through art making. Chicana artists articulate and make productive the ambiguity, tensions, and contradictions that occur when living in nepantla. "Border artists inhabit the transitional space of nepantla. The border is the locus of resistance, of rupture, and of putting together the fragments. By disrupting the neat separations between cultures, Chicana artists create a new culture mix, una mestizada" (47).

Nepantleando addresses embodied experiences through art. Special attention is given to the process of rupture and rebuilding. Performing in both formal and informal spaces of art education, including art museums, community programs, schools, and public spaces, nepantleando explores nepantla through art, teaching, and lived experience.

WORKS CITED

Anzaldúa, Gloria. *Borderlands / La Frontera: The New Mestiza.* 4th edition, Aunt Lute Books, 2012.

Anzaldúa, Gloria, and AnaLouise Keating. *Light in the Dark / Luz en Lo Oscuro: Rewriting Identity, Spirituality, Reality.* Duke University Press, 2015.

Christen Sperry García

///borderlands///arte///remezcla///pedagogy///entre/// el valle///HSI///san diego///

es una tortilla?

pero en tejas

en el valle

comemos tortillas de harina

pero en california

comemos tortillas de maíz

y los tamales?

la frontera

tú sabes

that place where many stay away

or border porn awaits
o first world *voluntarios* exploit
fear *miedo*

un lugar known as sub-par
matamoros
sidewalk school clases de arte
para asylum seekers
\team\brownsville\partnership\
fear of *barrio logan* chicano park san diego
pero that's where we're from, newton ave
no longer
;;;;crumbling stucco ghost town;;;;;;;;;;;;;;
now turned arts district
~~~~en el valle~~~ ~~~ ~~~~~~
la línea
esperando
para
siempre
it's~~~~~~~~~~~~~~~hot
pero~~~~~~~~~~~~
~~~~~~~~~~~*el*
aircon~~~~~~~~~~~~~~~~~~~~~~~*no funciona*
~~~~~~~~~~~~~~
~~~~~~~~~
~~~~~~~~~~
~~~~
~~~~~
~~
~
pero estoy yo
~~~~~

performeando latina faculty

HSI
HSI
HSI
HSI
HSI

Hispanic——————
——— Serving——————
——————Institution

——————resisting the mañana———
——————————stereotype
————————————————

perdón, mi español
is probably incorrect
it's mixed

entre english *y español*

teaching in place
donde
where we are not taught
to value the in between
visual art═══════════════*arte educación*

resisting
the arts as white property (Kraehe 20)
east coast / euro centric thought
void of borderland
perceptions of
chicana arte as

-exotic-
-primitive-
-too female-
-too ethnic-
(Davalos 13)
addressing race and///in///between
to a room full of conference empty
ears closed
bookended at the table
don't pose a threat
teacher-certification-tests
written away from the borderlands
so
we fail
over
and

over over
and
over

no hay una opción
en español

to speak tres languages>>>>>>>>>>.

perfectly>>>>>>
and imperfectly>>>>>>>
concurrently>>>>>>>>>>>>>>>>>

translating in——————————————
—————— >>>>>>>>>>>>
translating out———————————————————————————
—————-□>>>>>>>>>>>
>>>>>>>>>>>>>>>>>> or no translating

mis *estudiantes* no saben que
Gloria Anzaldúa
es del valle
taught to hate Spanglish
not
proper
not
real
*pero///troka///es/// truck
*lonche///es///lunch
*to google///es///googlear
*gualmar///es///walmart

la tamalada

watchale…
abuela controls *la masa*
pero en tejas la masa es roja
tortillas que hablan el in-between
pero no olvides
los fries con carne asada

ni los hotdogs con tocino

no me digas

pinche colloquial spanish

nepantlando

a way to address and validate self on

border

space

"no representation is representation . . .

not being represented generates a

silent loudness or a gaping hole"

(Sotomayor 134)

to practice art vs. doing art

practice teaching vs. doing teaching

entering space of *nepantla*

la frontera

not taken for granted

"the museum, like the borderlands, is

occupied space

border arte…tries to

decolonize that space"

(Anzaldúa and Keating 63)

an

image

can teach

border

migratory

self-made

mobile art museums

que viajan
museo me vale
chance to value
and see what we have
patriotic concha?
concha nepantla
texan o tejana
pero soy de
california
entre tejas
entre méjico

WORKS CITED

Anzaldúa, Gloria, and AnaLouise Keating. *Light in the Dark / Luz en Lo Oscuro: Rewriting Identity, Spirituality, Reality*. Duke University Press, 2015.

Davalos, Karen Mary. *Chicana/o Remix: Art and Errata Since the Sixties*. New York University Press, 2017.

Kraehe, Amelia M., Rubén Gaztambide-Fernández, and B. Stephen Carpenter II, editors. *The Palgrave Handbook of Race and the Arts in Education*. Palgrave Macmillan, 2018.

Sotomayor, Leslie C. "Uncrating Josefina Aguilar: Autohistoria and Autohistoria-Teoría in Feminist Curating of a Muñecas Series." *Studies in Art Education*, vol. 60, no. 2, 2019, pp. 132–143. https://doi.org/10.1080/00393541.2019.1600221.

Isaac Chavarría

POET'S STATEMENT

Anzaldúa's statement, "We have a tradition of migration" (33), connected me to the many migrants whose death ends their physical journey. Their story is seemingly complete. Yet, other lives are continuously honored through storytelling. The "other" is a mixture of figures; some are prominent, like Theodore Roosevelt, and others are archetypes: jaded lovers and innocent children. I liken this practice to Anzaldúa's reflection on the "ignoble death" (34) migrants encounter. In "Cases," I juxtapose the dignity bestowed upon some spirits while the undocumented are too easily forgotten. There is a spiritual borderlands in Brooks County. In a space with a population slightly above 7,000, it is estimated 2,000 migrants have died since 2008. Like the *muertos* from the Texas Ranger campaigns, the spirits of migrants are too often overlooked; even in death we are not seen as equal.

The remnants of the Río Grande Valley's land conversion into irrigated plots are a reminder of the departure of a way of life as much as a memory of Anzaldúa's days fishing (31). The canals exist still, simultaneously as feeders of crops and harvesters of lives. In "La Llorona del Valle," the antagonist is the canal system more so than La Llorona. The "Anglo agribusiness corporations

[that] cheated the small Chicano landowners of their land" (31) have passed on a mostly unaltered and unfenced irrigation system, which discreetly leads to deaths of residents. Although society transforms the fears and anger of existence into the demonized version of La Llorona, useful to deter horseplay along the canal system, it is the changes brought upon the Río Grande Valley ninety years ago that we should be protecting ourselves from.

The racism, violence, and manipulation the Río Grande Valley has endured—factored into Anzaldúa's and the community's development. By strengthening historical awareness, we improve responses to the still existing realities and systems in our environment. The taking of land, to create first borders and then an economic system, lingers in the departed lives.

WORKS CITED

Anzaldúa, Gloria. *Borderlands / La Frontera: The New Mestiza.* Third edition, Aunt Lute Books, 2007.

Cases

when immigrants die in brooks county brush, heading to san antonio, the bodies are buried in unmarked graves or left to decompose naturally above ground. in san antonio certain spirits reside near historical markers: the spirit of a king williams man gambling with love; ghost children guiding vehicles over train tracks.

unmarked texas graves use red ribbon crosses or personal artifacts. the spirit of an immigrant remembers their own name even if we don't. they live again at their place of death.

sightings by ranchers describe figures around a low flame, waiting. perhaps deciding between childhood memories or reconnecting with family last seen a decade ago. historical souls fill houses, one or a handful at a time. between the checkpoints of hebbronville and falfurrias there are 500.

sometimes it is a child drifting out of the brush, mute, hand held up, wanting you to take him home. to take responsibility and raise him. take him away from the coyotes y nopales. take them home. give them a home. find them family.

La Llorona del Valle

la llorona del valle
begins her summer
with two more.

the first she coaxed
during a game
of chicken,
along the edge
they sped until
one quit or died.

the second was gifted
by a father
drunk he believed
she was la virgen
and sacrificed la hija
in fatal baptism.

when our skin
peels off
from a summer burn
el valle fills her
with bodies
from the barrio-colonias.

she irrigates
para nuestra comida
for our lives
and in return
we provide
our children.

ETHAN TRINH

POET'S STATEMENT

I am standing in front of Gloria's picture at Alta Vista museum in San Antonio on November 2nd, 2019.

I am silent.

Gloria is smiling at me. Through the picture, she states, "Patroness of all nepantleras and nepantleros. Invoked by writers and those negotiating shifting identities." Under the picture shows a small note, "Santa Gloria de la Frontera, Courtesy of Norma Cantú." My legs are cramped. I cannot move. I am trying to catch and freeze time and space here.

I don't want to leave.

My heart is being squeezed right now. It's heartbreaking to hear the stories from Gloria's death from the El Mundo Zurdo conference. I am feeling useless.

All of a sudden, time and space change.

It's like I am standing in between worlds.

It's like I am seeing Gloria.

It's like I am witnessing her freedom.

It's like I am there with her.

All of a sudden, time and space change.

I am standing in front of her,
at Alta Vista museum in San Antonio on November 2, 2019.

Time and space intertwine whenever I have a conversation with Gloria. I found her when I started my doctoral journey. It has been three years since I started having multiple conversations with her. Gloria is a friend, a spirit, a writing counselor, a provider of camaraderie, who always comes to talk to me whenever I am feeling down or depressed. Gloria taught me that I need to listen to my true self, listen to the universe, listen to the wholeness of a being, listen to what truly matters to me, listen to the cracks-in-between of my worlds. I have been in a conversation with her every night since the first day we met. The conversation has never been boring; rather, it is such a privilege to talk with her. Deep down in my heart, I know she is listening to me attentively and is ready to guide me to the next step of my writing. Especially, she taught me one important thing in my writing: facing my fears to expose myself nakedly on an academic paper (Trinh, *Suicide, Resist, Photovoice, Split*). I did and will continue to do so; for it is now part of my writing philosophy. Gloria is sitting next to me, and asking, "What is next in your journey?" I respond, "Let's talk soon."

I was on the plane, flying back to Atlanta. I was looking at the clouds up in the air. All of a sudden, I had a feeling that Gloria was there with me. I had an urgent need to write. I wrote so I could continue a dialogue with her. So, here was the conversation:[1]

1 This poem was originally published in the *Society for the Study of Gloria Anzaldua Newsletter*, Dec. 2019, p. 6.

To You, Gloria E. Anzaldúa

I paused.
I did not want to enter the room where
Your body lays down
Alone.
I have always wanted to visit you,
To talk to you,
To ask you numerous questions.
I followed your words:
"Write to expose a self."
I
Exposed
Myself
Naked
            In writing.
I
Write to face
My lonely naked queer self.
I do not look for victory as I conquer myself.
I look for conversations,
A therapeutic conversation.
Like, there's a time we actually had a conversation.
You came and whispered to me:
"The act of writing is the act of making soul, alchemy."
I thought it was my illusion,
I thought I over-imagined,
I thought I was crazy,
But you were there.
You were whispering in my ear.
"The act of writing is the act of making soul, alchemy."
You gave me strength.
Your spirit went beyond the physical spaces.
We have not talked much, have we?
But I know you are always there for me.

I am sorry, Gloria.
I am sorry, my dear Gloria.
I could not enter the room.
Someone told me, "Let her go."

Deep down in my heart,
You left with peace.
The Aztec goddess has taken you
With her.
And now, you are free
Like a wind.
Like a moon.
Like a spirit.
That comes and goes with freedom.
That comes and sits with us,
To unite us, queer nepantleras,
Across borders,
Across languages,
Across histories.
You are never leaving us.
You are reborn in us.
Sleep well, Gloria!

WORKS CITED

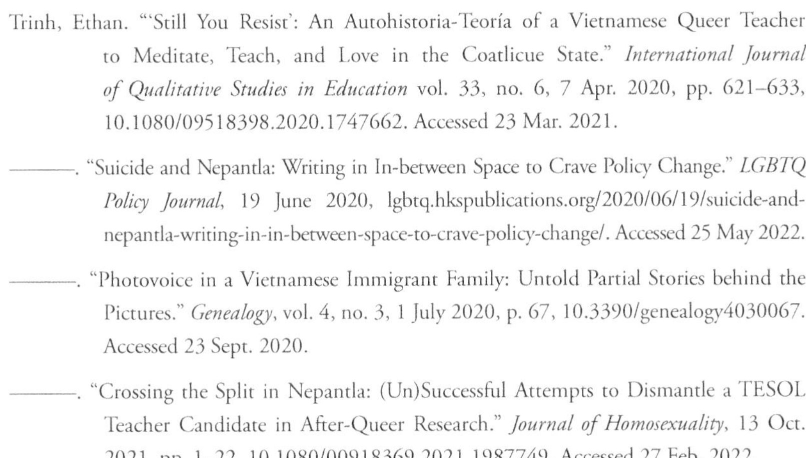

Trinh, Ethan. "'Still You Resist': An Autohistoria-Teoría of a Vietnamese Queer Teacher to Meditate, Teach, and Love in the Coatlicue State." *International Journal of Qualitative Studies in Education* vol. 33, no. 6, 7 Apr. 2020, pp. 621–633, 10.1080/09518398.2020.1747662. Accessed 23 Mar. 2021.

———. "Suicide and Nepantla: Writing in In-between Space to Crave Policy Change." *LGBTQ Policy Journal*, 19 June 2020, lgbtq.hkspublications.org/2020/06/19/suicide-and-nepantla-writing-in-in-between-space-to-crave-policy-change/. Accessed 25 May 2022.

———. "Photovoice in a Vietnamese Immigrant Family: Untold Partial Stories behind the Pictures." *Genealogy*, vol. 4, no. 3, 1 July 2020, p. 67, 10.3390/genealogy4030067. Accessed 23 Sept. 2020.

———. "Crossing the Split in Nepantla: (Un)Successful Attempts to Dismantle a TESOL Teacher Candidate in After-Queer Research." *Journal of Homosexuality*, 13 Oct. 2021, pp. 1–22, 10.1080/00918369.2021.1987749. Accessed 27 Feb. 2022.

JUAN C. ESCOBEDO

ARTIST'S STATEMENT

HouseMan Series

"My work explores liminal identities which are forced to maneuver through varying socioeconomic backgrounds and racial cultures. Specifically, the inadequacies that one feels when you are placed in a socioeconomic status outside of the one you were born into." These are two sentences taken directly from my artist statement, a piece of writing I developed after attending graduate school, where I completed a Masters Degree in Fine Arts. The school I attended was in Boston and primarily a White, middle-class (and above) institution—a very different racial and socioeconomic culture from the one I was raised in.

I am from Sunland Park, New Mexico, a stone's throw away from the city of El Paso, Texas, and a walk from the border of Ciudad Juárez. The people I grew up with are first-generation, working-class (or below) Mexican Americans who speak Spanish and English equally—a frontera similar to what Gloria Anzaldúa describes in *Borderlands*.[1] The funny thing is I had never heard of Anzaldúa until I

1 See Anzaldúa's *Borderlands / La Frontera*, specifically the first paragraph of the preface for physical and psychological descriptions of a borderland.

came to San Antonio in 2016. A coworker introduced me to the word *nepantla* and recommended *Light in the Dark.* When I read through the book, I realized I was grappling with what Analouise Keating describes as "space/time of chaos, anxiety, pain, and loss of control," but also a "liminal space where transformation can occur" (xxxiv).

For me, the anxiety and time of chaos was a result of infiltrating, maneuvering, and exiting an academic setting and field of study that, historically, is not made for individuals of my socioeconomic class and race. Additionally, after graduating, there was a time of reassimilation into my original background, during which I was confronted with the deficiencies of the community and family circumstances I grew up in. Years later, I still struggled with confusion and anger over the shortcomings of my background. I developed the idea of HouseMan, a creature that somehow finds itself in a new world and uses his homes as a protection (see figure 1). These homes, which were originally a source of comfort, become a burden because of the negative connotations their appearance exudes. Beneath HouseMan's façade exists a body, which is an amalgamation of the different components of his original environment. HouseMan's presence in a foreign environment causes a psychological and physical volatility which results in an ungrounded being who is searching for a steady space to exist in (see figure 2).

Originally, I thought of HouseMan's existence as something to pity because he would never have the ability to identify himself or acclimate to a space. Now I see him as fortunate because the ephemerality of his identity allows him to enter and exit spaces at will. It also allows him to collect components for his opulent anatomy. HouseMan exists in a place of constant tension but also a place "where the missing or absent pieces can be summoned back, where transformation and healing may be possible, where wholeness is just out of reach but seems attainable" (Anzaldúa, *Light* 2).

WORKS CITED

Anzaldúa, Gloria. *Borderlands / La Frontera: The New Mestiza.* Aunt Lute Books, 1987.

———. *Light in the Dark / Luz en lo Oscuro.* Edited by Analouise Keating, Duke University Press, 2015.

Figure 1. Juan C. Escobedo, *This is HouseMan. He just stepped out of time,* 2018
Collage, 8 ½ inches x 11 inches

Figure 2. Juan C. Escobedo, *This is HouseMan. He senses something wrong but doesn't know what it is,* 2018
Collage, 11 inches x 8 ½ inches

MARITZA TORRES

ARTIST'S STATEMENT

Maritza Torres is best known for her graphic style and portrayal of the empowered woman. The focus of her work explores themes of otherness and isolation, specific to her Xicana identity.

Torres grew up as the eldest daughter of a large Mexican American Mormon family. Although her family is strongly bonded, she herself is an atheist. In 2001 she moved to Los Angeles to study at the Fashion Institute of Design and Merchandising, and graduated with her associate's degree in Fashion Design. Maritza worked as a graphic designer but soon became disillusioned with the industry and embraced her real love, which was art.

Having had little exposure to Xicanx works growing up in the suburbs of Utah, Torres was stunned to find the deepest connection yet to her own feelings voiced in the pages of *Borderlands*. As a self-taught artist, Maritza could see the parallel narrative reflected in Anzaldúa's own isolation in small-town Texas. Torres has been greatly influenced to make space for herself to deeply examine her own feelings around identity and colonization as a way to bridge past and future.

Maritza Torres, *7 Layer Dip*, 2019
Ink and marker on paper, 3 feet x 3 feet
Photograph courtesy of the artist

JULIE TREVIÑO

ARTIST'S STATEMENT

This art piece is dedicated to ancestors of the past and to the future generations. For loss, hope and love.

Julie Treviño, *Eye Will See You Again,* 2019
Mixed media on metal frame, 32 inches x 32 inches

KIERAN MYLES-ANDRÉS TVERBAKK

ARTIST STATEMENT

Yo soy muchas cosas, which is why I first resonated with *Borderlands / La Frontera: The New Mestiza* (Anzaldúa). I create multimedia artwork exploring the various dichotomies in my experience as a first-generation Mexican-Norwegian-American who is also nonbinary transgender. Within my chosen materials and treatment are intentional metaphors that are critical to decoding the work. Anzaldúa's nonlinear approach to storytelling has directly influenced my own embodiments of a contemporary queer, trans*, Chicanx experience. *Sin Título* (figure 1) is a tapestry made of cotton twine, photographs of México taken by my father, and a piece of found wood. Using a gel medium, I transferred the images onto the flattened strings, which I later meticulously pulled apart and braided back together. Through this process, I emphasize the human hand in the composing of an image of a place or group of people. I explore the tactile possibilities for representation and reclamation through a range of materials including leather, wood, paper, textiles, nails, found objects, and my family's archives of photographs and VHS tapes. I spend intimate time learning their histories, potentials, and how I can transform them anew, creating visual poetry that embodies both the struggle and the beauty in being queer, trans*, and Chicanx.

WORK CITED

Anzaldúa, Gloria. *Borderlands / La Frontera: The New Mestiza.* Aunt Lute, 2007.

Figure 1. Kieran Myles-Andrés Tverbakk, *Sin Título,* 2019
Cotton twine, photo transfers, found wood, 30 inches x 43 inches x 1 inch
Photo courtesy of the artist

Figure 2. Kieran Myles-Andrés Tverbakk, *Sin Título,* 2019, detail

JESUSA MARIE VARGAS

ARTIST'S STATEMENT

My artwork is an interpretation of personal stories and shared oral histories that shape and form parts of my identity. The need to document and remember experiences inspires me and is the driving force that sparks my creative processes. Allowing myself the liberty to share stories through two-dimensional media, sculpture, or video also provides me the creative freedom to explore how best a story or memory can be shared. My admiration for artesanía, folk art, inspires the approach I take when beginning my work. This determines the material or process of creating the artwork that will best impact the overall visual narrative. Found objects are often incorporated because of the personal attachment or memory linked to them. Literature written by Dr. Gloria Anzaldúa and by Dr. Carmen Tafolla on Chicana cultural theory and experiences has been the emotional catalyst in how I approach my artwork.

In this body of work, I was evaluating my thoughts and feelings of otherness and the expectations imposed on me, of Mexican representation that existed in my childhood, of two separate entities existing in one person. *Mi Sombra* is a sculpture of wood and found objects, created in a rasquachismo way and influenced by artesanía. I commonly use tossed-out materials found throughout my community. I then begin to transform the discarded or found objects in a way that is influenced by Mexican woodcarving and by magical and imaginative creatures. *Mi Sombra* translates to my shadow; she is a "being" representing the Mexicanidad in me that is not always visible but always there. She is adorned with cactus antlers and sits on a makeshift cart with wheels and rope, influenced by children's pull toys. The series is a visual representation of a child embracing two cultures.

Figure 1. Jesusa Marie Vargas, *Mexicanidad and the Otherness (#8)*, 2018
Black and white film photograph on fiber paper, 8 inches x 10 inches
Photograph courtesy of the artist

Figure 2. Jesusa Marie Vargas, *Mexicanidad and the Otherness (#6),* 2018
Black and white photograph on fiber paper, 8 inches x 10 inches
Photograph courtesy of the artist

OCTAVIO QUINTANILLA

ARTIST'S STATEMENT

Frontextos—Visualizing Gloria Anzaldúa in the Borderlands

I was a graduate student in the Rio Grande Valley when I first read Gloria Anzaldúa's *Borderlands / La Frontera: The New Mestiza*. It was a book that, in many ways, lit my way into my own writing, a key that opened the doors to the place where she grew up, and where I grew up, and that, in many ways, illuminated my understanding of the Borderlands. Recently, I also became fascinated by her visual rhetoric—her notes, diagrams, and transparency drawings that inform her creative process. In addition to both of us growing up in the RGV, this is one more thing that Anzaldúa and I have in common: a love for the visual.

On January 1, 2018, I embarked on a creative journey to combine text and image and explore visual poetry. On that day, I challenged myself to create and post one visual poem to my social media platforms every day. On that day, the FRONTEXTO was born (*frontexto* is a blend of *frontera* and *texto*, border/text). In terms of content and materiality, the text in these poems is usually in Spanish and the medium is usually mixed.

"La columna vertebral de Gloria Anzaldúa" and "La de la falda de serpientes," the two frontextos published in this issue of *El Mundo Zurdo*, are part of a manuscript I've titled *Asemic Borderland*. In this collection of frontextos, I explore Anzaldúa's borderland, which is also mine, through the means of visual rhetoric. In these two frontextos in particular, I wanted to allude to Anzaldúa's image as well as to mythological images we encounter in her writing.

Octavio Quintanilla, *La columna vertebral de Gloria Anzaldúa*, **2020**
Mixed media on paper, 14 inches x 11 inches
Photo courtesy of the artist

Octavio Quintanilla, ***La de la falda de serpientes,*** **2020**
Mixed media on paper, 14 inches x 11 inches
Photo Courtesy of the artist

CONTRIBUTORS

Mariana Alessandri is an associate professor of philosophy at the University of Texas Río Grande Valley and is affiliate faculty in the Mexican American Studies and Gender and Women's Studies Departments. Dr. Alessandri is privileged to teach at Anzaldúa's alma mater. She has published in *The New York Times* and *New Philosopher*, among other places.

Stephanie Álvarez is an associate professor of Mexican American Studies at the University of Texas Rio Grande Valley. She was first introduced to Anzaldúa by Chicana author Denise Chávez while earning her PhD in Spanish at the University of Oklahoma. As a Cuban American born and raised in the U.S., she related very much to Anzaldúa's *Borderlands / La Frontera*. As a student of Spanish, she was particularly drawn to the concept of linguistic terrorism which changed her entire trajectory as a graduate student and then as an educator. As a professor at UTRGV she created the first ever course on Anzaldúa. She has dedicated herself to studying and documenting the intersection of Latinx literature, cultural studies, and educational experiences and providing students with a culturally and linguistically affirming education. She has been awarded the University of Texas Board of Regents Outstanding Teaching Award, the Association of Hispanics in Higher Education Outstanding Latina/o Faculty Award, and the Carnegie Foundation for Teaching U.S. Professor of the Year.

Sergio G. Barrera, a native of the Rio Grande Valley, is a doctoral candidate in the Department of American Culture at the University of Michigan and upon graduation in the summer of 2022, will attend the University of Texas at Austin as the Carlos E. Castañeda Postdoctoral Fellow in the Center for Mexican American Studies. Barrera's work expands the understandings of men of color through Latinx studies, intersectional masculinities, performance, and community (auto)ethnographies. His scholarship finds that men of color in homosocial spaces use brotherhood and performance as methods that intervene with heteropatriarchal structures that influence men to behave in hypermasculine ways. In addition, Barrera thinks through the value of community formations in inclusive spaces while practicing emotional well-being and expressive freedoms through scholarship, mentorship, and classroom dynamics. Barrera, a recipient of the 2017 NACCS Frederick A. Cervantes award for best graduate student paper, hopes to continue his work on the experiences of Latinx/Black/Asian American men and their masculinities during the COVID-19 pandemic, especially through digital platforms.

Chelsea R. Barron Dávila-Conaway is a doctoral student in Counselor Education and Supervision at the University of Texas at San Antonio. She is a licensed professional counselor intern serving children and families at Bluebonnet Trails Community Services, a local mental health authority. Chelsea's research interests include indigenous epistemologies and colonialism in academia. A proud Río Grande Valley native, Chelsea hopes to one day return to her hometown to strengthen mental health services for underserved Latinx populations.

Javier Alejandro Camargo Castillo studied at the Tecnológico de Monterrey and earned a doctorate and a master's degree in humanistic studies with a specialty in ethics, as well as a bachelor's degree in international relations. He also studied publishing and editorial design, creation, and literary criticism in different institutions. He is currently a professor and director of the Doctoral Program in Humanistic Studies at the Tecnológico de Monterrey, on the Mexico City Campus.

Jacqueline Cantú Contreras is a doctoral student in Counselor Education and Supervision at the University of Texas at San Antonio. She is a first-generation college graduate and earned her BA in psychology and MS in clinical mental health from the University of Texas at San Antonio. Her research interests include first-generation college students, LGBTQ issues in counseling, and student achievement and mental health of low-SES high school students.

Samantha Ceballos is a graduate of the MA/MFA program in Literature, Creative Writing, and Social Justice at Our Lady of the Lake University. She graduated from the University of Texas at San Antonio with a bachelor of arts in English, with a dual concentration in creative writing and professional writing.

Yvette Chairez is a Latina mother, writer, and scholar from San Antonio, Texas. Her research focuses on motherhood and the interplay of rhetoric, linguistics, and performativity. Trauma studies, gaze theories, and an acute interest in the strange and absurd also inform her work. She is cocreator of *Felize*, a zine for women of color defining their own damn happiness, and a PhD student in the Department of English at the University of Texas at San Antonio where she applies decolonial practices to the teaching of literature and writing.

Isaac Chavarría is a pocho from deep south Tejas. His work assisting nonprofit organizations has produced over 20 chapbook titles for workshop participants. His poetry book Poxo, from Slough Press, received the inaugural 2014 NACCS

Tejas Foco Poetry Award. His group affiliations include the Coalition of Nuevo Chican@ Artists, Chocholichex, and Carnelitx. He is the current coeditor of *Interstice*, the literary journal of South Texas College, and co-runs a mobile bookstore.

Angie Contreras is a second-year BA student studying political science, with a minor in Spanish language and culture at Mary Baldwin University. She currently lives in the vibrant city of St. Petersburg, Florida. She identifies as Latinx of Salvadoran origin and her research interests include immigration, identity, intersectionality, Latin American culture, and political trends.

César L. De León is an educator and poet-organizer for #PoetsAgainstWalls. His work has appeared in *Queen Mob's Tea House*, *Pilgrimage*, *The Acentos Review*, and the anthologies *Pulse/Pulso: In Remembrance of Orlando* and *Imaniman: Poets Writing in the Anzaldúan Borderlands*, among others. An active participant in the local literary scene, he lives and works in the Río Grande Valley of Texas. He also makes a delicious mole con arroz . . . a veces.

Candace K. de León-Zepeda is an associate professor of English at Our Lady of the Lake University in San Antonio, Texas. She earned her PhD in English from The University of Texas at San Antonio. She is a first-generation Chicanx scholar-activist whose publications contribute to the growing scholarship of culturally relevant pedagogies. She is coeditor of *Teaching Gloria E. Anzaldúa: Pedagogy and Practice for Our Classrooms and Communities*.

Juan C. Escobedo (b. 1985, El Paso, Texas) uses childhood memories, pop culture, and social class politics as the major catalysts for his artwork. He works with found materials transforming them into small spaces, headdresses, and collages. The work he makes creates visual instability which confronts the viewer with the dual realities and consequently with the concept of liminal identities. Liminality is emphasized by the materiality of the objects themselves and the sources that are used to construct them. His work has been described as surreal, dramatic, satirical, and nostalgic with a propensity to use low-brow materials. Juan Carlos studied at New Mexico State University (BFA, emphasis on painting, 2010) and acquired a master's degree in fine arts at Massachusetts College of Art and Design in 2015.

Christen Sperry García is an artist, writer, and cofounder of Museo Me Vale and Nationwide Museum Mascot Project (NWMMP), which has performed at Museo de Arte Contemporáneo, Lima, Peru; Museo Jumex, Mexico City;

Museum of Contemporary Art San Diego, CA; Hammer Museum, Los Angeles, CA; and Museo de Arte Moderno, Bogotá, Colombia. She is assistant professor of art education in the School of Art at the University of Texas Río Grande Valley.

María L. M. García is a poet and teacher, from Mexico, California, and Texas. She is currently working on her MFA in creative writing at University of Texas Río Grande Valley.

José David "Pepe" García Gilling is a Mexican filmmaker and writer from Tampico, México. His academic work centers on the lack and misrepresentation of Latinx in films of the US. He is currently a teaching assistant at University of Texas Río Grande Valley, where he teaches a course in Mexican American Studies. He is the chair and director of programming of the South Texas International Film Festival and is working on several film projects that focus on the Latinx experience.

Erika Garza-Johnson is a poet and instructor of English at South Texas College in McAllen, Texas. She is a mother, caregiver, wife, cat rescuer, editor, Chicanx, cabrona, and author of a collection of poetry entitled Unwoven.

Alia Hazineh is, like most Canadians, of mixed heritage: Palestinian and Ukrainian. Alia received her undergraduate degree in May 2020.

Theresa Jbeili is a Canadian-born Lebanese woman. Theresa is currently attending Schulich School of Law at Dalhousie.

Smadar Lavie is a professor emerita of anthropology at the University of California, Davis, and a visiting scholar in the Department of Ethnic Studies, University of California, Berkeley. She specializes in the anthropology of Egypt, Israel, and Palestine, emphasizing issues of race, gender, and religion. Lavie received her doctorate in anthropology from the University of California at Berkeley (1989) and spent nine years as assistant and associate professor of anthropology at the University of California, Davis. She authored *The Poetics of Military Occupation* (UC Press, 1990), receiving the 1990 Honorable Mention of the Victor Turner Award for Ethnographic Writing, and *Wrapped in the Flag of Israel: Mizrahi Single Mothers and Bureaucratic Torture* (Berghahn Books 2014; University of Nebraska Press 2018), receiving the 2015 Honorable Mention from the Association for Middle East Women's Studies Book Award Competition. *Wrapped in the Flag of Israel*'s first edition was also one of the four finalists for the

2015 Clifford Geertz Prize of the Society for the Anthropology of Religion. She also coedited *Creativity/Anthropology* (Cornell University Press, 1993) and *Displacement, Diaspora, and Geographies of Identity* (Duke University Press, 1996). Lavie won the American Studies Association's 2009 Gloria Anzaldúa Prize for her article, "Staying Put: Crossing the Palestine-Israel Border with Gloria Anzaldúa," published in Anthropology and Humanism (2011). In 2013, Lavie was awarded the Heart at East Honor Plaque for lifetime service to Mizrahi communities in Israel-Palestine.

Cecilia Amanda Macias holds an MA in English from Texas A&M University–San Antonio. Her research focuses on Chicana literature and performance, and her own Chicanidad. She was born in Grand Rapids, Michigan, in what she calls the Tejana diaspora. Cecilia grew up on enchiladas, arroz con pollo, frijoles, and dancing to Selena. She has fond memories of riding in the back of a pickup truck through flat Indiana during her family's once–annual pilgrimage to San Benito, Texas. Cecilia relocated to the San Antonio area with her immediate family in 2002, though her ancestors have lived and worked in South Texas and Northern Mexico for hundreds of years. A proud resident of San Antonio, she works supporting adult education and literacy.

Soph/Spencer Margulies, also known as Spence, is a master's student in the Communication Department at the University of South Florida. Their research interests focus on intercultural communication with a special interest in silenced US histories, as well as queer Latinx experience within im/migration, media representation, and their own experience as a third culture individual.

Mauricio Patrón Rivera (b. Ciudad de México, 1984) is a PhD student of creative writing in Spanish at University of Houston. He earned an MFA in independent studies from Museu d'Art Contemporani de Barcelona (MACBA), an MA in human rights at Ibero Ciudad de México, and a BA in journalism at UNAM. He recently received a scholarship from Fundación Jumex Arte Contemporáneo. He has published "Nunca más un México sin nosotras. La voz de las trabajadoras del hogar en su lucha por la ratificación del Convenio 189 de la OIT" in Revista Metodhos (Comisión de Derechos Humanos de la Ciudad de México [CDHDF] 2017) and "Hacía un cuerpo en la necropolítica" in Políticas, prácticas y pedagogías TRANS (Universitat Oberta de Catalunya [UOC], 2015). Until 2017 he took part in the Seminar in Gender and Visual Culture at Museo Universitario Arte Contemporáneo (MUAC, UNAM, 2015–2017), where he discovered Gloria E. Anzaldúa.

Emmy Pérez, Texas Poet Laureate 2020, is the recipient of a 2022 United States Artist Fellowship. She is the author of the poetry collections *With the River on Our Face* and *Solstice*. Her work has also appeared in anthologies such as *Ghost Fishing: An Eco-Justice Poetry Anthology*, *Other Musics: New Latina Poetry*, *What Saves Us: Poems of Empathy & Outrage*, and other publications. A volume of her new and selected works is forthcoming from TCU Press. She is a past recipient of poetry fellowships from the National Endowment for the Arts, CantoMundo, and the New York Foundation for the Arts. Pérez is a professor of Creative Writing and the associate director of the Center for Mexican American Studies at the University of Texas Rio Grande Valley (UTRGV). She also holds the Dr. Robert S. Nelsen Professorship in Mexican American Studies at UTRGV, 2021-2024. For her teaching and mentoring, she has received a UTRGV Excellence Award in Student Mentoring and a UT Regents' Outstanding Teaching Award. In 2021, she served as Consulting-Artist-in-Residence with UT San Antonio's Democratizing Racial Justice Mellon Foundation grant, and in 2017, she co-founded the Poets Against Walls collective.

Octavio Quintanilla is the author of the poetry collection, *If I Go Missing* (Slough Press, 2014),and the 2018–2020 Poet Laureate of San Antonio, Texas. His poetry, fiction, translations, and photography have appeared, or are forthcoming, in *Salamander*, *RHINO*, *Alaska Quarterly Review*, *Pilgrimage*, *Green Mountains Review*, *Southwestern American Literature*, *The Texas Observer*, *Existere: A Journal of Art & Literature*, and elsewhere. His Frontextos (visual poems) have been published in *Poetry Northwest*, *Gold Wake Live*, *Newfound*, *Chachalaca Review*, *Chair Poetry Evenings*, *Red Wedge*, *The Museum of Americana*, *About Place Journal*, *The American Journal of Poetry*, *The Windward Review*, *Tapestry*, *Twisted Vine Literary Arts Journal*, and *The Langdon Review of the Arts in Texas*. Octavio's visual work has been exhibited at Presa House Gallery, Equinox Gallery, AllState Almaguer art space in Mission, Texas, the Weslaco Museum, Our Lady of the Lake University, El Centro Cultural Hispano de San Marcos, The Walker's Gallery in San Marcos, Texas, the Emma S. Barrientos Mexican American Cultural Center / Black Box Theater, and the Southwest School of Art in San Antonio. He holds a PhD from the University of North Texas and is the regional editor for *Texas Books in Review* and poetry editor for *The Journal of Latina Critical Feminism*. Octavio teaches literature and creative writing in the MA/MFA program at Our Lady of the Lake University in San Antonio. Visit his website: octavioquintanilla.com, or find him on Instagram @writeroctavioquin-tanilla and Twitter @OctQuintanilla.

Verónica "Lady Mariposa" Sandoval is a doctoral candidate in the American Studies and Culture program at Washington State University. She grew up in the borderland of the Río Grande Valley, and is a spoken word artist who has been writing and performing poetry for over 20 years. Her poetry and academic scholarship have appeared in several anthologies and online publications from Routledge, Aunt Lute Press, University of Delaware Press, Lamar University Press, and Texas A&M University Press. Her research includes homegirl aesthetics, chola agency, and an emphasis on Chicana feminist epistemology that centers community knowledges and Chicana legacies of resistance.

Alexander V. Stehn is associate professor of philosophy, associate director of the Center for Bilingual Studies, and faculty affiliate in the Mexican American Studies Department at the University of Texas Río Grande Valley. He specializes in US American and Latin American philosophies. Publications include the 10,000-word entry "Latin American Philosophy" in The Internet Encyclopedia of Philosophy and "Teaching Gloria Anzaldúa as an American Philosopher" in a forthcoming volume on teaching Anzaldúa.

Kathleen Thomas-McNeill is the great-great-granddaughter of some of Canada's first European immigrants. Kathleen is pursuing her master's degree.

Maritza Torres is a Xicana artist based in Los Angeles. She was born in the suburbs of Murray, Utah, in 1983, into a large Mormon family. (She no longer practices and is atheist.) Torres and her work are in constant evolution, each influencing the other. Currently her work focuses on unraveling and understanding her own Xicana identity. She believes that by exposing the context of her own family's journey, she will hold a mirror to the viewer with the hope of creating space where the viewer can ask: What part of colonization have I been born into? How has this affected how I see myself? How am I being conditioned to perpetuate this cycle?

Julie Treviño is a self-taught artist and has been painting and drawing for most of her life. Recently she began to pursue art full time. Julie combines various art mediums to achieve textures and layers that express her vision of simple images.

Ethan Trinh (they/them) is a doctoral student at Georgia State University. Ethan is inspired to do research about the intersectionality of gender, LGBTQ, writing instruction, and English speakers of other languages (ESOL) through the lens of Chicana feminism. Ethan is a coeditor of TESOLer's Social Responsibility Interest Section (SRIS) and membership cochair of Queer Studies SIG at American Education Research Association (AERA). Originally from Mekong Delta in southern Vietnam, Ethan enjoys creative writing and having a cup of Vietnamese iced coffee in their free time.

Kieran Myles-Andrés Tverbakk is a first-generation Chicanx Norwegian artist originally from Houston, Texas. They live and work in the Twin Cities, Minnesota, where they have a studio and are codirector of the artist-run gallery and platform, Sure Space. Tverbakk received their BFA in 2016 from the Minneapolis College of Art and Design and they are a 2020 recipient of the Artist Initiative Grant, awarded by the Minnesota State Arts Board.

Jesusa María Vargas. Self-reflection and personal investigation of her cultural environment and cultural history are the subjects of Jesusa Marie Vargas's artworks. Working in a wide variety of mediums including sculpture, painting, and photography, she provokes reflection and conversation about the Mexican American folklore and identity that inspire her work. Her creative processes and techniques help preserve deep-rooted cultural traditions that are a part of her Chicana identity. Jesusa also works in digital media, creating short art and documentary videos that represent Mexican American ideas and personal narratives.

Gloria Vásquez Gonzáles is an adjunct professor of Mexican American studies at the University of Texas at San Antonio. After a previous career of more than eighteen years in the Tejano music industry, her research focuses on the invisible work that women have done in this business and their navigation through the patriarchal environment. She is currently working on obtaining more oral histories from women in the industry.

Bernardita M. Yunis Varas was born in Viña del Mar, Chile, and moved to the United States when she was 10 years old. She has lived in Miami, Florida, New York City, Pennsylvania, and Washington, D.C. Bernardita has been involved in social justice as a student activist and progressive leader, participating in the Young People For fellowship program where she gained experience as a mentor and trainer/facilitator supporting hundreds of youth activists around the country. Bernardita worked as a paralegal and a communication specialist at various nonprofits, and taught English to adult immigrants. She received her Masters in Communication Studies-Rhetoric from The Pennsylvania State University where she taught Public Speaking and Group Communication. At the George Washington University, she taught English for Academic Purposes, and First Year Writing with a course she developed herself on Latinx Identities and

Stereotypes. She also worked at the Writing Center assisting faculty, graduate assistants, and WC consultants in working with multilingual writers. She is currently in a doctoral program in Communication Studies at CU Boulder and hopes to graduate in 2023. There she has taught courses on Voice & Gender/ Communication & Gender, Communication through Literature, Intercultural Communication, and Human Communication.

Erika Zavala is a fronteriza from Juárez/El Paso. She received her PhD from the Department of Curriculum and Instruction at Texas Tech University. Her work focuses on bilingual education. Her other academic interests are multiculturalism/multilingualism, Latinx in education, Latinx/Chicanx feminism, and Latinx/Chicanx/Hispanic women writers and educators in the United States.

EDITORS

Norma E. Cantú is the Norine R. and T. Frank Murchison Distinguished Professor of the Humanities at Trinity University in San Antonio, Texas. She is the founder and director of the Society for the Study of Gloria Anzaldúa, and organized El Mundo Zurdo, a gathering of Anzaldúistas from 2007–2019. Her most recent publications include a novel, *Cabañuelas*, and four anthologies: *Teaching Gloria E. Anzaldúa: Pedagogies and Practices for our Classrooms and our Communities*; *Mexicana Fashions: Politics, Self-Adornment, and Identity Construction*; *Entre Guadalupe y Malinche: Tejanas in Literature and Art*; and *Meditación Fronteriza: Poems of Love, Life, and Labor*. She serves on the Esperanza Peace and Justice Center's Conjunto de Nepantleras and on the boards of the Macondo Writers Workshop and the American Folklore Society as past president. An activist, scholar, poet, writer, and folklorist, she has published widely in the fields of Chicanx studies and border studies.

Adrianna M. Santos (she/her/ella) is an associate professor of English at Texas A&M University-San Antonio, faculty adviser for the Mexican American Student Association, and co-coordinator of the Mexican American, Latinx, and Borderlands Studies interdisciplinary minor. Santos has published in the journals of Aztlán, Chicana/Latina Studies, Journal of Latina Critical Feminism, and Shakespeare Bulletin with chapters in *El Mundo Zurdo* (Aunt Lute 2015), *Teaching Mexicana and Chicana Writers of the Twentieth Century* (MLA 2020), *Nerds Goths, Geeks, and Freaks: Outsiders in Chicanx / Latinx Young Adult Literature* (Mississippi 2020), and *Shakespeare and Latinidad* (Edinburgh 2021). She is coeditor of *The Bard in the Borderlands: An Anthology of Shakespeare Appropriations en La Frontera* (Arizona Center for Medieval and Renaissance Studies

Press, 2023). She has volunteered at the Santa Barbara Rape Crisis Center, Martinez Street Women's Center, and Child Advocates of San Antonio.

Rita E. Urquijo-Ruiz (she/her/ella) is a Mexicana/Chicana queer educator, writer, activist, and performer born in Sonora, Mexico, and raised in Southern California. She is a professor of Spanish and Chicanx/Latinx cultural and LGBTQ+ studies. Her academic interests are Mexican, Chicanx, and Latinx literatures and cultures, gender and sexuality, as well as theater and performance studies. As a daughter of the Mexico-US borderlands, her approach to teaching and writing is interdisciplinary by nature. Her work centers the stories of socially and economically marginalized communities in these two bordering countries. She has taught courses on literature, culture, writing, first-year experience, Spanish grammar, leadership, LGBTQ+ studies, and women's and gender studies. She is proud to have directed the Mexico, Americas, and Spain (MAS) Program, under which she and Juan Sepúlveda, PhD, (Education Department) cocreated the first Latinx Leadership Institute in 2019. Under MAS, she also led the charge to create the Global Latinx Studies major and will serve as its inaugural director. She has served on the editorial board and national advisory board of Chicana/Latina Studies: The Journal of Mujeres Activas en Letras y Cambio Social.

OUR MISSION Founded in 1982, Aunt Lute Books is an intersectional, feminist press dedicated to publishing literature by those who have been traditionally underrepresented in or excluded by the literary canon. Core to Aunt Lute's mission is the belief that the written word is critical to understanding and relating to each other as human beings. Through the centering of voices, perspectives, and stories that have not been traditionally welcomed by mainstream publishing, we strengthen ties across cultures and experiences, promoting a broader range of expression, and, we hope, working toward a more inclusive and just future.

LAND ACKNOWLEDGMENT We, Aunt Lute Books, acknowledge that we do our work of uplifting marginalized voices and striving toward justice via the written word on the unceded ancestral homeland of the Ramaytush Ohlone who are the original inhabitants of the San Francisco Peninsula. As the indigenous stewards of this land and in accordance with their traditions, the Ramaytush Ohlone have never ceded, lost, nor forgotten their responsibilities as the caretakers of this place, as well as for all peoples who reside in their traditional territory. As Guests, we recognize that we benefit from living and working on their traditional homeland. We wish to pay our respects by acknowledging the Ancestors, Elders and Relatives of the Ramaytush Community and by affirming their sovereign rights as First Peoples.

You may buy books from our website.

www.auntlute.com

aunt lute books

P.O. Box 410687
San Francisco, CA 94141
books@auntlute.com

This book would not have been possible without the kind contributions of the Aunt Lute Founding Friends:

Anonymous Donor
Anonymous Donor
Rusty Barceló
Marian Bremer
Marta Drury
Diane Goldstein
Diana Harris
Phoebe Robins Hunter
Diane Mosbacher, M.D., Ph.D.
Sara Paretsky
William Preston, Jr.
Elise Rymer Turner